Never Trust a Skinny Cook

IAIN HEWITSON

Never Trust a Skinny Cook

HUEY'S CULINARY TRAVELOGUE

FOOD PHOTOGRAPHY BY **GREG ELMS**

A Sue Hines Book

ALLEN & UNWIN

Thanks
To Ruth and Charlotte, of course.
To Mosh, Donnelly, Mr Moon, Rob, Noel, Chris, Marty
and all the crew at Dreampool Productions.
To Ruth Allen and the guys at Tolarno.
To Sue and Andrea and the team at Allen & Unwin.
And, once again, to Greg and Virginia for making the
food look so good.

First published in 2005

A Sue Hines Book
Allen & Unwin
83 Alexander Street
Crows Nest NSW 2065
Australia
Phone: (61 2) 8425 0100
Fax: (61 2) 9906 2218
Email: info@allenandunwin.com
Web: www.allenandunwin.com

National Library of Australia Cataloguing-in-Publication entry:

Hewitson, Iain.
   Never trust a skinny cook : Huey's culinary travelogue.
   Includes index.

   ISBN 1 74114 692 5.

   1. Cookery. 2. Cooks - Travel. I. Elms, Greg. II. Title.

641.5

Cover and text design by Andrew Cunningham – Studio Pazzo
Food styling by Virginia Dowzer
Typesetting by Pauline Haas
Index by Fay Donlevy
Printed by Everbest, China

10 9 8 7 6 5 4 3 2 1

The author and publisher thank Moss Melbourne and Empire III
Vintage for their generous loan of dinnerware used in the food
photography.

When I dine in a restaurant
I don't know, I always ask to shake
hands with the chef. I know if he's
thin I'll probably eat poorly
and the only hope is to flee.

FERNAND POINT

Outside
Tables
Please Place
your Order
in
Le bar

Contents

INTRODUCTION ix

SOUPS 1

STARTERS
SNACKS
LIGHT MEALS 23

SALADS 59

FISH 87

SHELLFISH 121

MEAT 149

POULTRY 191

VEGETARIAN 221

DESSERTS 245

BASICS 279

GLOSSARY 282

PEOPLE &
PLACES INDEX 285

RECIPE INDEX 286

PICTURE CREDITS 293

Introduction

In the fourteen years since I began working on television, I have cooked in literally thousands of places. The majority of these segments have been filmed in Australia, although there have also been a fair number of visits to the more exotic parts of the world (not that Australia doesn't have its fair share of exotic destinations). But, in many cases, there has been little opportunity for me to play the tourist with early starts, heavy workloads and lots of travel taking up much of the time. (I did, however, always manage to make time for restaurant visits and the like – in the name of research, of course.)

So, taking that all into account, it is exciting to be now doing a new television series, *Never Trust a Skinny Cook*, where I not only have time to do the real touristy stuff, but in most places I also have the opportunity to veer from those paths and search out the little hidden treasures.

These include places such as the tiny cafe in Mauritius just down the road from the Sugar Beach Resort, which didn't even have a name, but served the most fantastic local food – a heady blend of Indian, Asian, French and Creole flavours. Or Zest Tours in Wellington, New Zealand, who not only introduced us to traditional Maori flavours at Kai in the Bay, but also took us to the beach where we ate freshly caught paua (New Zealand abalone) both in fritters and in a good old fashioned 'butty'. And the markets in Thailand where they whipped up a delectable spicy seafood pancake in about ten seconds flat over a wood-fired hot plate right there in front of us. And let us not forget the mother and daughter just outside Noosa who knew every goat in their herd by name and made some terrific fresh goat cheeses. Or our mates at the Waka Di Ume in Bali who created a special feast of Babi Guling (crisp skinned suckling pig) just for us and then attempted to teach me the traditional dance – an attempt which was an abject failure and fortunately never made it onto the show.

Actually, I could go on for pages about the delights of travelling in search of such special treats. But I won't and will instead leave you to enjoy this book and the many more shows, which I'm sure will appear on a screen near you.

Soups

Whenever I whip up a true classic (which, in typical Hewitson style, I can't resist mucking around with) the letters and emails flood in, each and every one of them pointing out what I've done wrong and, invariably, giving me the 'true' version. Interestingly, these so-called authentic versions always differ dramatically proving that there is no such thing as a truly authentic recipe, with even the classics varying from region to region and sometimes even village to village. And then, of course, there are the variations which happen over time and may be caused by seasonal constraints or even the flair and imagination of the cook. And then, there are my versions!

Vegetable 'Bouillabaisse'

Serves 4–6

– as cooked in a kitchen in Canberra

a good pinch saffron threads ¼ cup (2 fl oz) dry white wine	Preheat oven to 180°C (350°F). Combine and set aside.
2 tbsp (1 fl oz) olive oil 1 large onion, chopped 2 leeks, well washed & sliced 1 medium fennel bulb, cleaned, cored & sliced 2 garlic cloves, crushed	Heat oil in a large pot and sauté gently until tender.
8 baby waxy potatoes, peeled & cut into chunks 2 x 400 gm (13 oz) cans diced tomatoes, drained a little 1 medium carrot, cut in chunks 2 celery stalks, cut in chunks 1.5 litres (1⅕ quarts) vegetable stock (bought or homemade, see page 281) a piece of orange rind 2 fresh thyme sprigs	Add along with the saffron mix and cook until vegies are tender.
8–12 1 cm (⅜ inch) slices baguette (French bread)	Place on an oven tray and bake until golden brown.
Rouille (see page 239) 2 garlic cloves, crushed	Mix together and smear generously on bread.
freshly grated parmesan chopped fresh Italian (flat leaf) parsley	Ladle soup into bowls, top with bread and sprinkle with parmesan and parsley.

Australia: Canberra

Because of the cooler climate in Thailand's north, a lot more vegetables and herbs are available than in the south. Flavours tend to be hot and salty. Coconut milk, because of the lack of coconut palms, is rarely used and overall the food is not as spicy as that of the south. Also, until 1921 when the rail link was completed (up until then it had taken a month to travel from Bangkok via boat and elephant), the north had been fairly isolated with the influences of neighbouring China and Burma being strong. The food still reflects this. Sugar and Asian fish sauce are recent additions to the culinary repertoire with soy and bitter flavours from leaves and herbs being more traditional.

Sour Fish Soup with Morning Glory (Kaeng Som Pla Kup Phak Bung)

Serves 4

– as cooked at the Four Seasons Resort

½ tsp sea salt	Pound in mortar.
4 small red chillies, chopped	
½ red onion, chopped	
2–3 cm (¾–1¼ inch) knob galangal (or ginger), grated	
4 garlic cloves, crushed	
1 tsp shrimp paste	

vegetable oil	Heat a little oil in wok and sauté paste gently. Add rest and whisk well. Bring to boil and simmer for 10 minutes.
1 litre (32 fl oz) chicken or vegetable stock (bought or homemade, see page 281)	
2 tbsp (1 fl oz) tamarind water (see page 32)	
1 tbsp (½ fl oz) light soy sauce	
½ tbsp shaved palm sugar	

2–3 cups morning glory (see page 5), chopped	Add and cook for a few more minutes.
250–300 gm (8–10 oz) cubed, boneless, skinless, firm, steaky fish	

steamed rice	Check seasoning, adding more soy if necessary. Then place rice in bowls and ladle soup over the top.

'When I talk of steaky fish I am talking about firm fleshed varieties such as blue eye, groper, cod, monkfish etc.'

Thailand: Chiang Mai

This is the Thai version of the famous Chinese congee, a thick porridge-like concoction which is famed for its medicinal benefits. Whilst this variation has far more vegies than the original, in similar fashion it is believed that such a soup is easily digested and therefore is the perfect restorative for anyone even vaguely under the weather. (Obviously in a similar vein to that other magic elixir, Jewish penicillin – chicken soup.)

The soup is eaten at all times of the day and is often served with a selection of condiments such as chillies in Asian fish sauce, shredded ginger or even roasted peanuts.

Rice, Ginger & Green Vegetable Soup (Khao Tom)

Serves 4–6

– as served at Bangkok's Hualamphong Restaurant

1.2 litres (1 quart) chicken or vegetable stock (bought or homemade, see page 280 & 281)	Bring to simmer in wok or large pot.
160 gm (5¼ oz) steamed rice 1 tbsp freshly grated ginger 1 garlic clove, crushed 2 tbsp (1 fl oz) Asian fish sauce 1 tbsp (½ fl oz) light soy sauce 2 pinches freshly ground white pepper 2 small red chillies, finely sliced	Add, whisk and simmer for 5 minutes.
3 Chinese broccoli stalks, sliced 6 morning glory, chopped 2 baby bok choy (Chinese chard), sliced ¼ wonga bok (Chinese white cabbage), shredded 4 spring (green) onions, cut in 3 cm (1¼ inch) lengths	Add and toss until crisp-tender.
1 handful fresh coriander (cilantro) leaves	Check seasoning, then put into bowls and top with coriander.

'Morning glory, which is also known as kang kong, phak bung, ong choy and water convolvulus, is a variety of water spinach – normal spinach could be substituted.'

Thailand: Bangkok

'This can be prepared in advance up until the cheese. Only add the cheese at the last minute otherwise the soup will be gluggy.'

Chilli, Chicken & Cheese Soup

Serves 4–6

— as cooked on the balcony of the Auckland Hilton

1 tbsp (½ fl oz) olive oil 4 chillies, seeded & finely sliced 4 garlic cloves, crushed	Heat oil in pot and gently cook.
1 large onion, chopped 6–7 medium potatoes, peeled & neatly cubed 1.5 litres (1⅕ quarts) chicken stock (bought or homemade, see page 280) 2 x 400 gm (13 oz) cans diced tomatoes, drained a little freshly ground salt & pepper	Add, mix well and simmer gently for 15 minutes.
2 large skinless chicken breasts, cubed	Add and cook very, very gently for another 15 minutes.
2 cups (8 oz) grated tasty cheese 3 tbsp chopped fresh parsley	Add, turn off and stir until cheese has melted. Check seasoning.

New Zealand: Auckland

It is said that the perfect cure for a hangover is a Bloody Mary. I don't know whether that is true, I tend to go down the path of another bottle of what you were drinking the night before (but never before midday). Actually everyone seems to have a cure of their own from the truly horrible mix of Fernet Branca and Crème de Menthe which my former business partner Rudy Loenen swore by. Or the Berocca Milkshake which became chef Bill Marchetti's breakfast of choice. And I seem to remember Keith Floyd talking of Bull Shots (whatever they are) and he should know as he actually wrote a book on the subject of hangover cures.

That aside, this is a delicious soup which is not guaranteed to cure any hangover but is worth sipping nonetheless.

Bloody Mary Soup with Plumped Oysters

Serves 6–8

— as cooked on a boat in Rotorua when I did have a hangover

8 large ripe tomatoes, cored & halved
4 whole garlic cloves, unpeeled but smashed a little
12 fresh basil leaves
olive oil
freshly ground salt & pepper

Preheat oven to 180°C (350°F).
Place tomatoes, garlic and basil on an oven tray. Sprinkle with oil and seasonings, making sure that you moisten the basil. Cook until the tomatoes collapse, then whip skins off.

---

1 litre (32 fl oz) V8 juice
250 ml (8 fl oz) chicken stock
  (bought or homemade, see page 280)
a good slurp of Worcestershire sauce
a good slurp of balsamic vinegar
a good slurp of vodka
a good slurp of Tabasco
freshly ground salt & pepper
juice of 1 lemon

While tomatoes are cooking, bring to boil and gently simmer until tomatoes are ready. Then squeeze garlic out of the husk and chop along with peeled tomatoes. Add to the pot, whisk well and taste for seasoning.

2–3 freshly shucked oysters per person
snipped fresh chives

Place oysters in individual bowls. Pour over soup (the heat will 'plump' the oysters) and sprinkle with chives.

*'You, of course, can add other seafood such
as mussels, clams, scallops and oysters
but, obviously, not at the same time as
the fish, as they take less time to cook.'*

Italian Fish 'Soup'

Serves 4–6

— as cooked overlooking Bass Strait

1 tbsp (½ fl oz) olive oil 2 chillies, seeded & finely sliced 4 garlic cloves, crushed	Heat oil in wok and sauté gently.
2 x 400 gm (13 oz) cans diced tomatoes, drained a little 375 ml (12 fl oz) fruity white wine 5 or 6 waxy baby potatoes, peeled & cut in chunks a piece of orange rind 750 ml (24 fl oz) fish stock (bought or homemade, see page 280) sea salt freshly ground pepper 1 tsp sugar	Add, cover and simmer for about 15 minutes or until potatoes are tender, adding a little more stock if necessary.
600 gm (1¼ lb) various fish fillets, cut into chunks (blue eye, tuna, salmon, snapper, etc)	Add, cover and gently cook until ready, removing each piece as ready.
chopped fresh Italian (flat leaf) parsley	To serve, put potatoes in flat soup bowls, top with fish and 'soup' and sprinkle with parsley.

Australia: Great Ocean Road

A delicacy in New Zealand, the Green Lip Mussel has never been regarded very highly in Australia, mainly because, in comparison to the tender local black numbers, it has always seemed to be a tough rather tasteless relation. This actually can be blamed on the fact that in Oz, the Green Lips are almost invariably frozen – a process which is not sympathetic to any mussel.

But in New Zealand, the Green Lips are another kettle of fish entirely – tender, juicy, meaty and full of flavour. They are, like the famous clams of Boston, highly suitable for chowders or robust stew-type presentations. They can also, because of their size, be twice cooked successfully by steaming them first to open, then coating them on the half shell with any flavoured butter and/or fresh crumbs before bunging them under a hot grill until bubbling – delicious stuff.

Green Lip Mussel Chowder Serves 6–8
— as cooked overlooking the Hauraki Gulf

olive oil 3 rindless bacon rashers, diced 1 leek, well washed & sliced	Heat a good splash of oil and sauté.
1.5 litres (1⅕ quarts) fish stock (bought or homemade, see page 280) a large pinch of saffron threads 2 bay leaves 2 x 400 gm (13 oz) cans diced tomatoes, drained 2–3 large potatoes, peeled & diced freshly ground salt & pepper	Add, bring to the boil and simmer until potato is very tender (15 minutes or so).
1 kilo (2 lb) mussels, scrubbed & debearded (see below) 3–4 corn cobs (ear of corn), kernels removed	Add, cover and cook, removing mussels to bowls as they open (and discarding any that don't).
chopped fresh parsley crusty bread	Ladle soup over the top and sprinkle with parsley. Serve with plenty of crusty bread.

'To debeard the mussel, grasp the string-like substance that grows out the side of the shell and pull it towards the hinge until it comes away. And if fresh green lips are not available, substitute any large mussels.'

Duck, Noodle & Preserved Mustard Green Soup

– as inspired by Bangkok's Chinatown

1 litre (32 fl oz) chicken stock (bought or homemade, see page 280) 2 tbsp (1 fl oz) oyster sauce 4 tbsp (2 fl oz) duck stock/sauce (see below)	Bring to the boil.
1 good handful vermicelli noodles 1 good handful each bok choy (Chinese chard) & Chinese broccoli leaves	Add and cook briefly until noodles are just tender and vegies have wilted.
½ Chinese BBQ duck, boned & cut in thickish slices 1 can or packet of sour, pickled mustard greens	Put noodles, vegies and most of the stock in bowls. Top with duck and mustard greens and pour rest of the stock over the top.
4–6 small red & green chillies, sliced Asian fish sauce	Put chillies in a bowl and cover with Asian fish sauce – serve on the side.

'When you buy the duck from Chinatown ask for some of the duck sauce/stock. And the sour, pickled mustard greens are available in Asian grocers.'

Silverbeet 'Minestra'

Serves 4–6

— as cooked in Canberra's Commonwealth Park

olive oil 3 celery stalks, diced 2 large onions, diced 2 medium carrots, diced 3 garlic cloves, crushed	Heat a little oil in large heavy-bottomed pot and sauté until lightly coloured.
1.5 litres (1⅕ quarts) chicken stock (bought or homemade, see page 280) 3 x 400 gm (13 oz) cans diced tomatoes, drained freshly ground salt & pepper	Add, toss well and cook for 15–20 minutes until vegies are tender.
8 silverbeet (Swiss chard) stalks, sliced 2 x 400 gm (13 oz) cans cannelini beans, drained & rinsed well	Add, mix and gently cook for another 5–6 minutes.
freshly grated parmesan chopped fresh Italian (flat leaf) parsley	Check seasoning and serve sprinkled with parmesan and parsley.

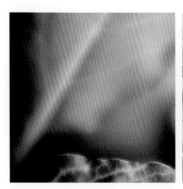 

Australia: Canberra

'This is the basis for almost any soup using root vegetables – carrots, sweet potatoes, etc. They all work just as well.'

A Simple Parsnip Soup with a little local honey   Serves 6–8
– as cooked by the lake at Daylesford

2 large onions, chopped

6–8 parsnips, peeled & chopped

1 large potato, peeled & chopped

1.5 litres (1⅕ quarts) chicken stock
   (bought or homemade, see page 280)

freshly ground salt & pepper

Place in a pot and cook until vegies are very tender.

---

a good splash of thickened cream

a good splash of honey

Add, check seasoning and then blend.

---

chopped fresh Italian (flat leaf) parsley

Sprinkle on the top.

Australia: Daylesford

Mauritius has about the best beaches and lagoons in the Indian Ocean and as Mark Twain said in 1896, 'Mauritius was created first, then heaven. And heaven was copied after Mauritius.' Maybe he got a little carried away but it certainly is a paradise. Only eight hours flight from Perth, the thing that strikes you the minute you arrive is how friendly the locals are. Genuinely pleased to welcome tourists, they are good natured and eager to have a chat (the official language of the Island is English, although you're bound to hear French, Indian and Creole – a mix of French and various African dialects).

Curried Dholl 'Soup' with Oysters & Coriander Raita

Serves 4–6

– as cooked on the beach at the Sugar Beach Resort

1½ cups dholl (yellow split peas)	Soak in cold water for 30 minutes. Drain and set aside.
1 tbsp (½ fl oz) vegetable oil 1 large onion, chopped 2 garlic cloves, crushed	Heat oil in large pot and sauté until tender. Add dholl and toss well.
2 heaped tsp curry powder ½ tsp ground cumin	Add spices. Cook for 1–2 minutes.
vegetable or chicken stock (bought or homemade, see page 280 & 281) 2 tbsp chopped fresh coriander (cilantro) 10 curry leaves freshly ground salt & pepper	Add along with stock to just cover. Stir and simmer for 20–25 minutes until dholl is tender.
150 ml (5 fl oz) coconut milk	Add and cook for a few more minutes (adding more stock if too thick).
¾ cup (6 oz) plain yoghurt 2 tbsp chopped fresh coriander (cilantro) 2 tbsp grated continental (telegraph) cucumber juice of ½ lemon	While soup is cooking, combine to make raita.
12–18 freshly shucked oysters	To serve, put soup in flat bowls, arrange oysters on top and sprinkle generously with raita.

'Closer in texture to the dhals of India than to a soup.'

Mauritius: Flic en Flac

This is one of the true Thai classics. The name means 'boiled galangal', which to me doesn't sound that appetising (although the soup itself is delicious). Unfortunately, in this recipe ginger is not a suitable substitute and unless the galangal is very young and fresh it is not eaten.

This soup in most parts of the world almost always features chicken. But in Thailand it is often also made with seafood (or a combination of both) and I once had a terrific vegetarian version with lots of different mushrooms.

In my version, I have cut back the coconut with stock, as otherwise I found it a little too coconutty (is there such a word, or did I just make it up?). But that may just be my western palate. Still, Mr Moon, who is a bit of a fan of Tom Khaa Gai, appeared to enjoy it because when I cooked it on the beach at Cape Panwa, by the time I turned around he had scoffed the lot.

Chicken, Coconut & Galangal Soup (Tom Khaa Gai)

Serves 4

— as cooked on the beach at Cape Panwa

1 litre (32 fl oz) chicken stock (bought or homemade, see page 280) 250 ml (8 fl oz) coconut milk 250 ml (8 fl oz) coconut cream 1 tsp shaved palm sugar a pinch of sea salt	Bring to the boil in a wok.
2 lemongrass stalks, white part only, smashed & finely sliced 3 red (French) shallots, sliced 3 small red chillies, chopped	Pound with a mortar and pestle until smooth and whisk into liquid.
2 tbsp (1 fl oz) Asian fish sauce 3 tbsp fresh lime juice 3 fresh kaffir lime leaves, shredded 5 cm piece galangal, peeled & finely sliced 1–2 skinless chicken breasts, finely sliced	Add and simmer very gently until chicken is cooked.
½ punnet (tub) cherry tomatoes, halved 1 x 250 gm (8 oz) can straw mushrooms, drained & rinsed 2 long red chillies, seeded & finely sliced	Add and cook for a minute. Put into bowls.
a small handful of fresh coriander (cilantro) sprigs	Scatter over the top.

Moroccan Lamb & Chickpea Soup

Serves 6–8

— as cooked at Garnisha in Boreen Point

1 tbsp (½ fl oz) olive oil 1 large onion, chopped 3 garlic cloves, crushed	Heat oil in large heavy-bottomed pot and sauté gently until tender.
2 tbsp harissa paste (Garnisha brand if available)	Add and toss for a few minutes to toast.
500 gm (16 oz) diced lean lamb	Add and toss until it changes colour, continually scraping the bottom of the pot as you do so.
1.5 litres (1⅕ quarts) beef stock 　(packet or homemade, see page 280) 2 x 400 gm (13 oz) cans diced tomatoes, drained a little 2 x 400 gm (13 oz) cans chickpeas, drained & rinsed 2 bay leaves a pinch sea salt 3 tbsp chopped fresh coriander (cilantro)	Add, mix well and simmer gently for about 50–60 minutes or until lamb is very tender, adding more stock as necessary. Taste for seasoning.
½ cup (4 oz) plain yoghurt harissa paste a squeeze of fresh lemon juice	Mix yoghurt with harissa and lemon to taste.
chopped fresh coriander (cilantro) warm pita bread	Ladle into bowls, sprinkle yoghurt and coriander over the top and serve with pita on the side.

*'Only one secret when making this simple soup –
because it is not being blended, the celery needs to
be neatly and evenly diced. And sambal oelek is an
Asian chilli paste that is available in most
supermarkets.'*

A Light Celery Soup

Serves 4–6

– as cooked by the pool on Hamilton Island

1 large onion, chopped

2 garlic cloves, crushed

3 x 400 gm (13 oz) cans diced tomatoes,
   drained a little

1 tsp sambal oelek

pale, inner stalks of 3 bunches celery, diced

1.5 litres (1⅕ quarts) vegetable stock
   (bought or homemade, see page 281)

freshly ground salt & pepper

Put in large pot and simmer gently for 30 minutes
or so until vegies are very tender. Check seasoning.

---

4 thick slices country-style bread

freshly grated parmesan

chopped fresh Italian (flat leaf) parsley

Put the bread in individual bowls, ladle soup over
the top and sprinkle generously with parmesan and
parsley.

The Food of Bali

To experience true Balinese food can be a difficult task. Dining out is not really a part of their heritage so therefore many restaurants are geared mainly to the tourists and are, in most cases, fairly Anglicised (for example instead of serving traditional spicy food with accompanying bowls of sambals, the food often tends to be bland with a commercial bottle of chilli sauce plonked alongside).

Of course there are exceptions. Interestingly it seems that the cheaper or more daggy a restaurant is the more authentic it will be. And if the owner hardly speaks a word of English then it's a good chance you're on a winner. There is also the local warungs which are very much a part of village life. Often more of a shop, or in many cases a lean-to, than a restaurant, they sell not only snacks but everything from soft drinks and beer to various grocery items. They are also the meeting place for the locals, a place to gossip, a place to catch up on what is happening in the village.

So while you can eat well in Bali, and so you should because the ingredients are often terrific, you do have to be careful. The main tourist areas often have restaurants trying to cater to everyone – Nasi Goreng and Gado Gado alongside burgers and pizza while a number of hotels tend to present 'Balinese' buffets which owe more to Club Med than they do to Bali. But in both Ubud and Legian we ate very well in a variety of styles and didn't feel we were being ripped off in the process. And Jimbaran Bay where there are a large number of restaurants serving seafood right on the beach, was a bit of fun. The entertainment is by wandering 'minstrels' who, for a small fee, play everything from Beatles covers to Van the Man and Cold Chisel numbers. And the food is rather good as long as you stand right next to the cooks and get them to take the seafood off the grill about half an hour before he or she normally would (to say they overcook is a bit of an understatement). Also unless you drink beer or bad local rosé, take along a bottle or two – in fact that applies to all of the casual eateries.

Actually, the way the Balinese eat in their homes is interesting. Rarely sitting down together for a meal they tend to snack throughout the day whenever they feel hungry. Lack of refrigeration means that the food purchases are made almost every day and, after the morning's trip to the market, rice and small portions of dishes such as spiced vegies, fish or meat and the aforementioned sambals are prepared and set out for the family to help themselves. Sort of like a Balinese tapas, even if they do eat at the same time the meals are rarely a sociable affair.

Festivals are a different kettle of fish (pardon the culinary pun). Here the food is lavish, is eaten as a group and is invariably beautifully presented. You can experience famous festival dishes such as Babi Guling (spit roasted suckling pig with a stuffing of chillies and fragrant herbs, roots and spices) and Bebek Betutu (duckling roasted in banana leaves) at some tourist restaurants or if you're lucky enough to be invited into a Balinese home on a special occasion. Another festival favourite is Lawar. A very spicy salad, it was traditionally made with turtle or pork and thickened with their blood but these days it is just as likely to be made from chicken or even seafood. Alongside are always served a large number of side dishes and condiments and this is, I suppose, what I expected all food would be like when I first came to Bali.

The Balinese, who are mostly Hindu, are also known for their elegant food offerings to the gods which may be as simple as small offerings of rice or as elaborate as 'tree offerings' that are eaten after the ceremony. These offerings are taken to the temple where they are purified by the priest who sprinkles holy water over them while chanting prayers. Once the 'essence' has been inhaled by the gods, the leftovers are eaten by the family who brought the food.

Every Asian country has a soup in this style – simple, easy and tasty. Almost a restorative in fact. This version leans more towards the Phos of Vietnam than anything else and, as such, is flavoured with plenty of herbs and vegies along with lightly cooked steak which, of course, doesn't need to be fillet but, gee, it does make the soup pretty classy. And just a hint: to make it easier to slice the steak thinly, throw it into the freezer for about 20 minutes before slicing.

Beef Soup Noodles

— as cooked on the beach at Lorne

serves 6–8

2 litres (1¾ quarts) chicken stock
  (bought or homemade, see page 280)
2 tbsp (1 fl oz) Asian fish sauce
1 heaped tsp grated fresh ginger
3 chillies, seeded & finely sliced

Bring to the boil and simmer gently for 15 minutes.

---

1 packet thick noodles
3 spring (green) onions, cut in 3 cm (1¼ inch) lengths
1 handful beanshoots
4 baby carrots, peeled & sliced on diagonal

Add, bring back to the boil and cook until noodles are just tender.

---

200 gm (6½ oz) fillet steak, trimmed of all fat & sinew
  and finely sliced
1 handful baby spinach leaves, stalks removed
1 cup (1 oz) fresh Vietnamese mint leaves
¼ cup (⅓ oz) fresh coriander (cilantro) leaves

Place in individual bowls, ladle soup over the top and mix to 'cook'.

'Vietnamese mint is available in every Asian market and some specialist greengrocers (normal mint could be substituted).'

Australia: Great Ocean Road

In Bali a soup is rarely (if ever) eaten at the beginning of a meal. In a country where dishes are rarely divided into courses, the soup is served as an accompaniment to other dishes (in similar vein to the Chinese whose noodle soups are always served amongst a number of other dishes, although they also have soups that are served, in the European style, to begin a meal). That said, this soup could be easily served at the beginning of the meal but in a communal bowl so each guest can help themselves to the 'meat' from the fish head.

Sour Spicy Fish Head Soup (Ikan Air Garam)

Serves 4–6

— as cooked on the beach at Jimbaran Bay

1 x 800 gm (26 oz) groper or snapper head 1 tsp white vinegar	Rub the head with vinegar and allow to sit for 30 minutes. Then wash and drain well.
vegetable oil 3 cm (1¼ inch) piece galangal (or ginger), peeled & sliced 5 garlic cloves, peeled & smashed a little 4 small chillies, sliced 1 lemongrass stalk, white part only, smashed & sliced 5 red (French) shallots, peeled & sliced	Heat a very lightly oiled wok and toss briefly until lightly charred. Pound with a mortar.
3 tomatoes, peeled, seeded & finely diced (see below) 2 tbsp (1 fl oz) kecap manis 2 tbsp (1 fl oz) Chinese black vinegar freshly ground pepper	Add to mortar and mix well, then put into a large pot.
1.5 litres (1⅕ quarts) fish stock (bought or homemade, see page 280)	Add to pot along with fish head and simmer for about 45 minutes until cooked.
3 large chillies, seeded & finely sliced juice of 1–2 limes	Add to taste and simmer for a few minutes.
steamed rice	Serve with rice on the side.

'To peel and seed tomatoes, core and put in boiling water. Count to 10 or 12 then remove and plunge into iced water. When cool, peel and cut lengthways into quarters. Remove pulp (and set aside to use for sauce or the like) and dice flesh.'

Starters, snacks
& light meals

George Biron – the Great Ocean Road Champion

One of the driving forces behind the resurgence in the Geelong and Great Ocean Road's food fortunes is chef George Biron. Champion of local produce, when he opened his restaurant, Sunnybrae, at Birregurra in the early nineties, the local growers found themselves with a sounding board who had a passion for anything they could and would produce. A keen vegetable grower himself, his big rambling kitchen garden also provided a source of inspiration for local farmers as he not only produced much for his kitchen but some weird and wonderfuls just for fun.

Sunnybrae, which he operated with his partner Diane Garrett, quickly became the ideal country restaurant (and this is not just talking about the sheer quality of the cooking), featuring a menu that changed daily and which reflected the seasons and what was available in the surrounding region. Anyone producing anything of interest in the area quickly found a spot on his menus and, through his cooking classes, he introduced such regional specialties to a whole new audience. (He also took them to visit the suppliers, to discover the source and, also, in season, mushroom foraging which I found fascinating).

Sadly, to the dismay of thousands, right at the height of its popularity George and Diane decided to close Sunnybrae and move on to other things. I was there for the 'Last Supper' along with my wife Ruth and many, many foodies such as Donlevy Fitzpatrick, Philippe Mouchel, Michael Trembath, Phillip Miles and Claude Forell. There were lots of tears and a sense that one of Australia's restaurant stars had disappeared.

But all is not lost. In his 'retirement', George has consulted to and has supervised the setting up of the nearby Pettavel Restaurant at the vineyard of the same name and an excellent country cafe at Heronswood on the Mornington Peninsula. (This is the home of Digger's Seeds, who also have a large kitchen garden and produce a huge range of exotic fruit and vegetable seeds including an unequalled range of heirloom tomatoes.)

He has also built a wonderful woodfired oven in his backyard, from which he produces terrific pizzas and other bits and pieces for all and sundry. In fact, in this day and age when the woodfired pizza has become an art form, these were the best I've ever eaten and I did spend a fair amount of time attempting to persuade him to open a kitchen 'table' where a dozen or so people could pay to come to lunch and sit around his kitchen table and watch as he weaves his magic over the wood oven (I'm sad to report I didn't get very far).

And, of course, above all he continues to champion the cause of the Great Ocean Road producers and recently, in a new role, finished a report on a Food and Wine Tourism Strategy for the Geelong Otway Tourism Board which, in a typical George understatement, he felt had ruffled a few feathers.

'This is more of a tapas style dish than an entrée.'

Mushrooms & Chorizo

Serves 2–4

– as cooked on the boardwalk at Geelong

olive oil ½ red onion, finely chopped 1 garlic clove, crushed	Heat a little oil in a pan and sauté gently until tender.
18–24 tiny button mushrooms 1 tsp smoked paprika	Add and toss well to toast paprika.
a good splash of sherry vinegar a good splash of dry white wine	Add and bubble briefly.
250 ml (8 fl oz) chicken stock (bought or homemade, see page 280) 1 tbsp chopped fresh parsley freshly ground salt & pepper	Add and cook down to a glaze (about 5 minutes).
2–3 chorizo, sliced on diagonal	Heat a little oil in another large pan and cook until crispy. Drain and toss with mushrooms.

George Biron's Pizzas

– as cooked at Birregurra

500 gm (16 oz) unbleached baker's flour 1 tsp Saf or Fermipan dried yeast, or 30 gm (1 oz) fresh yeast 2 tsp sea salt	Using your hands, mix together, combining thoroughly.
about 300 ml (10 fl oz) lukewarm water	Slowly add and knead for about 5 minutes until a little sticky but not really wet. Cover with a damp cloth and set aside in a warm spot until doubled in size (30–60 minutes – for a really crisp base, cover with kitchen wrap and refrigerate overnight). When ready, roll into 5–6 balls with lightly floured hands and roll out to desired shape leaving slightly thicker edges.
olive oil	Put one terracotta tile on base of oven and one on top. Heat oven to its highest degree. Place pizza base on lightly floured pizza tin, spread with topping of your choice, and slide onto bottom terracotta tile. Cook quickly until crisp and brown around the edges. Brush edges with olive oil and serve.

'In a domestic oven the tiles concentrate the heat and ensure the pizza cooks quickly and evenly.'

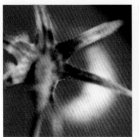

Basic Pizza Sauce

1 kg (2 lb) ripe tomatoes, peeled, seeded & chopped
 (see page 21), or canned
150 ml (5 fl oz) extra virgin olive oil
good pinch sea salt
1 chilli, finely chopped
2 garlic cloves, crushed
2 anchovies, chopped

Put all in a large pot and slowly simmer for about 20 minutes until thick and fragrant. (George adds the garlic and anchovies towards the end.)

Braised Fennel Topping

freshly ground salt & pepper
2 garlic cloves, finely chopped
1 chilli, finely chopped
1 pinch fennel seeds

Pound with a mortar and pestle.

---

250 gm (8 oz) fennel, cored & cut into thin strips
100 gm (3½ oz) red onions, finely sliced
50 ml (1½ fl oz) extra virgin olive oil
100 ml (3½ fl oz) water

Put in a pot and cook gently for about 20 minutes until tender. Then add spices and cook until soft and caramelised.

Caramelised Onion Topping

1 garlic clove, crushed
1 chilli, finely chopped
2 anchovies, finely chopped

Pound with a mortar and pestle.

---

500 gm (1 lb) red onions, finely sliced
extra virgin olive oil
freshly ground salt & pepper

Put in a pot, cover and cook for about 30 minutes until tender. Then add above and cook uncovered, stirring regularly until golden and very tender.

One of Australia's most passionate small producers is situated in Lara near Geelong. His name is Angel Cardoso, and his range of Spanish smallgoods are absolutely bloody marvellous, as good as any I have tasted in Spain. His ham and sausages are now to be found on some of the best tables in Australia.

Arriving in Australia in 1962 to work in the aeronautical industry, Cardoso's passion for food and, in particular, smallgoods, soon saw him experimenting with the local pork in an attempt to recreate the 'stars' of his homeland. In the typical overnight success story, it took him almost twenty years (and, I'm sure, thousands and thousands of dollars) before he was satisfied with the results. And he should be – the jamon is tender, soft and full of flavour, exactly as it should be, whilst his salamis and chorizo have the 'bite' and the depth of character that only the best achieve.

The only problem is that not every supermarket stocks his wonderful products (even in Geelong) so you may have to visit Lara or search out a good Spanish or Mediterranean deli. Or, if in Melbourne, go to the excellent Casa Iberica in Johnston Street, Fitzroy, which is well worth a visit and not just for Angel's smallgoods.

Chorizo & Vegie Stew with a Baked Egg   Serves 2–4
– as cooked in George Biron's woodfired oven

1 tbsp (½ fl oz) olive oil	Preheat oven to the highest degree. Place oil in an ovenproof dish, put in the oven and heat for 5 minutes.
2 red capsicum (bell peppers), cored, seeded & finely sliced 2 chorizo, sliced 4 large ripe, red tomatoes, cored & cut into wedges 2 garlic cloves, finely sliced freshly ground pepper sea salt	Add to dish, toss well and return to the oven. Cook until tomatoes collapse.
4 eggs chopped fresh parsley crusty bread	Remove dish from oven. Make four wells in the mix and break the eggs in. Return to the oven and cook until the eggs are set. Sprinkle with parsley and serve with bread.

'A terrific brunch or light lunch dish, which can also be cooked in a normal oven.'

About one hour's drive from Noosa in the hinterland at Kenilworth is the Coolabine Farmstead where Dee Dunham and her family produce terrific goat cheeses.

This is farmyard production to the highest degree. Every one of the ninety goats is individually named and, with all sincerity, Dee told me that apart from the fact that the Anglo-Nubian breed produces the best milk, they are also the most handsome goats (couldn't quite see it myself). Still, as they say, it's all in the eye of the beholder and the cheeses themselves were certainly excellent and included a two-day-old soft curd, white and ash mould cheeses, the Caprice which is marinated with olive oil, thyme and lemon, and both a traditional and marinated feta.

Potato, Goat Cheese Feta & Anchovy Tortilla

Serves 4

— as cooked at Coolabine Farmstead

¾ cup (6 fl oz) olive oil 4 large potatoes, peeled & sliced about ½ cm (¼ inch) thick 1 medium–large onion, finely chopped freshly ground salt & pepper	Heat oil in a large pan and gently cook until tender, turning every now and then. Remove vegies and pour off oil, setting aside.
½ cup (2½) cubed, marinated goat cheese feta 6 eggs, beaten	Add to potatoes and carefully mix. Season. Put 2 tbsp (1 fl oz) of the oil back in pan, heat and add potato mix. Cover and gently cook for about 10 minutes until just set (should still wobble in the centre). Turn out onto a plate, flip over and slide back into pan (adding a little more oil if necessary). Cook for a few minutes.
6–8 anchovies, sliced lengthways chopped fresh parsley	Arrange anchovies in a lattice pattern on top, sprinkle with parsley and serve hot or warm with a salad on the side.

Australia: Kenilworth

Grilled Bread with Smoked Chicken and a Mango & Avocado Salsa

— as prepared at Poacher's Pantry in ACT

1–2 mangos, peeled & diced 1 tbsp chopped fresh coriander (cilantro) juice of 1 lime ½ avocado, peeled & diced freshly ground salt & pepper	Toss together and set aside.
¼ cup (2 oz) plain yoghurt 1 tbsp diced telegraph (continental) cucumber 1 tbsp chopped fresh coriander (cilantro) a pinch of cayenne	Mix together.
4 thick slices country-style bread olive oil spray	Either toast or spray lightly with oil and grill.
2 smoked chicken breasts, sliced	Place bread on individual plates, top with chicken and then salsa and flick the yoghurt over the lot.

'A recipe derived from Maxine Clark's excellent book, Comfort Food.'

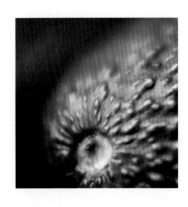

I was fascinated by the name of this dish and consequently couldn't wait to whip it up. The eggs were delicious and in about three seconds flat, the crew had devoured the lot. (The ultimate test for any of my dishes is how quickly the crew eat them – if the plate is cleared rapidly then I know I'm on a winner.) Traditionally served on New Year's Day or at weddings, they are also frequently taken as an offering to the monks at the temple.

Son-In-Law Eggs (Khai Luk Koei)

Serves 4

– as cooked on the beach at Cape Panwa

2–3 tbsp tamarind paste	To make tamarind water, mix with one cup of warm water and set aside for 10–15 minutes. Push through a fine sieve discarding solids.
2 dried long red chillies 1½ litres (1⅕ quarts) vegetable oil 2 cm piece ginger, peeled & julienned	Cut chillies into ½ cm pieces with kitchen scissors, removing seeds. Heat oil in a wok to 180°C (350°F), then deep fry chillies and ginger until crispy. Drain well.
8 boiled eggs, shelled & gently pricked all over with the prongs of a fork	Put in oil and cook for 5–6 minutes until golden brown.
6 tbsp shaved palm sugar 2 tbsp (1 fl oz) Asian fish sauce 3 tbsp (1½ fl oz) tamarind water (see above)	While eggs are cooking, put in a small pot and heat until sugar has dissolved. Taste, adding another tablespoon of Asian fish sauce if it needs a bit more of a tang.
deep fried red (French) shallots (bought or homemade, see page 52)	Serve eggs in a bowl, either whole or halved, and sprinkle generously with syrup, deep fried chillies, shallots and ginger.

'For this dish the eggs should be put in boiling water then when it comes back to the boil cooked for exactly six minutes before being removed and plunged into cold water.'

Thailand: Phuket

I often pick up ideas for dishes from restaurants and bars. I enjoyed a dish like this in a small cafe in Seminyak in Bali which didn't even have a name (the cafe that is). But the food was terrific and these spicy little numbers were a hit. So here is my attempt at replicating them and, if I must say so myself, the result isn't half bad.

Pork & Lime Patties with a Chilli-Lime Sauce   Serves 4
— as cooked by a pool in Seminyak

6 chillies, chopped	Whisk together and set aside.
3 garlic cloves, chopped	
200 ml (6½ fl oz) fresh lime juice	
2 tbsp (1 fl oz) kecap asin (or soy sauce)	
a good splash of kecap manis	
2 tbsp chopped fresh coriander (cilantro)	

300 gm (10 oz) minced (ground) pork (not too lean)	Mix together thoroughly.
grated rind of 1 lime	
½ tbsp (¼ fl oz) Asian fish sauce	
1 egg	
2 tsp (⅖ fl oz) sambal oelek	
¼ cup (⅓ oz) finely sliced spring (green) onions	
1 tbsp (½ fl oz) kecap manis	
2 garlic cloves, crushed	

rice flour	Form into smallish patties and dust with rice flour. Heat a thin layer of oil in a large pan and in 2 or 3 lots pan-fry until cooked and well coloured. Drain well and serve on banana leaves with the chilli sauce on the side.
vegetable oil	
banana leaves	

There are many influences evident in Balinese (and Indonesian) food. The famous Nasi Goreng and Mie Goreng (fried rice or noodles) certainly have similarities to the Ch'ao Fan and Ch'ao Mein of China's south. And Lumpia rolls are certainly recognisable to any lover of the good old spring roll. Satays which are to be found in different guises throughout the islands of Indonesia are deemed to have originated in the Middle East although anyone from that region would now be hard pressed to recognise them (see page 145). And even the rijstafel (rice table), which entails serving a number of different dishes all at once is a Dutch creation, although the dishes themselves are in most cases authentically Indonesian.

Vegetarian Lumpia Rolls with Sweet & Sour Sauce

Serves 4–6

— as cooked by chef Michael Blackie from the Bali Oberoi

1 tbsp (½ fl oz) vegetable oil ⅓ medium carrot, peeled & julienned 2–3 spring (green) onions, julienned ¼ small savoy cabbage, shredded 1 small handful bean shoots	Heat oil in a wok and sauté until fairly tender (yet still crisp).
60 ml (2 fl oz) chicken stock (bought or homemade, see page 280) a good splash of soy sauce freshly ground salt & pepper	Add and cook for a few minutes. Cool.
spring roll wrappers 50 gm (1¾ oz) flour mixed with 60 ml (2 fl oz) water	One at a time, put wrapper on board with one corner pointing towards you. Lay a thin cigar of the filling across the centre. Fold the edges in like an envelope and then roll up, sealing with a dab of flour mix. Refrigerate for at least 10 minutes.
1 tbsp (½ fl oz) vegetable oil 2 medium onions, finely sliced 3 small chillies, finely sliced 1 lemongrass stalk, white part only, smashed & finely sliced	Heat oil in a pan and sauté.
1 heaped tbsp sugar 60 ml (2 fl oz) white vinegar	Add and cook until reduced by half.
1 heaped tbsp tomato paste	Add and stir until well mixed.

Bali: Seminyak

60 ml (2 fl oz) chicken stock (bought or homemade, see page 280) 125 ml (4 fl oz) water ½ cup (3 oz) chopped fresh pineapple	Add and cook for a few minutes.
1 tbsp cornflour (cornstarch) mixed with 1 tbsp (½ fl oz) water	Slowly add, a little at a time, until lightly thickened. Strain.
1½ litres (1⅕ quarts) vegetable oil	Heat in a wok or deep sided pot to 180–190°C (350–375°F). Fry rolls without overcrowding, until golden brown. Drain on paper towels.
carrot julienne fresh coriander (cilantro) sprigs	Garnish with carrot and coriander and serve with sauce on the side.

'Julienned vegetables are fine slices of vegetables about 6 or 7 cm long. They can either be done by hand with a sharp, thin knife, or, far easier, on a mandolin (bench slicer).'

When I first went to Thailand, I must admit that I followed my normal practice of keeping clear of most street food (for hygienic reasons). But I soon corrected this error in my ways because this is one country where I would recommend eating on the street. Not only, in most cases, are the stalls' hygiene standards rather good, but some of Thailand's best peasant dishes are available. I ate the best Som Tam of my visit at a tiny stall in Bangkok, whilst in the night bazaar market I had a terrific mussel pancake stuffed with crispy beanshoots followed by a sweet pancake (roti), which was also pretty good (sort of a moveable feast). I also had some terrific noodles in Chiang Mai and was almost tempted to repeat the exercise in Bangkok after reading this story in the Lonely Planet guide: 'A vendor possessing a new angle to the perfect bowl of noodles can expect word to travel fast. Several years ago a rumour circulated around Bangkok that a particular noodle vendor was dosing his soup with aphrodisiacs whose miraculous effects were being celebrated by all those who consumed it.' The chef was an overnight success and quickly made a small fortune, but unfortunately for all his clients it soon became apparent that it was a hoax.

Gold Bags with Sweet Chilli Sauce (Thung Tong)

Serves 12–16

– as bought from a street vendor in Bangkok

vegetable oil ½ large onion, finely chopped 1 garlic clove, crushed	Heat a little oil in a wok and sauté gently.
150 gm (5 oz) minced (ground) chicken	Add and toss until it changes colour.
1 heaped tsp shaved palm sugar 1 tbsp grated fresh galangal (or ginger) 4 spring (green) onions, finely chopped 2 tbsp chopped fresh coriander (cilantro)	Add and mix well.
tamarind water (see page 32) Asian fish sauce	Add to taste. Cool a little.
square wonton wrappers toothpicks	Place one on top of another to form a star. Wet edges with a little water and place a teaspoon of mix in centre. Gather up corners to form pouch and put two toothpicks through crossways to seal.
1½ litres (1⅕ quarts) vegetable oil	Heat in wok or deep pot to 180°C (350°F) and fry 'bags' until golden.
sweet chilli sauce (see page 281)	Serve with sauce on the side.

Thailand: Bangkok

How can you resist a dish that is called Galloping Horses (Mar Hor)? I must admit I couldn't find out any reason or explanation for such a name – the finished dish certainly didn't look like a horse (except for maybe the one which I backed in last years' Melbourne Cup and which I think is most probably still running). But jokes aside, it is a terrific starter in the Thai style which encompasses the typical sweet and salty flavours. It can be served on fruit such as pineapple or orange, but can also be served on betel leaves if you prefer.

Galloping Horses (Mar Hor)

Serves 4–6

– as cooked at Bangkok's Sukothai Hotel

2 tbsp (1 fl oz) vegetable oil 4 garlic cloves, crushed 3 small red chillies, finely chopped	Heat oil in a wok and briefly cook.
250 gm (8 oz) finely minced (ground) pork	Add and cook, mashing as you do so to seal and separate.
2–3 tbsp shaved palm sugar 3 tbsp (1½ fl oz) Asian fish sauce 3 tbsp pan-roasted peanuts (see page 50), coarsely chopped 4 spring (green) onions, chopped 6 cherry tomatoes, quartered chicken stock (bought or homemade, see page 280)	Add, along with a little water or stock and cook gently until thick and fragrant (adding more liquid if necessary).
2–3 tbsp chopped fresh coriander (cilantro)	Add, mix in and taste for seasoning.
1 small ripe pineapple, sliced & cored 1 long red chilli, seeded & finely sliced	Arrange pineapple slices on platter, mound pork mix in centre and sprinkle with chilli.

'The easiest way to prepare pineapple slices – cut into slices and with a pastry cutter that fits just inside the skin, cut into rounds. Then with a small cutter, remove core.'

Thailand: Bangkok

I have always loved caviar but these days cannot afford it and, even though last year it was allowed back into Australia for about one minute, in recent years have been unable to purchase it. (Because the sturgeon, the fish from which true caviar is harvested, was deemed to be an endangered species, the government banned its importation.)

But all is not lost. There is a farmed version from the States that is pretty good, although still expensive. And while salmon caviar may not be a substitute for 'the real thing', it does have its own distinctive personality. For a start it pops in your mouth just like the real stuff. And, secondly, the Yarra Valley Salmon Company in Victoria is producing lots so it's super fresh, freely available and reasonably priced to boot.

Add to that the fact that the salmon are farmed in crystal-clear water diverted from and then returned to the Rubicon River (one of the main problems with sturgeon is the fact that the Caspian and Black Seas are so polluted that numbers are dramatically down).

Hashbrown Cakes with Sour Cream & Salmon Caviar

Serves 4–6

— as cooked on the banks of the Rubicon

4 large potatoes, peeled	Cook in plenty of lightly salted boiling water until almost tender. Drain, cool and grate.
a slurp of sweet chilli sauce (see page 281)	Add and mix well (adding another egg if too dry or a little flour if too wet). Then form into cakes either free form or using a pastry cutter.
2 corn cobs (ear of corn), kernels removed	
2 eggs	
3 tbsp snipped fresh chives	
4 spring (green) onions, finely chopped	
freshly ground salt & pepper	
olive oil	Heat a thin layer of oil in a heavy-bottomed pan and cook, on both sides, until a crust has formed.
sour cream	Drain and top with a generous dollop of sour cream and caviar.
salmon caviar	

Australia: Yarra Valley

Little Popovers with Salmon Caviar & Sour Cream

— as prepared in a Daylesford Hotel Kitchen

70 gm (2½ oz) plain (all-purpose) flour, sifted 125 ml (4 fl oz) milk ¼ tsp salt 1 egg, lightly beaten 1 tbsp (½ oz) melted butter	Using a wooden spoon, mix together.
oil spray	Lightly oil baby muffin trays. Add mix to ⅔ full, place into a cold oven, turn on to 200°C (400°F) and cook for 15–20 minutes until golden and risen. Allow to cool a little in the trays.
sour cream salmon caviar	Top with sour cream and salmon caviar and serve at room temperature.

'This delicious recipe is from my New Zealand mate Ruth Pretty's book, The Ruth Pretty Cookbook.'

One of my favourite cheeses is the Persian feta from the Yarra Valley Dairy. Developed originally in conjunction with leading cheesemaker–consultant Richard Thomas, it is packed in olive oil with fresh herbs and is soft and rich with lots of flavour. Perfect in salads or just smeared on good bread, I also discovered that it is a delicious addition to scrambled eggs.

Scrambled Eggs with Persian Feta
Serves 4
— as cooked at the Yarra Valley Dairy

8 eggs 2 tbsp (1 oz) cream freshly ground salt & pepper	Beat together, to just combine, with a fork.
a good dollop of butter	Melt in a large pan (don't brown). Add egg mix and scramble lightly, pulling edge of eggs into centre continually. When <u>soft</u> curds form, remove from heat.
2 tbsp cubed Persian (or any soft) feta	Add, off the heat, and stir until melted.
4 thick slices country-style bread, toasted or grilled 2 tbsp chopped fresh chives	Put toast on plates, top with eggs then sprinkle with chives.

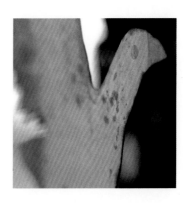

Australia: Yarra Valley

BBQ Prosciutto Wrapped Figs Stuffed with Feta

Serves 4

– as cooked at the Yarra Valley Dairy

wooden skewers	Soak in cold water, to avoid burning, for at least 30 minutes.
12 fresh figs 12 cubes of feta 12 slices prosciutto	Cut figs in cross shape from top almost through to the bottom. Stuff with cheese and tightly wrap a slice of prosciutto around the outside. Place 3 figs on each skewer.
olive oil spray	Preheat BBQ or ridged grill. Spray figs with oil and cook until heated and prosciutto is slightly crispy.

Australia: Yarra Valley

I must admit that I'm not the greatest golfer in the world. In fact the only time I actually hit a half decent shot was when I was about ten and I made a wonderful drive right through our neighbour's front picture window. But even I was tempted to get out on the greens when I visited the Sebel Lodge in the Yarra Valley. Designed by Jack Nicklaus, this is the golf course to end all golf courses, but after slicing my first shot I left it to the pros and went back to cooking with chef Marc Brown (who makes the most fabulous black pudding amongst other good things).

Prawn, Trout & Sesame Toasts

Serves 4–8

– as cooked by Marc Brown at the Sebel

6 large green prawns (shrimps), peeled, de-veined & chopped 1 fillet smoked trout, chopped 4 red (French) shallots, finely sliced a pinch of sea salt	Pound in a mortar, or process, until smooth.
4 slices country-style bread, halved 25 gm (¾ oz) sesame seeds vegetable oil	Spread evenly on bread, sprinkle with sesame seeds then shallow fry in hot oil for 2 minutes on each side. Drain well on paper towels.

'Marc served this on a salad of cucumber or homemade cucumber pickles and leaves with a dressing spiked with harissa and fresh wasabi.'

Croque Monsieur is one of the great sandwiches of the world (along with New York's Reuben and Bill Granger's lobster numbers). Basically, it is little more than a ham and cheese sanga, pan-fried. But in France, it is the ingredients that set it aside – hand-sliced ham off the bone, a good tasty cheese such as gruyère, the best country-style bread and, if you're lucky, a generous smear of Dijon mustard.

This version which, as you may notice, has nothing whatsoever to do with the original, is also a ripper, and if I remember correctly, came from New Zealand's *Cuisine* magazine.

Smoked Salmon Croque Monsieur
Serves 6

– as cooked at Walter Peak High Country Farm in Queenstown

170 gm (5½ oz) gruyère	Slice finely either by hand or on a mandolin.
12 slices toast bread 350 gm (11 oz) sliced smoked salmon	Lay six slices of bread on a board and top with cheese and then the salmon. Place other piece of bread on top and cut off crusts.
soft, unsalted butter	Spread on both sides and pan-fry until golden brown in a non-stick pan over moderate heat. Drain on paper towels and cut into quarters.

New Zealand: Queenstown

Jamon, Roasted Capsicum & Cheese Toasties
Serves 4

– as cooked on the boardwalk at Geelong

8 thick slices country-style bread pesto, bought or homemade (see page 281)	Lightly smear four slices of bread with pesto.
8 pieces roasted red capsicum (bell pepper), see page 133 8 slices gruyère (or other tasty cheese) 4–8 slices of jamon (or prosciutto)	Lay on top, then press other pieces of bread firmly on top.
soft, unsalted butter	Spread both sides evenly with butter then pan fry or cook on a ridged grill with a weight on top (use another pan or a brick wrapped in foil) until golden brown on both sides. You can also cook in a sandwich grill.

Australia: Great Ocean Road

In Australia, particularly in Melbourne, there has been a boom in pizza outlets. And, finally, we are getting close to the original little number which started off as little more than a way to use the leftover bread scraps – maybe smeared with a little fresh tomato sauce and a couple of olives or even just a sprinkling of good olive oil and maybe some fresh herbs. Since those humble beginnings we have seen everything from 'the lot' which involves every so-called Italian ingredient known to man, to the Hawaiian (which, I hate to say, I quite enjoy as long as the ham is from the bone and the pineapple is fresh) and, in more recent times, the so-called gourmet which even includes a Tandoori Chicken version whose creator deserves to be hung, drawn and quartered.

But I digress. Sure there are still many pizza joints serving such abominations, but the current trend leans towards crisp, thin bases topped with limited amounts of the very best ingredients (the limited topping ensures that the base will remain crisp). The best I have ever had was cooked by the admirable George Biron (see page 26) but just to prove that you maybe should do as I say not as I do, here is my pizza pie which, although it is rather tasty, would make any Italian cringe.

Huey's Pizza Pie Serves 4–6
– as cooked while George Biron wasn't watching

olive oil spray
2 sheets bought puff pastry
Italian tomato-based cooking sauce
12 slices salami

Preheat oven to 200°C (400°F).
Spray a baking sheet lightly and place one sheet of pastry on top. Smear with tomato sauce, leaving an edge all around and top with a layer of salami.

½–1 punnet (tub) cherry tomatoes, quartered
4–6 anchovies, chopped
8–10 pitted black olives, chopped
6 fresh basil leaves, torn
freshly grated mozzarella
freshly grated parmesan

Scatter over the top.

---

1 egg
60 ml (2 fl oz) milk

Beat together and paint the rim. Top with the other pastry sheet and crimp edges with a fork. Paint the lot with the egg wash and bake for about 20 minutes until risen and golden brown. Serve in wedges with a salad on the side.

The Wizard of Oz

The man behind the Great Barrier Feast on Hamilton Island is none other than the esteemed Len Evans. Regarded by many as the father of the Australian wine trade, every year this supreme enthusiast puts together a great team for this highly enjoyable weekend. In his words he 'just rings up a few friends and invites them to a party', which may explain the party atmosphere but, in the typical Evans manner, may be a little bit of a simplification of the whole process.

Actually, when we were putting together the first series of Never Trust a Skinny Cook there were a few people who we wondered whether they would be recognised or even understood on the world stage. This was certainly not a problem with our Mr Evans. Apart from being Australia's first wine columnist in 1962 and writing the first major wine book in 1973 he has also been a senior wine judge at every major Australian wine show and, these days, is chairman of a number of them. And, along the way, he has managed to pick up a few awards including an OBE in 1982, the Chevalier de L'Ordre Merite Agricole from the French government in 1993, was judged to be Decanter Magazine's (UK) 'Man of the Year' in 1997 and was also awarded an Order of Australia in 1999.

Oh, and I almost forgot, he just happens to have been a champion of the wines of the Hunter Valley, first of all with Rothbury Estate and now with Tower Estate where one of his partners is superstar chef Rick Stein.

'Just a few notes. Poritake is available at Japanese markets, but if not available you could use togarashi which is a Japanese spice mix. This and the lotus chips are available in most Asian markets, while sashimi grade tuna is the absolute highest grade and is available only in specialist fishmongers.'

Tuna Tataki

Serves 4–6

— as prepared at the Great Barrier Feast by Paul Wade from the Little Nell Restaurant in Aspen

250 ml (8 fl oz) soy sauce 125 ml (4 fl oz) water 60 ml (2 fl oz) fresh lemon juice 60 ml (2 fl oz) fresh lime juice 1–2 garlic cloves, crushed 1 knob ginger, peeled & grated 1 tangerine, portioned	To make ponzu dressing, mix together, set aside for 24 hours, then strain.
450 gm (14¼ oz) sashimi grade tuna, cut into square blocks	Either using a blow torch or a very hot grill, sear quickly on all sides.
poritake (a mixture of toasted seaweed & sesame seeds, see note above)	Roll tuna in this and then slice neatly and evenly into thin slices.
3 cups wonga bok (Chinese white cabbage) shredded ½ cup (2½ oz) red capsicum (bell pepper) julienne ½ cup (2½ oz) carrot julienne ½ cup (2½ oz) pea shoots sweet chilli sauce (bought)	Gently toss with sweet chilli sauce to taste.
250 ml (8 fl oz) mirin (Japanese rice wine) 1 cup (6 oz) pickled ginger	Process.
fried lotus chips	Mound salad on plates. Spoon a little more sweet chilli sauce around, then arrange tuna on top, garnish with lotus chips and spoonfuls of the pickled ginger mix. Sprinkle with ponzu.

'I always make more mayonnaise than is needed as it keeps well and is delicious on everything from sandwiches to salads and even my breakfast eggs.'

Dill-flavoured Egg Salad with Smoked Salmon

Serves 4

– as cooked on the beach at Hamilton Island

6 eggs	Place in boiling water and when they come back to the boil cook for exactly 7 minutes. Drain, cool and peel. Chop coarsely.
1 heaped tsp Dijon mustard 2 eggs 2 egg yolks a pinch of salt a little ground pepper	Put in a food processor and whiz up for 1 minute.
500 ml (16 fl oz) vegetable oil fresh lemon juice 1 heaped tsp chopped fresh dill	Add oil little by little, through the feeder tube. Then add lemon juice to taste and the dill. Add mayonnnaise to taste, to chopped eggs and mix well.
4 thick slices country-style bread 4–8 slices smoked salmon mustard cress	Toast or grill bread. Put on plates and top with salmon then a mound of egg salad. Garnish with mustard cress.

Australia: Hamilton Island

Raw Tuna with Shredded Apple, Ponzu Dressing & Wasabi Flavoured Roe

– as cooked by Geoff Lindsay at the Great Barrier Feast

300 gm (10 oz) sashimi grade tuna (see page 47)	Dice into 5 mm (¼ inch) cubes.
5 cm (2 inch) daikon (white radish), shredded	Gently toss with the tuna.
5 cm (2 inch) carrot, shredded	
1 Granny Smith apple, shredded	
1 tbsp roasted sesame seeds	
1 tbsp roasted pine nuts	
1 heaped tsp grated fresh wasabi (or wasabi paste)	
50 gm wasabi tobbiko (flying fish roe)	
80 ml (2½ fl oz) light soy sauce	
120 ml (4 fl oz) extra virgin olive oil	
a squeeze of fresh lime juice	
4 fresh wasabi leaves (see below), or banana leaves	Mound salad on leaves.

'Fresh wasabi is now being grown in Tasmania – it's expensive but, wow, what a taste sensation. And the flying fish roe, which is becoming increasingly popular, is available in specialist fishmongers or delis.'

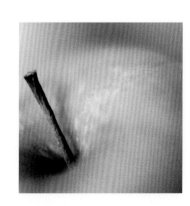

I was invited to a cocktail party at the Bali Oberoi. I thought I was rather special until I arrived and discovered that every guest in the hotel, including Mr Moon, had been invited. (What was that old Groucho Marx quote: 'If any club allows me to be a member then I don't want to join'. Well, I felt a little like that.) Anyway, grumbling aside, the finger food was delicious. Lumpia (spring) rolls with a sweet and sour sauce (see page 34), Satay Lilit with Sambal Tomat (spiced minced seafood satays, see page 145) and my favourite, Rempah, which are the tastiest meat patties with a rather pungent sauce flavoured heavily with kecap manis, the Indonesian sweet soy. After making an absolute pig of myself and eating about 4000 of the blessed things, I thought I better have a shot at making them myself and here is the result (and talking of snacks, the fried peanuts that they served in the bar were pretty terrific too, see page 52).

Beef Patties with Coconut (Rempah)   Serves 4–6

– as cooked by the pool at the Bali Oberoi

150 gm (5 oz) grated fresh coconut
400 gm (13 oz) lean minced (ground) beef
1 tbsp (½ fl oz) kecap manis
1 tsp ground coriander
1 tsp ground cumin
2 garlic cloves, crushed
freshly ground salt & pepper

Mix together thoroughly. With wet hands, form into small patties.

---

vegetable oil
rice flour

Heat a good layer of oil in a large non-stick pan. Flour the patties and fry until well browned. Drain well on paper towels.

---

3 chillies, finely sliced
4 tbsp (2 fl oz) kecap manis
4 tbsp (2 fl oz) fresh lime juice

Mix together.

---

banana leaves
¼ cup (1½ oz) pan-roasted peanuts (see below)
grated fresh coconut

Put a square of banana leaf on individual plates or platter. Pile patties on top, sprinkle generously with sauce then with peanuts and coconut.

'To pan roast peanuts (or any nuts), just rub the skins off then toss them in a dry hot pan until a fragrant smell appears.'

*'A terrific snack – normal celery leaves could be used,
as long as they are small'*

Fried Peanuts with Garlic & Chinese Celery
(Kacang Tojin)
– as cooked on the beach at Legian

500 gm (16 oz) whole raw peanuts	Rub skins off.
6 garlic cloves, crushed 1 tsp sea salt flakes	Mix together. Rub into peanuts and set aside for 15 minutes.
6 cups (1⅕ quarts) vegetable oil	Heat oil to 180–190°C (350–375°F) in a wok or deep sided pot. Add peanuts and fry for about 10 minutes until golden brown. Drain well in fine sieve then scatter over paper towels.
8 large red (French) shallots, finely sliced Chinese celery leaves (see page 237)	Then fry shallots for about 2–3 minutes until crisp. Remove and drain as above. Repeat process with celery leaves. Allow all to cool then toss together.

Bali: Legian

'A recipe derived from Kiwi author Annabel
Langbein who, to my mind, produces just about
New Zealand's best cookbooks.'

Smoked Mackerel Fritters with
Avocado Salsa

Serves 4

— as cooked in Lord of the Rings country just outside Queenstown

1 ripe avocado, sliced	Mix together and set aside.
1 small red onion, sliced	
2 tbsp chopped fresh coriander (cilantro)	
grated zest & juice of 2 limes	
sea salt	
pinch of cayenne	
a good splash of olive oil	

200 gm (6½ oz) self-raising flour	Whisk until smooth.
2 eggs	
1 tsp salt	
125 ml (4 fl oz) soda water	
freshly ground pepper	

350 gm (11 oz) flaked smoked mackerel	Add and mix through.
¼ cup (⅓ oz) chopped fresh coriander (cilantro)	
grated zest of ½ lime	

vegetable oil	Heat a thin layer in a pan and drop in dessertspoons of the mix (don't overcrowd pan). Cook until golden brown then drain well on paper towels and serve with the avocado salsa.

New Zealand: Queenstown

The Oberoi Hotel which is situated on the Pte aux Piments in North Mauritius (on the north side of the Baie de L'Arsenal) has to be one of the world's great hotels. Described as a garden with rooms, the individual pavilions have been designed in a mix of African and Asian styles which reflect the richness of Mauritian culture. There are a couple of terrific pools, a luxurious spa centre and a great restaurant (see page 122) which is situated in a large open sided pagoda. The bar and private dining areas are in a similar style and the staff are both friendly and highly professional. (My daughter Charlotte was going through her spaghetti bolognese stage and it wasn't until late in our stay that we realised it wasn't on any menu in the resort but the chef had whipped up a pot of ragu just in case after we had mentioned it in passing – she ate it every day.) One of the waiters also told me of a favourite local dish, chilli eggs, which often appeared in the staff canteen. Needless to say I didn't quite make it to the canteen but, following his directions, I cooked them and had a most enjoyable lunch.

Mauritian Hot Chilli Eggs

Serves 4

– as cooked by the pool at the Oberoi

8 large eggs	Put in boiling water and when they come back to the boil cook for exactly 6 minutes. Plunge into cold water and when cold, drain and peel. Gently prick all over with a fork.
vegetable oil 2 onions, finely chopped 1 lemongrass stalk, white part only, smashed & finely sliced 3 chillies, finely sliced 2 garlic cloves, crushed 1 heaped tsp grated fresh ginger	Heat a little oil in a pot or deep pan and sauté gently until tender.
½ tsp shrimp paste 1 heaped tsp turmeric ½ tsp tamarind paste 2 cups (16 fl oz) water	Add and mix well.
1–2 tsp hot chilli sauce 2 fresh thyme sprigs 8 curry leaves 2 pinches sugar 2 ripe tomatoes, seeded, peeled, & chopped (see page 21) freshly ground salt & pepper	Add, stir and rapidly cook for about 10 minutes, adding more water if necessary.
1½ litres (1⅕ quarts) vegetable oil a small handful of fresh coriander (cilantro) leaves steamed rice	Heat oil in a wok or deep sided pot to about 180°C (350°F) (see page 223). Add eggs and cook to golden brown. Drain well. put in sauce and cook very gently for 5 minutes or so, turning regularly. Fold in coriander and serve with rice on the side.

Mauritius: Baie de L'Arsenal

Nasi Goreng has to be about Bali's most popular dish. Served at every meal, including breakfast, I am surprised that the American fast food joints don't have it on their menus (but, then again, maybe they do because I certainly didn't darken their doors).

As a man who began his whole Chinese experience by eating 'No. 93: Fried Rice with BBQ Pork' on a regular basis, I enjoyed the odd plate of Nasi Goreng. But not as much as producer Michael Dickinson who ate it morning, noon and night and became such an expert that he started criticising the way the egg was cooked. (There are two schools of thought here: some like it crispy in the manner of the crispy-crunchy Chinese home-style eggs, while others appear to like it more in the Anglo-Saxon style, slowly cooked and just set.) Anyway, ignoring the instant expert (after all, a little bit of knowledge is a dangerous thing), I turned to the kitchen staff at Waka Padma Hotel. None could quite agree on the egg but they did give me some hints as to cooking my first ever Nasi Goreng, and then, to my horror, turned up to watch as I made my first attempt for the camera.

Indonesian Fried Rice with an Egg (Nasi Goreng)

Serves 2

— as cooked by the pool at Waka Padma

3 tbsp (1½ fl oz) vegetable oil 3 red (French) shallots, finely sliced 2 garlic cloves, finely sliced 2–3 red chillies, finely chopped	Heat oil in a wok and sauté gently for a few minutes.
1 large skinless chicken breast, cubed	Add and toss until sealed.
2 ripe tomatoes, finely chopped ¼ small wonga bok (Chinese white cabbage), finely shredded 1–2 tbsp (½–1 fl oz) kecap manis 4 cups (20 oz) cooked jasmine rice	Add along with rice, a little at a time, and cook, continually stirring, until heated through.
2 eggs	At the same time, fry the eggs to the desired degree.
fried red (French) shallots (bought or homemade, see page 52)	Mound rice on plates, top with eggs and sprinkle with shallots.

'The rice should be cooked at least the day before (about 2 cups raw = 4 cooked) and, before using, break up any lumps with your hands. And the reason the recipe is only for two — so you don't overcrowd the wok, otherwise it will stew not fry.'

After the Grand Marque champagne tasting at the Great Barrier Feast in Hamilton Island, I ended up at the Night Club. As I was about to leave, fellow TV chef Geoff Jansz was just arriving. So what could I do? Being the nice sort of fellow that I am I stayed for a few more and the rest of the night is a blur. Except when I got home I whipped up a bit of a snack. (I know this because the next morning you should have seen the state of the kitchen – where is Mr Moon when you need him?) I also returned to the club the next night, to be welcomed with open arms by the bouncers, so I obviously hadn't misbehaved. But I was a bit worried when I got inside to be greeted by the band who asked whether I was going to come up and sing 'Sweet Home Alabama' just like I did last night. To my assertion that I didn't even know the words I was dismayed to be told that 'last night you did'. The moral of the story – don't drink with TV chefs (myself included).

Muffin Melts

Serves 4

— as cooked late at night, in my hotel room at Hamilton Island

1 tbsp (½ fl oz) vegetable oil
1 tbsp (½ oz) butter
4 rindless bacon rashers, halved
honey

Preheat overhead grill. Heat oil and butter in a pan and fry bacon until just crispy. Add a good splash of honey and toss to coat.

4 English muffins, halved
2 handfuls grated tasty cheese

Place muffins, cut side up, on an oven tray. Top with bacon and then cheese and grill until golden brown. Serve with some bacon cooking juices over the top.

Australia: Hamilton Island

When we were in Chiang Mai between dodging buckets of water (see page 102), we stayed at the amazing Four Seasons Chiang Mai Resort. Designed by noted Thai architect Chulathat Kitibutr, the fantastic pavilions are set around a working rice paddy complete with water buffalos and workers garbed in traditional dress. There are also a number of pools, a highly rated spa, two tennis courts and a health centre. And for those of us who are less physically minded, two excellent restaurants and a bar where the *Skinny Cook* team were often to be found (doing research, of course). And during that 'research', I discovered these delicious sweetcorn cakes which I, of course, just had to try.

Corn Cakes with Cucumber Pickles

Serves 4

– as served at the Elephant Bar

2 chillies, seeded & finely sliced	Whisk together to dissolve sugar.
¼ red onion, finely sliced	
3 tbsp (1½ fl oz) Asian fish sauce	
3 tbsp (1½ fl oz) cold water	
3 tbsp (1½ fl oz) fresh lime juice	
2 tbsp shaved palm sugar	

1–2 continental (telegraph) cucumbers, sliced	Add to above, toss well and leave for 30 minutes, tossing every now and then.

2 cups fresh corn kernels	Mix to combine well, then refrigerate for 30 minutes.
1 egg	
2 tbsp chopped fresh coriander (cilantro)	
1 tbsp red curry paste	
3 tbsp rice flour	
1–2 chillies, seeded & finely sliced	
2 tbsp finely chopped spring (green) onion	

vegetable oil	When ready, heat a thin layer of oil in a large pan. Drop tablespoonfuls of mix into pan and cook until golden on both sides (don't overcrowd pan). Drain well on paper towels. To serve, arrange cakes on plate and top with pickles.

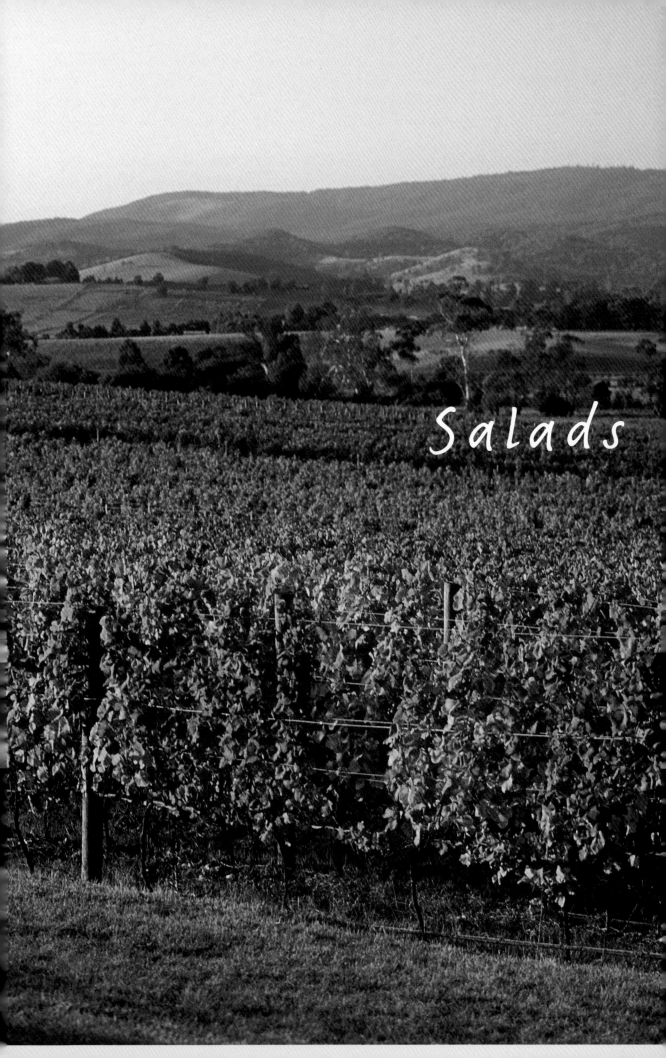

Salads

Peter Howard (chef, author, raconteur and former presenter on Channel Nine's *Today Show*) is one of Noosa's movers and shakers. Ensconced on a property just outside town he is the man I turn to for advice on everything concerning Noosa's food scene. And, in fact, it was he who first mentioned Coolabine Farmstead at Kenilworth where they are producing some terrific goat cheeses (see page 30) and also mentioned the ripper food that new arrival, Matt McConnell, was whipping up.

A true enthusiast, he is past president of Australia's Food Media Club, has often travelled overseas as an ambassador for Aussie food, is a highly regarded cheese judge and has written a number of books.

Thai Beef Salad

Serves 4

— as cooked by Peter Howard on the boardwalk at Noosa Heads

500 gm (16 oz) porterhouse, rump (sirloin), or fillet (tenderloin)	Trim off all fat and sinew and cut into 2 cm (¾ inch) thick slices.
olive oil spray	Spray grill or BBQ and cook steak to desired degree.
1 chilli, seeded & finely sliced 2 kaffir lime leaves, shredded grated zest & juice of 1 lime 1 tsp brown sugar 2 tbsp (1 fl oz) Asian fish sauce	Whisk in a bowl.
½ cup mixed lettuce leaves ½ cup fresh coriander (cilantro) leaves ½ cup fresh mint leaves ½ cup fresh Thai basil leaves 2 spring (green) onions, cut into 2 cm (¾ inch) lengths	Toss with beef and dressing to taste. Mound on plates.
2 tbsp pan-roasted peanuts (see page 50)	Sprinkle over the top along with a little more dressing.

Australia: Noosa

Hamilton Island is one of the 74 tropical islands in the Coral Sea. It is the largest inhabited island in the Whitsunday group. Discovered by Captain James Cook in 1770, the group was so named because the *Endeavour* passed through their waters on White Sunday (the seventh Sunday after Easter).

It is situated halfway between the Queensland coast and the Great Barrier Reef which is one of Australia's premium tourist destinations. The most extensive reef system in the world, it is also the largest World Heritage Area.

And although the resort itself is the largest in the Whitsundays (with accommodation for over 2000, its own airport, a 200 berth boat marina and many restaurants, shops and bars), over 80 per cent of the island remains in its natural state and is home to many Australian animals and birdlife.

Greek Lamb Salad

Serves 4

— as cooked overlooking the Whitsunday Passage

2–3 lamb backstraps (boned loin), trimmed of all fat & sinew olive oil freshly ground salt & pepper 1 lemon	Preheat a ridged grill or BBQ. Cook oiled lamb to desired degree, seasoning once sealed and squeezing lemon juice over the top as it cooks. Remove, sprinkle with more lemon juice and rest for a few minutes.
125 ml (4 fl oz) olive oil 1–2 tbsp (½–1 fl oz) red wine vinegar a squeeze of fresh lemon juice 2 garlic cloves, crushed freshly ground salt & pepper	Whisk together.
½ cup (4 oz) plain yoghurt 2 garlic cloves, crushed a squeeze of fresh lemon juice	Mix together.
3 ripe, red tomatoes, cored & cut into wedges ½–1 continental (telegraph) cucumber cut in thick slices then halved 2–3 tbsp pitted black olives ¼ cup (1¼ oz) crumbled feta ½ red onion, finely sliced 3 tbsp fresh oregano leaves	Toss with dressing to taste. Mound on individual plates. Slice lamb and place on top, sprinkling with a bit more dressing. Then flick the yoghurt over the top.

What is it that Queenslanders have with BIG edifices? If you have never been to this part of the world you won't have the faintest idea what I'm talking about, but not far from Noosa at Nambour is THE BIG PINEAPPLE a so-called theme park based around, you guessed it, pineapples. Kitsch as all get out, this is no Disneyland and, in fact, is little more than a bloody huge pineapple (which you can climb), a miniature train and lots of pretty tacky souvenirs. But I must say the pineapple-based sundaes and the like aren't bad although the place has never inspired me to then race off to THE BIG PRAWN and other similar Queensland icons (I think there may even be a BIG COCKROACH, but I may have imagined this).

Vietnamese Chicken Coleslaw
— as cooked in a Queensland pineapple field

Serves 4

1 lemongrass stalk, white part only, smashed & finely sliced 2 star anise 6 whole black peppercorns 3 fresh kaffir lime leaves, shredded a pinch of rock salt 2 cups (16 fl oz) chicken stock (bought or homemade, see page 280)	Place in a pot and bring to the boil.
2 skinless chicken breast breasts	Add and cook very, very gently for 4–5 minutes. Turn heat off, cover and set aside until cooked turning every now and then. Remove chicken and shred.
¼–½ wonga bok (Chinese white cabbage), shredded ½ cup (3 oz) pan-roasted peanuts (see page 50) 1 medium carrot, grated 2 chillies, finely sliced a good handful each of fresh coriander (cilantro) & mint leaves 1 cup chopped fresh pineapple	Put in a bowl with chicken.
2 tbsp (1 fl oz) Asian fish sauce 1 tbsp (½ fl oz) Asian rice wine vinegar 2 tbsp (1 fl oz) vegetable oil juice of 2 limes 1 garlic clove, crushed 1 tbsp shaved palm sugar	Put in a separate bowl and whisk to dissolve sugar. Add to salad to taste. Mound salad in bowls and sprinkle a little more dressing over the top.

Australia: just outside Noosa

Victoria's *Age Good Food Guide* recently awarded the Lake House in Daylesford two hats and gave them 17/20 points. It also said 'Lake House has made special occasions an art form. But then every occasion here is special. There's the sublime setting. Then there's the impressive wine list and the service provided by well trained staff who anticipate every whim. And, of course, there's the food: carefully prepared but not overworked. To say the menu is seasonal is an understatement.'

Sounds good, doesn't it? Well, it is good. Owned and operated by Alla and Allan Wolf-Tasker, The Lake House began as a small restaurant with a few rooms and has now developed into a major country player with a large, well fitted out restaurant, conference rooms, spacious, classy suites of different shapes and sizes and, above all, the good, fresh food which has always been its forte. As they say in the *Michelin Guide* – well worth a journey.

Carpaccio of Beetroot with Baked Feta, Rocket, Walnuts & Pear

Serves 6

— as cooked by Alla Wolf-Tasker at the Lake House

300 gm (10 oz) plain yoghurt 2 fresh chives, finely chopped freshly ground pepper	Drain yoghurt in a coffee filter or very fine sieve overnight in the fridge. Next day mix with chives and a little pepper.
20 cubes of feta, about 2 cm (¾ inch) in diameter 200 gm (6½ oz) plain (all-purpose) flour 4 eggs, beaten 200 gm (6½ oz) breadcrumbs, dried	Preheat oven to 200°C (400°F). Place flour in one bowl, eggs in another and crumbs in a third. Lightly coat feta with flour, then egg, then crumbs.
olive oil spray	Place feta on a lightly oiled baking dish and cook in oven until golden brown on all sides.
juice of ½ lemon 60 ml (2 fl oz) extra virgin olive oil freshly ground salt & pepper	Whisk.
2 medium beetroot (beets), peeled & sliced very finely on a mandolin or bench slicer	Dress with some of the above and place on individual plates in the round.
a good handful of well washed rocket (arugula) a good handful of pan-roasted walnuts (see page 50)	Toss with a little of the lemon oil and mound on top of beetroot.
2 ripe pears, very finely sliced	Mound most on top then place feta around. Top salad with a dollop of yoghurt and then a little more pear.

Australia: Daylesford

The Daylesford–Hepburn Springs region reflects the influence of the Swiss–Italian miners who originally settled here in the last century. Names, architecture and even some of the food shows this heritage. A perfect example of this is the Bullboar Sausage which is still only made in this area. Different to any other sausage I have seen in Australia it is – surprise, surprise – made from bull and boar and, in typical European manner, is a heady mix strongly flavoured with red wine, garlic and a number of spices. They are to be found in most local butcher's shops, on many of the menus and are a feature of the Swiss–Italian Festival, which is held every year.

Bullboar, Potato & White Bean Salad

Serves 4

– as cooked at Daylesford

3–4 Bullboar sausages (or any thick well-flavoured sausage)	Blanch in gently simmering water until just firm when squeezed. Drain.
6 kipfler (or any waxy baby) potatoes, peeled sea salt	At same time, boil potatoes in lightly salted water until tender. Drain and halve lengthways.
olive oil spray	Preheat ridged grill or BBQ. Cook sausages and potatoes spraying with oil and turning every now and then.
6 tbsp (3 fl oz) olive oil 1 tbsp (½ fl oz) sherry vinegar a squeeze of fresh lemon juice 1 garlic clove, crushed	Whisk together.
½ red onion, finely sliced 1 punnet (tub) cherry tomatoes, halved 1 x 400 gm (13 oz) can cannelini beans, drained & rinsed well 2 heaped tbsp fresh Italian (flat leaf) parsley	Slice sausages and toss with potatoes, rest of ingredients and dressing to taste.

When you think of Australia's Yarra Valley what do you think of? You think of wine. World renowned vineyards such as Mt Mary, Yarra Yering, Fergusson's, Coldstream Hills, Di Stasio and Yeringberg producing fabulous cool climate chardonnays, pinots and cabernets.

But the Yarra Valley is not just about wine. Like many other regions in Australia and New Zealand, we are witnessing small producers springing up all over this fertile valley – each of them dedicated to producing the very best and, in many cases, succeeding.

Michael Kennedy from the Healesville Hotel is a great supporter of such producers. Apart from having about the Valley's best wine list and a terrific, highly rated restaurant, his produce store is a haven for local foodies. Actually it was here that I was introduced to the wonderful lettuces, cresses and herbs from his parents-in-law's Harvest Farm. They were so fresh that they almost sang so I wasn't surprised to discover that they are grown just down the road and are harvested and delivered twice a day. (I was reminded of a meal at Robert Carrier's Hintlesham Hall in Sussex in the seventies when the salad was the star of show – made from nine different leaves and herbs all of which were grown in his huge kitchen garden and which were harvested to order.)

BLT Salad with a Poached Egg
– as cooked at Harvest Farm

Serves 4

6 tbsp (3 fl oz) extra virgin olive oil 1 tbsp (½ fl oz) white wine vinegar 1 garlic clove, crushed 1 tbsp (½ fl oz) fresh lemon juice 1 tbsp Dijon mustard freshly ground salt & pepper	Whisk.
2 good handfuls lettuces, cresses & fresh herbs, washed & dried ½ punnet (tub) cherry tomatoes, halved	Tear lettuces and leaves into a bowl and add tomatoes.
8 slices prosciutto olive oil	Pan-fry or grill until crispy and drain well.
white vinegar 4 large eggs	Put a large pan on the heat. Fill to ⅔rd with water and bring to a gentle simmer. Add a splash of vinegar. Break eggs into cups, swirl water with large spoon and float eggs in one at a time. Cook until just set. Toss leaves with dressing to taste and place on individual plates. Top with prosciutto and poached eggs.

Australia: Yarra Valley

There are fledgling industries in both New Zealand and Australia dedicated to the cultivation of truffles. Proving quite successful so far, I wonder whether these countries will eventually provide their own truffle oil (and hopefully it will be cheaper to boot). But until then we will need to use it sparingly as it is certainly expensive.

A Fennel & Mushroom Salad with Truffle Oil   Serves 4
— as cooked at Canberra's National Museum

2–3 medium fennel bulbs	Remove outer and damaged layers and cut out core. Using a mandolin or bench slicer, slice very finely.
1 lemon freshly ground salt & pepper	Place fennel neatly in a bowl or on a platter and squeeze some lemon juice over the top. Season.
12–15 firm button mushrooms, wiped with a damp cloth olive oil truffle oil fennel greens	Slice finely and scatter over the top. Sprinkle with a little more lemon juice, some olive oil and 1–2 tsp of truffle oil. Scatter fennel greens over the top.

'Serve as part of an antipasto selection or with simply grilled meat.'

When you travel throughout Europe, every village and town, no matter how small, appears to have a group of artisan producers making superb handcrafted foods. Until recent times in Australasia, this has been a bit of a rarity. But I am pleased to note this is all changing. Small producers are realising that a premium will be paid for the very best and growers and farmers are cutting out the middleman and value adding by, say, making cheeses from their own milk. In this vein, Poacher's Pantry at Hall (about an hour's drive from Canberra) produces a range of excellent smallgoods from its own and local livestock – everything from bresaola (air-dried beef) and peppered sirloin to hot smoked poultry, garlic and tomatoes.

Prosciutto, Avocado & Orange Salad with a Hot Tomato Vinaigrette

Serves 4

– as cooked at Poacher's Pantry

4 tbsp (2 fl oz) olive oil 12 thin slices prosciutto	Heat oil in a large non-stick pan and fry prosciutto until crisp. Drain well on paper towels.
1 punnet (tub) cherry tomatoes, quartered juice of 2 lemons	Add tomatoes and lemon to the pan and stir for 1 minute. Turn off.
2 large oranges, peeled & segmented 1 large handful rocket (arugula) 1 avocado, peeled & cubed 8 fresh basil leaves, torn freshly ground pepper	Toss in a bowl with the tomato vinaigrette. Place prosciutto on plates, top with salad and pour extra dressing over the top.

Smoked Peppered Sirloin and Pesto Asparagus Salad

Serves 4

– as cooked at Poacher's Pantry

2 bunches asparagus sea salt	Snap woody end off and discard then lightly peel new end. Blanch in a large pot of lightly salted boiling water until just tender. Drain well.
2–3 tbsp pesto (bought or homemade, see page 281) 2 tbsp (1 fl oz) olive oil freshly grated parmesan 6–8 semi-dried tomatoes, sliced	Toss asparagus with pesto, oil, some parmesan and tomatoes.
8–12 slices smoked peppered sirloin (or bresaola) olive oil	Lay a few asparagus spears on individual plates and top with a slice of sirloin. Repeat process, finishing with any leftover pesto on the top and a sprinkling of oil around the plate.

The plantation houses of Mauritius, or those that are left, remind you of days gone by when slaves worked the sugar cane and their French masters sat on the porches being fanned, a la days of the Raj, and drinking, I suppose, rum punch (or maybe champagne). We visited a couple that have survived. First of all, La Maison Eureka at Moka which is also known as the 'mansion of 109 doors' for obvious reasons. Another imposing structure is Le Saint Aubin. Also known as the Maison de Vanille, once again for obvious reasons, this plantation house was built with reclaimed wood from sailing ships and basically operates as a tourist restaurant although it is still surrounded on all sides by working cane fields and a large vanilla plantation.

A Fish Salad with a Spicy Lime & Vanilla Dressing
Serves 4
– as cooked at the Maison de Vanille

125 ml (4 fl oz) fresh lime juice 2 tbsp soft brown sugar 2–3 vanilla beans, split lengthways	Put in a small pot and cook until sugar is dissolved, whisking continually. Turn off heat.
2 chillies, finely sliced 1 tsp grated fresh ginger a splash of Asian fish sauce grated rind of ½ lime 1 small–medium carrot, halved lengthways & finely sliced 125 ml (4 fl oz) peanut oil freshly ground salt & pepper	Add, mix well and set aside.
8 x 100 gm (3½ oz) fish fillets (whiting, dory or sole) peanut oil	Heat a thin layer of oil in a large pan and when almost smoking cook fish in 2 or 3 lots until well coloured. Drain.
1 red onion, finely sliced ¼–½ continental (telegraph) cucumber, finely sliced ½ cup diced ripe pineapple small handful fresh coriander (cilantro) leaves 1–2 tbsp chopped fresh parsley	Put in a bowl. Remove vanilla beans and toss dressing through salad. Place on individual plates.
chopped fresh parsley 4 lime wedges	Place fish on top, sprinkle with parsley and serve with lime on the side.

Steak & Sweet Potato Salad with a Tomato & Chilli Relish

Serves 4

— as cooked in the Mauritian highland

2 sweet potatoes, washed well but unpeeled	Blanch until just tender when pierced with a skewer. Drain well and when cool cut into thick slices (don't overcook).
1 tbsp (½ fl oz) sesame oil 2 tbsp (1 fl oz) kecap manis 2 tbsp (1 fl oz) mirin (Japanese rice wine) grated rind & juice of 1 lime	Whisk.
2 x 180 gm (6 oz) porterhouse, rump (sirloin), or fillet (tenderloin) steaks trimmed of all fat & sinew	Add to marinade, toss well and leave for 30-plus minutes, tossing every now and then.
olive oil 1 large red capsicum (bell pepper), cored, seeded & diced ½ large red onion, finely chopped 2 chillies, seeded & finely chopped 1 heaped tsp grated fresh ginger	Heat a little oil in a pot and sauté.
1–2 x 400 gm (13 oz) cans diced tomatoes, drained a little ½ cup (4 oz) chicken stock (bought or homemade, see page 280) 2 tbsp (1 fl oz) oyster sauce 2 tbsp (1 fl oz) sweet chilli sauce (bought) freshly ground salt & pepper	Add and gently cook for about 10 minutes until thick and fragrant, adding more stock if necessary.
olive oil spray	Preheat a lightly oiled BBQ or ridged grill and cook steaks to desired degree brushing with marinade as you do so. When ready, remove and rest for 5 minutes. At same time cook sliced sweet potato until well coloured.
a handful of baby tatsoi (or baby spinach) leaves, well washed crème fraiche (or sour cream)	To serve, arrange sweet potato on individual plates and top with leaves. Then slice steaks and place on top along with a spoon of relish and a dollop of crème fraiche.

'Very much in the Mauritian style because of the different influences. And tatsoi is a slightly bitter leaf that is available in the lettuce section of specialist greengrocers.'

Mauritius: Central plateau

Smoked marlin is a very popular, rather expensive, Mauritian delicacy. And one of this island's most famous dishes involves both smoked marlin and hearts of palm. It is called Millionaire's Salad and is so named because the ingredients are so bloody expensive. (To get a palm heart you first of all need a three-year-old palm tree. This is then cut down and the trunk is trimmed until you get to the heart which, at the most, would glean enough for six salads – no wonder it's so expensive.)

Smoked Marlin Salad

Serves 4

– as cooked overlooking the Indian Ocean

125 ml (4 fl oz) Asian rice wine vinegar 70 gm (2½ oz) sugar 3 chillies, finely chopped 3 garlic cloves, finely chopped juice of 1 lemon	Combine in a pot and boil for 5 minutes whisking regularly. Set aside to cool.
½ red onion, finely sliced ½ cup diced ripe pineapple small handful bean shoots 2 tbsp fresh coriander (cilantro) leaves a good handful of mixed lettuces, washed & dried ¼ continental (telegraph) cucumber, finely sliced 2–3 tbsp grated fresh coconut	Toss in a bowl and add cooled dressing to taste.
12–16 slices smoked marlin	Place on individual plates, put a mound of salad in the centre and drizzle with a little more dressing.

You can use other smoked fish in this recipe but something oily like eel or mackerel would work best. And if you happen to be a millionaire, you can also add hearts of palm.'

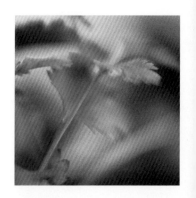

Mauritius: Ile aux Cerfs

Out and about in Queenstown

Queenstown is not just about jumping off bridges and skiing down the side of mountains.

But that said, if that is your want, there are now four bungee jumping sites in Queenstown including the truly scary Nevis Highwire, which at a 134 metres, is New Zealand's highest (Mr Moon screamed all the way down). You can also experience jet-boating or whitewater rafting on the Shotover and Kawarau Rivers, travel down the Skyline Luge, go river boarding through the Roaring Meg section of the Kawarau which includes grades two and three rapids, or leap off Bob's Peak in a hang-glider. And if that's not enough, to crown it all off you can go skydiving where you will be dropped out of an aeroplane to fall at speeds of up to 200 kph.

A visit to nearby Arrowtown is also a must. Once the hub of Central Otago's gold boom, it sprang up when gold was first discovered here in 1862. Many of the original buildings still stand and a feature is the partially restored Chinese Camp, which reflects the strong Cantonese presence in the Central Otago Goldfields. Arrowtown is also home to the very highly rated Saffron Restaurant (listed amongst Conde Nast Travellers 100 Best Tables in the World), who also operate the more casual Pesto and the quirky Blue Door Bar.

Speaking of gold, the 'new gold' of this region is wine. Formerly renowned for its stonefruit orchards, the climate and soil has also proven successful in the production of top end quality cool climate wines. To my mind, the most successful varieties in this area are pinot gris, chardonnay and pinot noir, but I also tasted some terrific crisp, dry rieslings.

Vineyards to visit include Gibbston Valley, Peregrine, Felton Rd, Mt Difficulty and my favourite, Chard Farm. Located just over the road from the Kawarau Bungee Bridge, Chard Farm is perched on the side of a mountain up a rather precarious track (if like me, you tend to over-imbibe in such situations, may I suggest a designated non-drinking driver). Established by one of the regions pioneers, Rob Hay, in 1987, it is only 20 minutes drive from Queenstown itself (and right next door to the Gibbston Valley Vineyard).

And for those of us with a passion for wine, may I also suggest a visit to 'The Big Picture'. Situated just outside Cromwell about 40 kilometres from Queenstown, it is a fascinating concept. Developed by Phil and Cath Parker, it incorporates the Aroma Room where you are introduced to the many smells and aromas associated with wine and an 18 minute virtual flight across the vineyards of Central Otago. During this flight, you enjoy a tasting, tutored by Phil and the winemakers themselves as you 'land' at their vineyards.

Last but not least, this is Lord of the Rings country and there are many tours dedicated to this modern-day phenomenon.

Lamb's Liver & Zucchini Salad
with Sage Butter

Serves 4

— as cooked overlooking Queenstown's Remarkable Mountain Ranges

olive oil 3–4 small zucchini, finely sliced on a mandolin or bench slicer 2 garlic cloves, finely sliced	Heat a little oil in a wok and sauté until lightly browned tossing regularly. Put in a bowl.
12 fresh mint leaves, finely sliced a good splash of mint vinegar a good splash of olive oil sea salt freshly ground pepper	Add to bowl and toss gently. Set aside.
2 lamb's fry (liver), trimmed & sliced plain (all-purpose) flour sea salt freshly ground pepper	Heat a thin layer of oil in a large pan and, in 2 or 3 lots, cook floured, seasoned liver until crusty on the outside but pink within.
100 gm (3½ oz) unsalted butter 12 small fresh sage leaves	Add to pan and heat to light brown. Place zucchini salad on individual plates, top with liver and then pour sage butter over the lot.

New Zealand: Queenstown

I remember my first taste of smoked eel. It was in the late sixties in an Auckland restaurant long since forgotten. But I do remember who produced it – the Van der Drift family from the South Island's West Coast, who pioneered the sale of smoked eel in New Zealand. (Interestingly, when I first came to Australia, I bought eel from their brother-in-law, Joe Fokker, who had the eel fishing rights in Camperdown.)

Still, that aside, after the first taste I was hooked. And it was a real pleasure to come up with this simple salad which, to my mind, works as it cuts through the eel's inherent fattiness perfectly.

Smoked Eel with Watermelon & a Balsamic Glaze

Serves 4

– as cooked on the shores of Lake Wakatipu

½ cup (4 fl oz) balsamic vinegar	Put in a small pot and over high heat, reduce to a glaze. Set aside.
¼–½ watermelon (either seedless or with white seeds)	Remove skin and cut 8 triangles. Place 2 in a square on 4 individual plates.
1 small handful baby tatsoi leaves 1 Granny Smith apple, cored & sliced olive oil	Toss leaves and apple with a little oil.
4 boneless, skinless smoked eel fillets	Place on the watermelon then mound the salad on top. Drizzle balsamic over and around.

'If tatsoi, a rather bitter leaf, is not available use small wild rocket leaves. In similar vein, you could replace the eel with smoked trout fillets.'

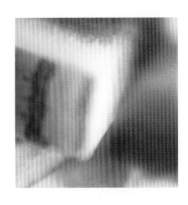

New Zealand: Queenstown

There could be perceived to be a certain degree of bias in this (although surprisingly, I don't think so), but on my visit to New Zealand I thought the quality of the ingredients all across the spectrum was outstanding and appeared to have gone up a notch since my last visit. Wonderful sparkling fresh seafood, tender flavoursome meat (and not just the lamb), and great fruit and vegies. In fact, just about the only criticisms I could make are that the oysters all appeared to be pre-opened and missing that wonderful salty brine which gives them their magic, and that the local wild trout is, sadly, not available commercially.

Crudités with Salmon & an Anchovy Vinaigrette

Serves 6–8

– as cooked on the foreshore at Napier

1 garlic clove, crushed 1 heaped tsp Dijon mustard 2 tbsp (1 fl oz) fresh lemon juice 4–6 anchovies, finely chopped	Whisk.
250 ml (8 fl oz) olive oil	Add little by little, whisking continually.
sea salt 6 baby potatoes, scrubbed 12 baby carrots, peeled 12 medium asparagus tips 12–18 baby beans, halved	In a large pot of salted boiling water, cook spuds until almost tender. Then add carrots and when both are cooked, add beans and asparagus briefly. Drain well and arrange in separate mounds on a platter.
½ punnet (tub) cherry tomatoes 6 baby radishes, halved ¼–½ continental (telegraph) cucumber, cut in thick slices 12 baby spring (green) onions, cleaned	Pile in mounds.
olive oil 2 x 200gm (6½ oz) salmon steaks, skinned & boned	Grill or pan-fry over high heat until crispy on all sides and opaque in the centre. Place in the centre of platter and sprinkle the lot generously with dressing.
2–3 tbsp chopped fresh Italian (flat leaf) parsley crusty bread	Sprinkle with parsley and serve with plenty of crusty bread.

'You, of course, can alter the vegies (or fish) to suit yourself.'

New Zealand: Hawke's Bay

The floating markets or 'talaat naam' of central Thailand are, these days, more of a tourist attraction than the genuine farmers' markets they once were. Originally they were local events where the farmers from the banks of the nearby canals would bring their boats down laden with their wares.

But I still enjoyed my visit to Damnoen Saduak Market in Ratchaburi Province which is about 100 km outside Bangkok. I don't think I've experienced a traffic jam on the river before and, of course, there were lots of shops selling T-shirts and 'antique' carvings. There was also plenty of super fresh produce being sold from the boats and some pretty good snacks too, including some delicious coconut pancakes and the ubiquitous noodle dishes.

Noodle Salad with Prawns & Pineapple

Serves 4

— as enjoyed in a nearby cafe

2 cm (¾ inch) knob of ginger, grated	Whisk.
125 ml (4 fl oz) Asian fish sauce	
2 tbsp shaved palm sugar	
6–8 small red chillies, sliced	
125 ml (4 fl oz) fresh lime juice	
2 packets thin noodles	Bring large pot of water to the boil. Add noodles and baby carrots and when almost tender, add greens just to wilt. Drain well.
4 baby carrots, peeled & sliced on the diagonal	
4 baby bok choy (Chinese chard), sliced	
6 spring (green) onions, cut into lengths	
¼–½ small fresh pineapple, peeled, cored & chopped	Put noodle mix into individual bowls, top with pineapple and prawns and then ladle a generous amount of the sauce over the top.
18–24 cooked, peeled small prawns (shrimps)	

'If any of the dressing is left over, the cafe owner suggested that it makes a great, albeit spicy, salad dressing.'

Thailand

Squid & Snake Bean Salad Lawar (Cumi Cumi)

Serves 4

– as cooked at the Waka di Umi in Ubud

4 cups (32 fl oz) water

400 gm (13 oz) squid tubes, cleaned

6 long (snake) beans, chopped into ½ cm
  (¼ inch) pieces

Bring water to boil. Add squid and cook for 2 minutes adding beans towards the end. Remove squid and continue to cook beans until crisp-tender. Drain well.

3–4 red (French) shallots, finely chopped
  (or ½ small red onion)

3 chillies, finely chopped

6 spring (green) onions, finely chopped

2 garlic cloves, crushed

2 tbsp (1 fl oz) lime juice

¼ cup (1 oz) grated fresh coconut

¼ tsp shrimp paste, crumbled

freshly ground salt & pepper

Add to beans and toss well. Dice the squid finely and toss in. Taste, adding more lime juice if necessary.

---

banana leaves

lime wedges

Cut into squares, place on individual plates and top with salad. Serve lime on the side.

David Thompson's Thai Passion

It is interesting to realise that the man who is regarded as the world's foremost authority on Thai cooking is actually an Australian, David Thompson. His book Thai Food is, these days, seen as the Thai culinary bible.

I remember meeting him for the first time many, many years ago at the first Darley St Thai in the Sydney suburb of St Peters. Situated in the upstairs dining room of a rather seedy pub, Sydney produce guru Barry McDonald had told me that this was a restaurant worth the trek. The food was masterful, fascinating and, above all, absolutely delicious. And the enthusiasm of the man himself was infectious – at the drop of a hat (I think I had asked where the fresh green peppercorns had come from) I was dragged off to the coolroom to discuss the amazing array of produce which was being sourced throughout Australia, Asia and the Pacific. At that time, I and many others realised that here was a chef who would go far. And, as they say, the rest is history. First of all success with the very swish 'new' Darley St Thai in Kings Cross then Sailor's Thai in The Rocks, and finally Nahm in London which achieved the first ever star for a Thai restaurant in Europe in the Michelin Guide – a guide not overly renowned for its understanding of Asian food, let alone David's very in-your-face blend of true Thai flavours.

But I must point out that his passion for Thai food is not a recent aberration and certainly not a jump on any bandwagon in search of the next fusion food. Instead, his love affair had begun many years before when he had visited Thailand 'by mistake', as he said. Falling in love with both the food and culture, he moved to Bangkok where initially, as a French trained chef, he was disconcerted by the looser, less regimented approach to cooking, but soon came to see this was actually 'a responsive and intimate way of cooking and seasoning'.

At this time, he also began researching the history and traditions of Thai food and, whilst not discounting regional and peasant cooking, came to realise that the heights of Thai cuisine were most probably reached in the late 19th Century when 'the development of Thai Cuisine was clearly driven by those who did not have to cook or sully their hands with manual labour, otherwise they would not have demanded so much'. Fascinated by what is loosely known as 'royal cuisine', this is the food and culinary experience he has attempted to recreate both through his books and restaurants. Not that his food isn't up-to-date – it certainly is – but at the same time he has dedicated himself to describing and demonstrating this ancient cuisine before it is 'eroded, altered and modernised'. A wonderful sentiment from a man with a great passion.

Sour Hot Fish Salad (Yam Plaa Yaang)

Serves 4

– as cooked on the deck of the Cape Panwa Hotel

500 gm (1 lb) firm fish fillets vegetable oil spray fresh lime juice	Preheat BBQ or grill. Spray the fish and cook over high heat, squeezing juice over as you do so until crusty and brown. When cool enough to handle, flake into a bowl in largish chunks.
2 lemongrass stalks, white part only, smashed & finely sliced ¼ red onion, finely sliced 1 tbsp grated galangal (or ginger) 2 spring (green) onions, shredded 4 fresh kaffir lime leaves, shredded handful fresh mint leaves handful fresh coriander (cilantro) leaves	Add to bowl.
4 small red chillies, finely sliced 4 tbsp (2 fl oz) fresh lime juice 1 tbsp (½ fl oz) Asian fish sauce 1 tsp shaved palm sugar	Whisk, add to salad and toss well.

Green Papaya Salad (Som Tam)

Serves 2

— as eaten at a street-side stall in Phuket

2 tbsp shaved palm sugar 2 tbsp (1 fl oz) Asian fish sauce 1 tbsp (½ fl oz) tamarind water (see page 32)	Mix together to dissolve sugar then set aside.
2 garlic cloves, crushed 2 tbsp dried shrimps 4 small red chillies, chopped pinch of sea salt 1 heaped tbsp pan-roasted peanuts (see page 50)	Pound in a mortar to a coarse paste.
6 cherry tomatoes, quartered 2 long (snake) beans, blanched briefly then chopped	Add and continue to pound.
1 cup (6 oz) grated unripe, green papaya 1 lime	Add papaya together with sugar syrup and the lime juice and skin. Pound softly using spoon to scrape down side. Mound on plate with all the juices.

'Som means sour and Tam means to pound.'

Thailand: Phuket

While in Phuket we also made a trip to Phang Nga Bay about 90 minutes north of the city.

First of all we went to see the Sea Gypsies at Koh Panyi, whose picturesque village is perched on stilts over the water. The inhabitants, mostly Muslim, are basically fishermen, but in recent years have developed a nice little sideline with up to 3000 people per day visiting their restaurants (and buying the odd souvenir to boot). The quality and sheer freshness of the seafood was stunning.

Then it was off to meet John Gray from John Gray Sea Canoes, who took us out to visit the hongs (caves) which riddle the outer islands. Prehistoric in appearance, the many islands have been formed from raised coral reef limestone and the hongs are collapsed cave systems surrounded by towering walls with many of them open to the sky. They were first discovered by John in 1989 and access to them is only by sea canoe and only at low tide.

On a slightly more modern note, film buffs will recognise the bay because this was where the James Bond movie *The Man with the Golden Gun* was filmed.

Raw Beef Salad (Pla Neua Sot) Serves 4

— as cooked on John Gray's boat on Phang Nga Bay

2 x 180 gm (6 oz) porterhouse, rump (sirloin), or fillet (tenderloin) steaks, trimmed of all fat & sinew	Finely slice across the grain and place in a bowl.
3 small red chillies, finely chopped ½ tsp shaved palm sugar ½ tsp sea salt	Pound in a mortar (or in a processor).
3 tbsp (1½ fl oz) Asian fish sauce 4 tbsp (2 fl oz) fresh lime juice	Add to mortar and mix very well. Then add to beef, toss well, and set aside for 10 minutes for beef to 'cook'.
3 fresh kaffir lime leaves, shredded (or ½ tsp grated lime zest) 1 handful fresh coriander (cilantro) leaves 1 handful fresh mint leaves 5 red (French) shallots, finely sliced (or ¼ red onion)	Toss with beef then mound in individual bowls.
1 long red chilli, finely sliced 2–3 spring (green) onions, shredded	Scatter over the top.

'You can, if you like, sear the meat over very high heat just until rare, before slicing.'

Bali is definitely a fruit lover's paradise. Everything from guavas, lychees and mangosteens, to persimmons, pomegranates and rambutans thrive, as do a large number of interesting, rather strange numbers – like the durian. One of South East Asia's most popular fruits, it is banned from aeroplanes, hotels and even some buses and trains because of its overpowering smell. But it is delicious nonetheless, although it must be eaten within hours of harvesting because its flesh deteriorates very rapidly once exposed to the air. Another favourite is the jackfruit. The largest fruit in the world (some grow to 50 kg) when ripe it can either be used in fruit salad, be eaten by itself or, as suggested by Toby Anderson (see page 213) dipped in a rice flour batter before being deep fried and served with a palm sugar syrup. The smaller unripe or green ones are either simmered in spiced coconut milk and served as a side dish, or as part of a curry (see page 213). I also enjoyed the salak which is a little like a lychee in appearance but is crisp with a fairly sharp 'bite', the water apple which is similar to a nashi in flavour but not as watery, the pomelo which is the largest member of the citrus family and which is often used in savoury salads and the soursop which is normally made into mousses or jellies or the like.

Vegetable & Fruit Salad with Palm Sugar Syrup (Rujak)

Serves 4–8

– as prepared on the beach at Seminyak

125 gm (4 oz) shaved palm sugar 125 ml (4 fl oz) water 2 tbsp tamarind pulp 1 tsp shrimp paste 3–4 small chillies, whole	Put in a pot, bring to the boil, whisk and cook for 5 minutes. Set aside and when ready to use, strain.
¼–½ small papaya, peeled, seeded & diced ¼–½ pomelo (or grapefruit) peeled & segmented 1 water apple (or nashi) cored & finely sliced ½ cup (3 oz) diced, ripe jackfruit ½ cup (3 oz) shredded green unripe mango ¼ continental (telegraph) cucumber, finely sliced ½ punnet (tub) small cherry tomatoes, halved	Toss in a bowl with dressing to taste.
banana leaves 2 spring (green) onions, shredded	Cut banana leaves into squares, place on individual plates and top with salad. Sprinkle with a little more sauce and spring onions.

'You can use whatever fruit you like but, remember, because the sauce is sweet a percentage of the fruit used needs to be crisp and tart, as this is an appetiser or side salad rather than a dessert.'

In Bali, Gado Gado is served at room temperature (which, of course means the dish is warm) so although I don't recommend you serve it the second the sauce is made and the vegies are cooked, do think of it as a warm not cold dish.

Also any peanut butter will do as long as it is the crunchy not smooth variety. In Bali I used the 'Skippy' brand which, being a bit of a simpleton, I thought came from Australia. It turned out to be from Indonesia – which obviously means that they have kangaroos in Indonesia too (or is it possible that they just 'borrowed' the name?).

Tofu & Vegetable Salad with Peanut Sauce (Gado Gado)

Serves 4

– as cooked on the beach at Legian

4 waxy baby potatoes, well scrubbed & halved	Cook until tender in lightly salted water. Drain and set aside.
100 gm (3½ oz) firm tofu, cubed vegetable oil	Heat vegetable oil in a deep pan and fry tofu until golden brown on all sides. Drain well.
1 tbsp (½ fl oz) vegetable oil 1 tbsp Thai red curry paste 300 ml (10 fl oz) coconut cream	Heat oil in a wok and fry paste for a minute or two. Then add coconut cream and mix well.
2 heaped tbsp crunchy, peanut butter 1 tbsp (½ fl oz) soy sauce 1 tbsp shaved palm sugar 60 ml (2 fl oz) water	Add, stir and cook for 5 minutes or so to thicken.
juice of 1 lime	Add and taste for balance. Take off heat and cool.
sea salt ¼ small cauliflower, cut in florets 1 medium carrot, peeled & finely sliced 6 long/snake beans, cut in lengths (or green beans) ¼ small wonga bok (Chinese white cabbage), shredded	While making sauce cook cauli and carrot until almost tender in lightly salted water. Then add beans and wonga bok and after a couple of minutes drain very well.
4 hard-boiled eggs, quartered bean shoots sliced continental (telegraph) cucumber deep fried red (French) shallots 　(bought or homemade, see page 52)	Place cooked vegies on a platter or in a large bowl. Top with potatoes, tofu, eggs, a small handful of bean shoots a little cucumber. Then top with a generous amount of sauce and shallots and serve with extra sauce on the side.

Fish

Noosa, these days the playground of the rich and famous, first gained fame as a surfers' destination in the sixties. Surfboards are still in evidence, particularly on Sunshine Beach but the yuppies have almost taken over. Restaurant and property prices are high and the souvenirs tend to have designer labels.

But there are still some old Noosa pleasures. The National Park has excellent walks, terrific views and is easily accessible from the end of Hastings Street. And Fraser Island, a huge sandbank which is about 120 kilometres in length, is not that far away. This is wild, rugged four-wheel drive country which has some quite amazing scenery, great fishing and lots of lakes for swimming (which is lucky because you would be a braver man than me if you tackled the currents and sharks in the open sea). And let us not forget the famous Maleny Folk Festival which runs for the five days prior to New Year in nearby Woodford. Camping grounds are available on site and, while this is not quite Woodstock, if you are a fan of both progressive and traditional folk, Irish or even aboriginal music then this is the place to be. (I think these days there may have been a name change to the Woodford Folk Festival but the locals still refer to it as the Maleny Festival.)

Mahi Mahi with a Potato & Chorizo Salad & Sauce Vierge

Serves 4

— as cooked on the beach at Noosa

8 baby potatoes, scrubbed well	Cook in boiling water until just tender. Drain well and cut in half lengthways.
4 ripe, red tomatoes, peeled, seeded & diced (see page 21) 125 ml (4 fl oz) olive oil juice of 1 lemon 8–10 fresh basil leaves, sliced sea salt flakes freshly ground pepper	Mix together and set aside in a warm spot.
olive oil 2 chorizo, sliced	Heat a thin layer of oil in a large pan and sauté potatoes until golden. Push to the side and cook chorizo until crispy. Drain well and place on individual plates.
4 x 180 gm (6 oz) mahi mahi steaks (or swordfish or marlin) olive oil spray sea salt freshly ground pepper	Spray with oil, season and cook fish on a BBQ or lightly oiled grill. Place fish on potatoes and spoon tomato oil over the top.

'Mahi mahi is dolphin fish which is not to be confused with the cute and cuddly dolphin.'

Noosa is famed for its restaurants. Seemingly there are thousands of the blessed things and most are very good too. There is a definite regional cuisine happening here with lots of fresh, clean flavours, Asian influences and, above all, terrific ingredients.

A couple of Noosa's finest are owned and operated by Jim Berardo (Berardo's, and Berardo's on the Beach) who somehow lured Matt McConnell (the *Age Good Food Guide*'s Best Young Chef 2002) from Melbourne to take the helm. Apart from cooking some terrific food for us, Matt also introduced me to the people at Prime Fish at Mooloolaba who are exporting the most superb line caught mahi mahi and swordfish.

Sadly, Soleil at Sunshine Beach (which I judged to be Noosa's finest in a restaurant competition a few years ago) has gone, as has Eddie Brunetti's famous Jetty out at Boreen Point where a lunch normally went on late into the night. There are still many to choose from, but like most tourist towns the industry is in a continual state of flux so a little bit of consultation may be necessary to discover whether the latest hot chef or owner is still in residence.

Swordfish Kebabs with Spiced Chickpea Salad

Serves 4

– as cooked by Matt McConnell at Berardo's

3 garlic cloves	Blend until smooth and set aside.
juice of 2 lemons	
150 ml (5 fl oz) olive oil	
freshly ground salt & pepper	

½ cup (4 fl oz) olive oil	Heat oil in a pot and sauté until softish.
2 onions, finely sliced	
2 garlic cloves, crushed	
1 tbsp ground coriander	
1 tbsp ground cumin	
1 tsp saffron threads, lightly roasted	

2 cups cooked chickpeas (or canned)	Add and stir to just wilt herbs. If using canned chickpeas, first rinse and drain very well.
12 green beans, blanched & chopped	
2 tbsp each of chopped fresh coriander (cilantro), parsley & mint	

500 gm (16 oz) swordfish cut into 1 cm (3/8 inch) thick pieces	Place 2 or 3 pieces of swordfish on each skewer. Sprinkle with salt and the lemon dressing then grill or barbecue. To serve, mound chickpea salad on plates and top with fish. Drizzle with the lemon dressing.
wooden skewers, soaked in cold water for 30 minutes	
sea salt	

Another one of Noosa's superstar chefs is Gary Skelton. When he first arrived from Sydney he opened a restaurant called Season smack bang on Hastings Street. Many at the time, including me, felt that this was just what Hastings Street needed – another restaurant. But within days his hole in the wall had queues halfway down the street waiting to enjoy his simple, fresh, clean food.

These days, Season is a far grander affair. It has moved across the road, is situated right on the beach and, because of the increased seating capacity, you no longer have to queue around the block. But the food's still as good as ever – crisp, classy pizzas, spotlessly fresh fish and lots of the best local ingredients.

Tuna with Roasted Eggplant & Tomato Vinaigrette

Serves 4

– as cooked by Gary Skelton on the beach at Noosa Heads

olive oil 3 red (French) shallots, finely sliced	Heat a little oil in a pan and sauté shallots until soft.
1 x 400 gm (13 oz) can whole, peeled tomatoes, drained	Add and gently cook for 15 minutes. Remove from heat and strain through muslin.
100 ml (3 fl oz) balsamic vinegar freshly ground salt & pepper	In another pan, reduce vinegar by half and then add to tomato mix along with seasonings. Set aside.
4 x 180 gm (6 oz) tuna steaks, trimmed of bloodline freshly ground salt & pepper	Heat a thin layer of oil in a pan and cook tuna (no more than medium rare).
4 slices roasted eggplant 4 tbsp baba ghannouj (bought or homemade) 16 baby capers 8–12 pitted olives, chopped 1–2 tbsp chopped fresh chives	To serve, put tomato vinaigrette on plates, top with baba ghannouj, roasted eggplant and then fish. Garnish with capers, olives and chives.

Australia: Noosa

Barramundi with a Radicchio, Witloof & Walnut Slaw

Serves 4

— as cooked at the Great Barrier Feast

olive oil

4 x 180 gm (6 oz) barramundi fillets

plain (all-purpose) flour

freshly ground salt & pepper

Heat a thin layer of oil in a large pan. Flour and season fish and pan-fry until golden brown and almost cooked. Place on plates (it will continue to cook once removed from the heat source).

---

1 witloof, cleaned & finely sliced

½–1 radicchio, cleaned & finely sliced

3 heaped tbsp pan-roasted walnut halves
  (see page 50)

olive oil

balsamic vinegar

freshly ground salt & pepper

While fish is cooking, toss witloof, radicchio and walnuts in a bowl with oil, vinegar and seasonings to taste.

---

100 gm (3½ oz) unsalted butter

juice of ½ lemon

2 tbsp chopped fresh parsley

Remove most of the oil from the pan and add butter, lemon and parsley. Cook until lightly browned and pour over fish. Mound slaw on the side.

'Barramundi is a superb, mildly flavoured fish from Australia's Northern Territory. Any firm fleshed fish will do as a substitute. Witloof is also known as chicory or Belgian endive.'

Tuna with a BBQ Fennel Salad

Serves 4

– as cooked in Wellington's Botanical Gardens

juice of ½–1 lemon 60 ml (2 fl oz) olive oil sea salt freshly ground pepper	Whisk.
4 x 180 gm (6 oz) tuna steaks, trimmed of bloodline	Preheat ridged grill or BBQ. Put in shallow dish, pour over marinade. Turn over a few times then leave for 20 minutes.
2–3 small fennel bulbs	Clean off any damaged or coarse outer leaves. Cut out core in V shape and then cut into thin wedges.
1 small red onion, cut into wedges olive oil spray	Spray fennel and onion generously and grill until lightly charred and tender. Put in bowl.
1 punnet (tub) cherry tomatoes, halved 10 fresh basil leaves, torn olive oil balsamic vinegar sea salt freshly ground pepper	Add tomatoes and basil to bowl then dress to taste with oil, balsamic and seasonings. When ready, cook tuna to desired degree, brushing with marinade as you do so. Then put on plates and mound salad on the side.

'Treat tuna as the steak of the sea and cook no more than medium (surprise, surprise I like mine rare) otherwise it will be dry and tasteless.'

Napier is a New Zealand city that has been greatly affected by a natural disaster. In 1931 a massive earthquake demolished the whole of Napier and nearby Hastings, killing hundreds of people. On new land lifted from the harbour by the earthquake, Napier was rebuilt in the popular architecture style of the time, Art Deco. Most of these buildings still survive and Napier is now regarded as having the world's largest collection of buildings in this style. Add to that the sea, surf and great vineyards and you have a very special place.

Gurnard with Asparagus, Mushrooms & Ponzu Dressing

Serves 4

– as cooked on the foreshore at Napier

60 ml (2 fl oz) fresh lemon juice
125 ml (4 fl oz) Asian rice wine vinegar
80 ml (2½ fl oz) soy sauce
3 tbsp (1½ fl oz) mirin (Japanese rice wine)
2–3 spring (green) onions, finely chopped

Make ponzu dressing by whisking together.

4 x 180 gm (6 oz) gurnard steaks
sesame oil
sea salt

Brush fish with oil, season and grill or barbecue, brushing generously with ponzu as you do so.

1 bunch asparagus, sliced
2–3 handfuls mushrooms, a variety either sliced or
   halved as necessary
vegetable oil

Heat oil in wok and toss asparagus and mushrooms until crisp-tender. Place on plates, top with fish and sprinkle with more ponzu dressing.

'Gurnard, a New Zealand fish, is similar in texture to groper/harpuka. It would be a good substitute as would blue eye, snapper, cod or, in fact, any steaky fish.'

New Zealand: Hawke's Bay

Poached John Dory with a Vegetable Sauce

Serves 4

— as cooked overlooking the Great Ocean Road

1 tsp saffron threads	Soak saffron in wine for 5 minutes.
60 ml (2 fl oz) dry white wine	
1 tbsp (½ fl oz) olive oil	Heat oil in a large pan and sauté gently until tender.
1 garlic clove, finely sliced	
1 small fennel bulb, cleaned & finely sliced	
1 leek, well washed & sliced	
4–5 baby carrots, peeled & sliced on the diagonal	
4 green beans, sliced on the diagonal	
375 ml (12 fl oz) fish stock	Add along with the saffron-wine mix. Simmer for 3–4 minutes.
(bought or homemade, see page 280)	
1 bay leaf	
1 piece orange peel	
freshly ground salt & pepper	
4 x 180 gm (6 oz) John Dory (or whiting) fillets	Lay on top, cover, turn heat off and leave for 4 minutes. (Check if ready by making a small cut with a knife.)

'The success of cooking the fish in this manner depends on the thickness of the fish. If thicker than normal simmer, covered, for 2–3 minutes before turning off the heat.'

Salmon Pan-fried in Rice Paper with Sweet Chilli Sauce

Serves 4

– as cooked on the shores of Lake Burley Griffin

250 ml (8 fl oz) white vinegar 140 gm (4½ oz) caster (superfine) sugar ½ tsp sea salt	Combine in a pot, bring to the boil and simmer for 2 minutes until the sugar dissolves. Remove from heat.
3 chillies, seeded & finely chopped 3 garlic cloves, finely chopped ¼ cup drained, canned crushed pineapple 1 tsp grated fresh ginger	Add and mix well.
400 gm (13 oz) salmon fillet, finely sliced 1 tsp grated fresh ginger 2 tbsp (1 fl oz) soy sauce	Place in a bowl and gently mix.
8–12 rice paper rounds 2–3 spring (green) onions, finely sliced	Soften rice paper individually in warm water then drain on a clean towel. Place on bench and top each one with 2–3 pieces of salmon and a little spring onion. Fold up like an envelope.
vegetable oil paper towels	Heat a thin layer of oil in a large pan and in 2–3 lots fry packets until golden brown (seam side down first). Drain well on paper towels and serve with sauce on side.

Australia: Canberra

The Ocean Road coast was once known as the Shipwreck Coast. The Split Point Lighthouse at Airey's Inlet, was built in 1891 to alleviate this problem (it was one of a series of navigational aids built around Australia's 36,700 kilometre coastline during that period). It was manned until 1990 when the government discovered that its rather creative lighthouse keeper had rigged up a system to keep it working so he could pop off to the local pub – obviously this gave them the idea to automate it themselves and he was given the chance to permanently base himself at the bar.

This was also where I caught up with Andrew McIldowney who had served his apprenticeship with me at Clichy in the seventies. A very fine chef, at that time he was working at the Airey's Foodhaven (which I notice has now been taken over by Kosta and Pam Talihmanidis, brother and sister-in-law of Chris – see page 143 – and the former owners of the famed Kosta's in Lorne).

Salmon in Miso Broth
Serves 2

– as cooked by Andrew McIldowney at Split Point Lighthouse

20 gm (¾ oz) dried shiitake mushrooms	Soak in warm water for 30 minutes then cut off and discard stalks and slice caps.
300 ml (10 fl oz) dry white wine 1 heaped tbsp dark miso paste	Bring wine to the boil in a large frypan, then stir in the miso and mix well.
2 x 200 gm (6½ oz) boneless salmon fillets, skin on a little extra virgin olive oil 1 tsp finely diced preserved orange zest (or preserved lemon)	Add salmon skin side up along with shiitakes, orange zest and oil. Gently cook for 6–7 minutes turning salmon once.
150 gm (5 oz) baby spinach leaves washed well freshly ground salt & pepper	When fish is almost ready, add spinach and seasoning. Cook until lightly wilted. Serve in large flat soup bowls.

'I have seen preserved orange in a few delis but preserved lemon is a lot more freely available – if you can't find either just use a teaspoon of grated orange zest. And the dark miso paste is available at any Japanese or many Asian supermarkets.'

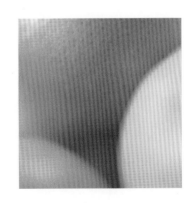

A Thai Tongue Twister

In 1782 Rama I moved the nation's capital to Bangkok (the village of the Hog Plum). Upon its completion, a new name was conferred which goes something like this: 'Krungthep mahanakhon bowon rattanakasin mahintara ayuthaya mahadilok popnoppaut ratchathani burirom – udomratch aniwet mahasathan – amonpiman – aratantathir – sakkathatitya – visnukamp rasit.' Which, according to David Thompson's Thai Food, translates as (although, interestingly, the *Lonely Planet Guide* has a rather different translation): 'City of angels, the great city, the residence of the Emerald Buddha, the impregnable city of the God Indra, the grand capital of the world endowed with nine precious gems, the Happy City, abounding in grand palaces that resemble the heavenly abode of the incarnated God, a city dedicated to Indra, built by Vishnu.'

A name which, I'm sure you will admit, flows off the tongue, doesn't it? But fortunately, for all and sundry, it is more commonly known as 'Krung Thep' or 'City of Angels'.

It maybe wasn't the greatest idea I've ever had, but I wanted to watch some Super 12 Rugby Union action and the only place that appeared to be showing it was the Aussie Bar at Patong Beach. The problem wasn't really anything to do with the fact that this is a rather sleazy part of town (although the Aussie Bar was an exception), but to do with the fact that HMAS Melbourne was in town just back from the Gulf and this maybe had the potential to not be the safest spot to be. Thankfully nothing happened and I had a great time with the friendly crew but sadly, I have to report that my team lost.

Grilled Salmon with Thai Spicy Apple Salad (Yang Pla Yum Poodza)

Serves 4

— as cooked at Patong Beach

2 coriander roots, cleaned & chopped finely	Pound in mortar (or process).
2 garlic cloves, crushed	
2 tsp sea salt flakes	
4–6 small green chillies, finely chopped	Add and continue to pound until smooth.
1 tbsp shaved palm sugar	Add and mix well to dissolve sugar.
3 tbsp (1½ fl oz) fresh lime juice	
1–2 splashes Asian fish sauce	
2 heaped tbsp chopped fresh coriander (cilantro)	
3 limes	Oil ridged grill or BBQ plate. Cut 2 limes in half and put on, flesh side down. At same time cook salmon, skin side down first, squeezing with the juice of the third lime as you do so.
4 x 180 gm (6 oz) salmon steaks, skin on	
vegetable oil spray	
3–4 poodzas (or green apples), skin on, cored & finely sliced	Toss in bowl with dressing to taste.
6 red (French) shallots, sliced lengthways (or ¼ red onion)	Mound salad in large flat soup bowls, top with salmon, sprinkle with a little more dressing and serve with grilled limes on the side.
3 spring (green) onions, shredded	
¼ cup fresh mint leaves	
¼ cup fresh coriander (cilantro) leaves	
½ cup pan-roasted cashew nuts (see page 50)	

'Poodzas or jujubes are known as Thai apples.
Obviously rather difficult to find outside Thailand,
Granny Smiths or similar are a good substitute.'

On 10 June 1886, Mt Taraweru erupted. New Zealand's greatest natural disaster, it not only destroyed the Pink and White Terraces (the eighth wonder of the world) but it buried the surrounding countryside under two metres of mud and ash.

The Buried Village of Te Wairoa is testament to this fury. Partially restored, these days it is still off limits to many Maoris who feel that it signifies the wrath of the gods, the desecration of holy ground.

On Lake Tarawera itself there is little evidence of 1886, but there is still evidence of volcanic activity as I found out when Craig Armstrong from Clearwater Charters suggested I cook a trout in the hot sand by the Lake. It worked perfectly.

Whole Rainbow Trout with Moroccan Flavours Serves 4
— as cooked in the sand at Lake Tarawera

¼ cup chopped fresh coriander (cilantro) ¼ cup chopped fresh parsley 125 ml (4 fl oz) olive oil 1 tsp turmeric 1 tsp sambal oelek ½ tsp ground cumin 1 tbsp (½ fl oz) lemon juice a good splash of honey sea salt freshly ground pepper	Whisk.
1 large whole trout or salmon	Lay large sheet of aluminium foil on bench. Top with fish. Cut a few slashes in each side of the fish then pour over the marinade. Wrap up tightly.

'If you don't happen to have some boiling sand nearby, cook in the oven or on the barbie.'

New Zealand

Fish with a Warm Gazpacho Salad

Serves 4

– as cooked in Queenstown

olive oil 4 x 180 gm (6 oz) fish steaks plain (all-purpose) flour freshly ground salt & pepper	Heat a layer of oil in a large pan and cook floured, seasoned fish steaks over moderate heat.
olive oil ½ red onion, diced 1 red capsicum (bell pepper), cored, seeded & diced 1 yellow capsicum (bell pepper), cored, seeded & diced 1–2 zucchini, diced 1 garlic clove, crushed 2 chillies, seeded & sliced	Heat oil in another pan or wok and sauté vegies until crisp-tender.
½ punnet (tub) cherry tomatoes, quartered ¼ continental (telegraph) cucumber, diced freshly ground salt & pepper	Add to vegies and toss. Remove from heat.
olive oil balsamic vinegar	Dress salad to taste and put in flat soup bowls. Place fish on top and sprinkle with a little more olive oil.

One of the most popular Thai festivals is the New Year festivities (Songkran). Originally a gentle, laidback affair to welcome in the lunar year, these days it has developed into a boisterous water festival. So what began as a gentle washing of hands in preparation for greeting the New Year cleansed, has now degenerated into a street 'riot' where bands of Thai, good naturedly roam the streets intent on soaking everyone with buckets of water and over-sized water pistols.

Unfortunately, when we visited Chiang Mai our mates at Thai tourism had forgotten to mention that it was even more over the top in this northern city than in any other part of Thailand. Consequently, not only did it take us hours to simply travel down the road, but on more than one occasion I got absolutely soaked attempting to do my show introductions. So what did I do? Being a mature type of fellow, I simply bought myself an even larger water pistol.

Deep Fried Fish with Three Flavoured Sauce (Plaa Thawt Sahm Rot)

Serves 2

– as cooked in Chiang Mai

1 plate-sized fish, well scaled	Make three deepish slashes crossways on each side.
3 long red chillies, chopped 4 garlic cloves, crushed 1 tsp sea salt 3 red (French) shallots, chopped 1 tbsp coriander roots, scraped & chopped	Pound to a rough paste in a mortar.
vegetable oil 3 tbsp (1½ fl oz) fresh lime juice 2 tbsp (shaved palm sugar 2 tbsp (1 fl oz) Asian fish sauce 125 ml (4 fl oz) water 2 tbsp tamarind water (see page 32)	Heat a little oil in a pan and sauté chilli paste. Mix briefly, then add the rest and taste for balance. Set aside.
1½ litres (1⅕ quarts) vegetable oil rice flour or cornflour (cornstarch)	Heat oil in wok to 180°C (350°F). Dust fish lightly with flour, shake off excess and gently place into oil (make sure it is covered with oil). Cook for about 15 minutes until lightly browned.
fresh coriander (cilantro) leaves	Put the fish on a plate, pour sauce over the top and garnish with coriander.

'To me snapper would be the perfect fish for this recipe.'

Thailand: Chiang Mai

Spicy Steamed Fish (Plaa Neung)

– as cooked by the pool at Cape Panwa Hotel

4 garlic cloves, crushed 2 coriander roots, cleaned & chopped 1 tsp sea salt flakes 6 small green chillies, finely chopped	Pound with a mortar (or process) until a rough paste is formed.
3 tbsp (1½ fl oz) fresh lime juice 1 tbsp caster (superfine) sugar 2 tbsp (1 fl oz) Asian fish sauce	Add and mix to dissolve sugar.
1 plate-sized fish	Make three deepish slashes on top side of fish. Put on plate that will fit into steamer then pour liquid over. Steam over simmering water until almost cooked (to check, just lift the flesh in the slashed area).
2–3 spring (green) onions, shredded good handful fresh coriander (cilantro) sprigs	Put on top, steam for another minute then carefully place on platter and pour liquid over.

'Once again snapper would be perfect for this. But I have also used baby barramundi and even a small flounder with great success.'

Thailand: Phuket

One of the most famous Mauritian Creole recipes is the Vindaye of Fish. Although some feel that its name comes from the French for garlic wine (vin d'ail) it is probable that it owes more to the Indian–Portuguese Vindaloo. A recipe that comes from Goa, Vindaloo is always exceedingly hot and involves vinegar as does this dish. This is most probably where the similarities end but it does bear out the feeling (see page 168) that much of the Creole food has strong Indian influences.

Creole Vindaye of Fish

Serves 4 as an entree

– as cooked at Eureka Plantation House

vegetable oil 4 x 120 gm (4 oz) delicate fish fillets plain (all-purpose) flour freshly ground salt & pepper	Heat a thin layer of oil in a pan and pan-fry floured, seasoned fillets until golden brown. Drain and put in gratin dish.
4 tbsp (2 fl oz) vegetable oil ½ red onion, finely sliced ¼ medium carrot, finely sliced ½–1 celery stalk, finely sliced 3 chillies, seeded & finely sliced 3 garlic cloves, crushed	Pour off oil and heat fresh oil then sauté vegies gently until tender.
1 heaped tsp turmeric ½ tsp mustard seeds	Add, toss briefly.
½ cup (4 fl oz) white wine vinegar	Add, bring to boil and taste for seasoning. Pour over fish and refrigerate for up to 48 hours, turning regularly.

'Try a Creole fish butty – put it between bread – delicious.'

Fish with Rougaille de Tomate

— as cooked at the Port Louis Markets

Serves 4

3 tbsp (1½ fl oz) olive oil	Heat oil in a sauté pan and sauté.
1 small red onion, finely chopped	
3 garlic cloves, finely chopped	
2 chillies, finely chopped	
1 heaped tsp grated fresh ginger	
3–4 large ripe, red tomatoes, cored & cut in thin wedges	
125–250 ml (4–8 fl oz) vegetable stock (bought or homemade, see page 281)	Add half of the stock and the rest. Cook until the tomatoes collapse adding more stock as necessary.
a splash of soy sauce	
freshly ground salt & pepper	
2 tbsp chopped fresh parsley	
1 tsp fresh thyme leaves	
4 x 180 gm (6 oz) salmon or ocean trout fillets	Lay fish on top of sauce, cover tightly and cook gently until fish is cooked (also adding more stock if necessary).
fresh thyme sprigs	Remove fish, check sauce for seasoning, then spoon into large flat soup bowls, top with fish and garnish with thyme.

'For this we used some local lemon pickles but preserved lemon or even grated zest will do.'

Pan-fried Fish with a Pickled Lemon & Smoked Marlin Sauce

Serves 4

— as cooked in the Mauritian hinterland

4 large potatoes, scrubbed sea salt	Cook in lightly salted water until tender. Drain and when cool enough to handle, peel and cut into thick slices.
olive oil 4 tomatoes, cored, peeled & sliced thickly (see page 21) 1 garlic clove, crushed freshly ground salt & pepper	While potatoes are cooking, heat a little oil in a pan and add tomatoes, seasoning and garlic. Cook until tomatoes collapse a little. Keep warm.
olive oil 4 x 180 gm (6 oz) fish fillets (snapper, groper, blue eye, etc) freshly ground salt & pepper	At the same time in another pan heat a thin layer of oil and seal fish on both sides. Remove and set aside.

100 ml (3 fl oz) cream
1 tsp sliced pickled lemon (see above)
200 gm (6½ oz) diced smoked marlin
  (or other smoked fish)
150 ml (5 fl oz) fish stock
  (bought or homemade, see page 280)
a pinch of cardamom
	Pour off oil, add and reduce by half. Then return fish and gently cook, turning once or twice.
	
	Put potatoes on individual plates, top with tomato and then fish and pour the sauce over the top.

'The name 'Flic en Flac' is thought to have come from its old Dutch name Fried Landt Flaak which means free and flat land.'

Mauritian Squid Curry

Serves 4

— as cooked on the beach at Flic en Flac

1 tbsp (½ fl oz) vegetable oil 1 large red onion, finely chopped 2 chillies, seeded & finely sliced 2 garlic cloves, crushed 1 heaped tsp grated ginger 1 lemongrass stalk, white part only, smashed & finely chopped 1 tsp finely sliced, cleaned coriander (cilantro) root	Heat oil in a wok and sauté until tender.
2 tsp curry powder 1 tsp ground cumin 1 tsp ground coriander	Add and toss briefly to release aromas.
500 ml (16 fl oz) chicken, vegetable or fish stock (bought or homemade, see page 280 & 281) 60 ml (2 fl oz) coconut cream 2–3 ripe red tomatoes, cored & cut into eighths 8 curry leaves	Add, mix well and simmer for about 10 minutes until tomatoes begin to collapse.
600 gm (1¼ lb) cleaned squid or calamari tube, sliced in rings 2 tbsp chopped fresh coriander (cilantro) steamed rice	Add squid and coriander. Check seasoning and simmer very gently for a few minutes. Serve on beds of steamed rice.

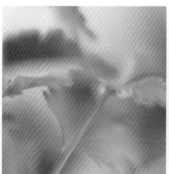

Mauritius: Flic en Flac

When you travel to the Klungkung Markets in East Bali (see page 213) make a detour to Kasamb a on the coast. And not just for the fish market which is pretty good and the local salt which is excellent. Also visit the local Bat Cave Temple (Pura Goa Lawah) which is interesting to say the least. Jam packed with bats, local legend has it that the cave also contains a giant snake (Naga Basuki). I didn't venture inside to find out whether that is true or not but I did taste the local specialty – Bat and Snake Soup, an acquired taste I think. And, speaking of the fish market, I bought some very good tuna (a lot more palatable than bat or snake).

BBQ Tuna with Pineapple Sambal

Serves 4

– as cooked by the pool in Seminyak

4 x 180 gm (6 oz) tuna steaks, trimmed of bloodline
vegetable oil
juice of 1 lime
freshly ground salt & pepper

Preheat BBQ or ridged grill.
Sprinkle tuna with oil, lime and seasonings and set aside.

4–6 slices fresh, very ripe pineapple, finely diced
1–2 garlic cloves, crushed
2 green chillies, finely sliced
2 red chillies, finely sliced
2 heaped tsp grated fresh galangal (or ginger)
juice of 2–3 limes

Toss together, taste for seasoning and balance and set aside for 15 minutes or so to develop flavours (can add a little oil if too tart).

---

vegetable oil
lime wedges

Cook tuna to desired degree, brushing with a little oil as you do so. Serve with a good spoonful of the sambal on the side and a lime wedge.

'As I have said on the show about 40 times, this is more of a salsa than a sambal but, if you like, you can chop the lot together to make it a bit finer and more authentic.'

Bali: Seminyak

Fish with Chilli & Galangal Sauce
(Ikan Bakar Rica)

Serves 1–2

— as cooked at Jimbaran Bay

1 plate-sized fish, snapper or similar sea salt juice of 1 lime	Preheat BBQ or ridged grill. Cut diagonal slashes in each side of the fish almost to the bone. Rub well with salt and lime juice and set aside for 15–20 minutes.
4 chillies, finely chopped 2 garlic cloves, finely chopped 2 red (French) shallots, finely chopped 1 tbsp grated fresh galangal (or ginger) 2 tbsp (1 fl oz) vegetable oil juice of 2 limes	Whisk and set aside.
aluminium foil oil spray	Cut a large piece of foil. Place shiny side down on bench. Spray lightly with oil, top with fish and massage chilli mix into it. Pour any excess over the top and wrap up tightly. Cook for about 15–20 minutes on the BBQ turning once. (To check, just peel a little of the flesh back from the slashes with a sharp knife.)
steamed rice steamed greens	Serve with all the juices over the top and rice and greens on the side.

Bali: Bukit Peninsula

To be honest, Canberra used to be a culinary desert. Of course there were a few exceptions – including anything owned and operated by Alby Sedaitis, a terrific restaurateur. But, all in all, Canberra was not a gourmet's destination (and I always felt this had a lot to do with the fact that a huge number of the diners were politicians who have never been renowned for their fine palates).

Still I'm pleased to report that the food scene in Canberra is now alive and well and terrific restaurants such as Artespresso, Ottoman and the Ginger Room are well worth a visit if not a journey. I also enjoyed a great night at the Benchmark Wine Bar which not only has an amazing wine list but the talented Melbourne refugee, Laurent Rospar, whipping up some French classics in the kitchen. Another terrific meal was at Aubergine in the suburb of Griffith. James Mussillon is a very talented young chef who has worked with both Joel Robuchon and Sydney's Guillaume Brahimi and his food style reflects this.

Aubergine's Mixed Fish with Provencale Vegetables, Pesto & Aioli

Serves 6

— as cooked outside the National Museum

vegetable oil
6 x 100 gm (3½ oz) fillets of snapper, skin on
6 x 100 gm (3½ oz) fillets of red emperor
   (or blue eye), skin on
24 scallops in the half shell, cleaned
sea salt flakes

Heat a thin layer of oil in a large pan. Season fish with a little salt and pan-fry skin side down first until crispy. When almost ready remove and quickly sear scallops on both sides.

1 eggplant, thickly sliced
1 red onion, sliced
1–2 zucchini, thickly sliced
fresh lemon juice

While fish is cooking, heat a little more oil in another pan and sauté vegies until golden brown and tender. Remove, place on fish and squeeze a little lemon juice over the top. (You could cook the vegies first and, if need be, keep them warm in a low oven.)

a dollop of butter
200 gm (6½ oz) baby spinach leaves, well washed
freshly ground salt & pepper

Put butter in vegie pan and briefly sauté seasoned spinach until wilted.

½ cup (4 oz) mayonnaise (see page 281)
2 garlic cloves, crushed

Combine and set aside.

pesto (bought or homemade, see page 281)
1 roasted capsicum (bell pepper), cut into strips

To serve, place a little spinach in the centre of individual plates. Top with onion and then red emperor. Layer with eggplant, snapper and zucchini. Place a dollop of aioli on top along with the roasted capsicum. Scatter scallops around the plate and sprinkle with pesto.

Snapper with a Green Vegetable Stew

Serves 4

— as cooked on Auckland Harbour

250 ml (8 fl oz) fish or chicken stock (bought or homemade, see page 280) 125 ml (4 fl oz) cream freshly ground salt & pepper	Put in a pan and reduce by one third.
4 x 180 gm (6 oz) boneless, skinless snapper fillets olive oil plain (all-purpose) flour freshly ground salt & pepper 1 lemon	Heat a thin layer of oil in another pan. Flour and season fish and pan-fry until almost cooked (to check make a small cut). Squeeze lemon juice over the top.
2 good handfuls prepared green vegies such as green beans, asparagus tips, double peeled broad beans, sugar peas, spring (green) onions etc. sea salt	While fish is cooking, blanch briefly in a large pot of rapidly boiling, lightly salted water. Drain well.
2 tbsp chopped fresh tarragon or chervil leaves a good knob or two of butter	Add to cream reduction with vegies. Toss well and when butter has melted put in flat soup bowls and top with fish.

'You can use any steaky fish (see page 4) for this dish.'

A visit to Auckland's new fish market which opened in June 2004, was an absolute must (I just love markets). Interestingly, in similar vein to Melbourne's Victoria Market, the second the camera came out, the sales assistants just disappeared. I will, of course, just presume they were simply shy. But when I finally found someone who would serve me I bought some absolutely terrific, spotlessly fresh seafood including New Zealand whitebait which is a completely different fish to its Australian and European namesakes and which, to my mind, is one of the world's great delicacies (especially when cooked in patties with the odd egg to just hold it together).

Sybil Hewitson's Whitebait Patties
– as cooked on Auckland Harbour

Serves 4

500 gm (1 lb) New Zealand whitebait
2 eggs
freshly ground salt

Add beaten eggs to whitebait along with a little salt.

---

vegetable oil
a good knob of butter

Heat a thin layer of oil in a large pan along with butter. In 3 or 4 lots, drop heaped tablespoons of whitebait mixture in and cook, turning once until lightly coloured.
Drain well.

---

2 chopped gherkins (sweet dill pickles)
2 tbsp chopped fresh parsley
1 tbsp finely chopped red onion
1 tbsp chopped capers
1 cup (8 oz) mayonnaise (see page 281)
a good squeeze of lemon juice

Mix together and serve on the side.

'New Zealand whitebait is sometimes available in specialist fishmongers or markets. Unfortunately this recipe doesn't really suit other varieties of whitebait.'

At the Auckland Fish Market there is also a terrific deli which had, amongst other goodies, bags of tiny, multi-coloured spuds. I had never seen anything like them before so couldn't resist grabbing a bag and partnering them with an excellent Lemon Flounder.

Lemon Flounder with an Exotic Potato Salad   Serves 2–4
— as cooked on Waiheke Island

400 gm (13 oz) baby potatoes, scrubbed well	Cook until almost tender. Drain.
olive oil 1 large red onion, sliced freshly ground salt & pepper	Heat a good splash of oil in pan and sauté onion until lightly coloured. Add potatoes, season and cook gently until tender.
125 ml (4 fl oz) olive oil 1 tbsp Dijon mustard 1 garlic clove, crushed a good splash of red wine vinegar freshly ground salt & pepper	Put in bowl and whisk.
olive oil 2 plate-sized flounder plain (all-purpose) flour freshly ground salt & pepper	Heat a thin layer of oil in a large pan. Flour and season flounder and pan-fry until cooked (one at a time, if necessary keeping the first hot in a low oven while cooking the other).
chopped fresh parsley	When flounder and potatoes are cooked, toss dressing to taste through potatoes along with parsley, then put flounder on plate with a pile of the salad.

'You can, of course, use any baby waxy potatoes.'

At the National Zoo in Canberra it was suggested that I might like to visit the lions and tigers inside their enclosure. Having just fed the lions with their afternoon snack (chicken wings) and having nearly lost my fingers in the process I quickly declined. But, being a nice sort of fellow, I offered the services of my assistant Mr Moon (working on the assumption that where there's no sense there's no feeling). Coward that I am, I then retired to the monkeys' enclosure where I made a complete fool of myself by cooking this Cuban-influenced dish for what turned out to be South American (not Cuban) monkeys – who in turn decided that pawpaw was not to their liking.

Swordfish with Pawpaw Salsita

Serves 4

– as cooked at Canberra's National Zoo

60 ml (2 fl oz) olive oil 3 chillies, seeded & finely sliced ½ small red onion, finely chopped	Put in a pan and gently cook, without colouring, until tender.
½ medium pawpaw (papaya), peeled, seeded & finely diced grated zest & juice of 2 limes grated zest & juice of 1 orange 12 fresh mint leaves, finely sliced freshly ground salt & pepper	Put in a bowl and pour hot oil mix over the top. Toss gently.
4 x 180 gm (6 oz) swordfish steaks, cleaned olive oil spay juice of 1–2 limes seasoning	Season and spray swordfish with oil and cook on a preheated grill or BBQ, squeezing lime juice over as you do so. To serve, put salsita on plates and top with fish.

Australia: Canberra

'Garnisha' is another one of Australia's relatively unsung cottage industries. Situated at Boreen Point just north of Noosa, Tim and Claire Warren make a ripper range of curry pastes, masalas, Indian style pickles etc.

A former builder with a passion for cooking, Tim also has a mean golf slice (he appears to spend half his day practising his golf swing using kaffir limes instead of balls). He also, during the filming of the show, just missed my ear with one of his mistimed shots. But apart from Tim's lack of aptitude as a golfer, this is a 'sea change' that has definitely worked.

The produce, including fresh turmeric, cardamom, galangal, mangos, papayas, various chillies and the aforementioned kaffir limes, are all grown on the property; the products are made, bottled and labelled on the premises and Claire handles the marketing. And when asked about the next step both answered with alacrity that there was no next step – this was the perfect sized business which gave them time to also enjoy a reasonably relaxed lifestyle (and to practise that golf swing).

Grilled Swordfish with a Green Bean & Corn Salad

Serves 4

— as cooked in the grounds of Garnisha

60 ml (2 fl oz) olive oil 60 ml (2 fl oz) fresh lime juice 2–3 tsp curry paste or masala freshly ground salt & pepper	Whisk together and set some aside for use as a dressing.
4 x 180 gm (6 oz) swordfish steaks	Pour over marinade and leave for up to 30 minutes. Then grill or barbecue brushing with marinade as you do so.
sea salt 24–30 green beans, topped, tailed & halved crossways 3 corn cobs (ear of corn), kernels removed ½ red capsicum (bell pepper), cored, seeded & diced 3 spring (green) onions, chopped 3 tbsp chopped fresh coriander (cilantro)	Blanch beans and corn in a largish pot of lightly salted boiling water for a minute or two. Then drain and put in a bowl with rest of ingredients. Toss with reserved marinade and put on plates. Top with fish and drizzle with a little more of the reserved marinade.

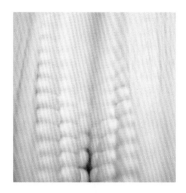

'The Jambu Air Apple is a member of the water apple family (see page 84) and the Singapore berries are rather sharp therefore gooseberries would be the perfect replacement.'

Sesame Seared Tuna with Cherry Tomato, Jambu Air Apple & Singapore Berry Salad

Serves 4 as an entree

— as cooked by chef Chris Salans at Mosiac Restaurant in Ubud

½ punnet (tub) small cherry tomatoes, halved

1 Jambu Air Apple (or nashi), sliced finely

¼–½ punnet (tub) Singapore berries (or gooseberries)

½ tbsp chopped fresh herbs (basil, chervil, tarragon, chives)

1 large knob fresh ginger, grated & squeezed to extract juice

extra virgin olive oil

balsamic vinegar

freshly ground salt & pepper

Toss together with oil, vinegar and seasonings to taste.

---

4 x 80 gm (2¾ oz) slices sashimi grade tuna (see page 47)

sesame seeds

Season tuna and lightly coat with sesame seeds.

---

vegetable oil

Heat in a large pan and sear tuna. Mound salad on individual plates and top with tuna.

Bali: Ubud

Jim Frangos would have to be deemed to be the Crown Prince of Daylesford. A long-time business operator, he first arrived in town on returning from the Vietnam War, when he bought the Belvedere Hotel. At that time, as he describes it, this was 'redneck' territory. Intolerant, introverted, highly critical of anything outside the norm and also fairly rough – he called the front bar of the Belvedere 'The Swinging' Arm purely and simply because of the number of fights.

These days Daylesford is certainly a very different place. Not only has the Swinging Arm transformed itself into the very sophisticated Frangos and Frangos coffee palace-wine-bar-restaurant, it would be hard to find a more tolerant, welcoming place. For example, Jim tells of his famous Breakfast Club where more than eighty people gather, many of whom have been married or involved with others in the group but are still on good terms (and no, we're not talking duelling banjo type scenarios). Visitors are also always welcome and nary a word is spoken in anger unless, of course, it concerns Victoria's new land taxes which appeared to have the locals, when I was there, talking rebellion in the streets.

Local Trout with Salsa Verde
— as cooked by the lake in Daylesford

Serves 4

1 garlic clove 8–10 capers, rinsed 2–3 baby gherkins (sweet dill pickles) 2–3 anchovies	Chop together to a fine paste (or process).
½ cup fresh basil leaves ½ cup fresh mint leaves ½ cup fresh parsley	Add and continue chopping until well mixed.
125 ml (4 fl oz) olive oil a good splash of red wine vinegar 1 tsp Dijon mustard freshly ground salt & pepper	Add, mix well and taste (should be fairly sharp). Set aside.
olive oil 4 small whole baby trout plain (all-purpose) flour freshly ground salt & pepper	Heat a layer of oil in a large pan. When hot add floured, seasoned trout and cook over fairly high heat until crisp and cooked almost through.
1 small red onion, finely sliced 1 red capsicum (bell pepper), cored, seeded & finely sliced 6 vine ripened tomatoes, cored & quartered ½–1 continental (telegraph) cucumber, sliced	Toss with a little oil and mound on individual plates. Top with trout and serve with a good dollop of the salsa verde on the side.

'When cooking fish always remove from the heat source just before it's finished as it will continue to cook.'

Shellfish

Dining out in Mauritius

While there are a number of interesting restaurants in Mauritius, the best ones tend to be situated in the resorts. This has a lot to do with the fact that most tourists stay in the resorts on the full or half board systems (full means all meals are included while half means breakfast and dinner). So it takes a pretty keen foodie to venture outside and pay extra for meals. But that said, the hotel food does tend to lean more towards France than Mauritius and to experience the true food of the island one needs to escape from the compound.

The queen of Mauritian food is said to be Jacqueline Dalais who operates five or six restaurants including La Clef des Champs at Floreal. I also ate well at a number of more casual eateries in Port Louis and, in most cases, found the Indian food to be excellent all over the island. But don't go looking for upmarket establishments. Outside the resorts they are few and far between so just look for the busy little number full of locals.

Speaking of upmarket, one night we dined at the ultra expensive Spoon des Iles at Le Saint Geran Hotel in Belle Mare. A concept from leading French chef Alain Ducasse, this idea has been repeated in many parts of the world. It's an interesting concept. Basically the menu is made up of three lists. One is the prime ingredients, the second the accompaniments and the third the sauces. You then mix and match to suit yourself (although each line itself, crossways, is the chef's suggestion). I stuck to what the chef recommended so I can't say whether the system works or not, but it does seem a little gimmicky and fraught with danger. But, that aside, the service was highly professional, the experience was most enjoyable and the food was both classy and delicious.

Another resort restaurant that was highly recommended, although we just plain and simply ran out of time, was Safran at Le Touessrok Hotel at Trou d' Eau Douce. I am told it serves the most stunning modern Indian food under the direction of leading London chef Vineet Bhatia.

But a more hands-on chef is to be found in the Oberoi's superb restaurant. Brit Andrew Skinner produced some of the best food of our stay with ever-changing menus which had real flair and subtle Mauritian influences.

Mauritian Spiced Scallops on a Palm Heart Salad

Serves 4

— as cooked by chef Andrew Skinner at the Oberoi

1 tsp paprika 1 tsp ground cumin 1 tsp ground coriander 1 tsp turmeric	Mix together and set aside.

1½ large tomatoes, peeled, seeded & diced
  (see page 21)
8 snowpeas, topped, tailed & shredded
1 medium chilli, seeded & sliced
a good pinch of sea salt
freshly ground pepper
juice of 1 lemon
½ palm heart, sliced (or 1 can heart of palm or
  finely sliced fennel)
1 tbsp chopped fresh coriander (cilantro)
1 tbsp pumpkin seeds, toasted
	Put two thirds of the tomato and rest of ingredients in a bowl and toss well.

olive oil 12–16 large fresh scallops, cleaned	Heat a little oil in a heavy-bottomed pan. Toss scallops well in spice mix and when oil is very hot sear quickly in pan on both sides.
baby lettuce leaves	Place some in a circle on individual plates. Put a pastry ring or similar in middle and fill with the salad. Top with scallops.
olive oil a little chopped onion 1 tbsp chopped fresh coriander (cilantro)	Return pan to heat. Add a little olive oil, onion, coriander, left over tomato and a good pinch of spice mix. Pour around the edge of a plate.
deep-fried celery leaves (or basil)	Place on top.

In a day and age when a restaurant that survives for five years is deemed to be a huge success, Antoine's in Auckland stands out from the crowd. Owned and operated by my mates Tony and Beth Astle since 1973, it is still regarded as one of this restaurant-mad city's finest. And no wonder – Tony is a workaholic who is at the stoves morning, noon and night and is definitely not au fait with the term delegation. The food reflects this care and attention and I particularly like the section of the menu dedicated to 'Antoine's Classics' which features the most popular dishes from over the years. He is also renowned for his treatment of offal. (He once shocked one of New Zealand's supposedly knowledgeable wine and food groups by serving a dish featuring every part of the pig including, I think, the tail.)

Sautéed Watermelon with Scallops, Wasabi Flying Fish Roe & Pink Peppercorn Vinaigrette

Serves 4

– as cooked by Tony Astle in the courtyard at Antoine's

1 tbsp dry mustard powder ¼ tbsp sugar ¼ tbsp salt 2–3 tbsp (1–1½ fl oz) garlic water (1 garlic clove blended with water)	Mix, in a bowl, to a paste.
125 ml (4 fl oz) vegetable oil	Whisk in, little by little, to mayonnaise consistency.
60 ml (2 fl oz) vegetable oil 125 ml (4 fl oz) water	Mix together then carefully whisk in, being careful not to curdle.
60 ml (2 fl oz) vegetable oil 125 ml (4 fl oz) malt vinegar	Mix together and whisk in.
freshly ground salt 1 tsp ground pink peppercorns	Add to taste. Set aside.
vegetable oil 4 largish squares of seedless watermelon Cajun spices, bought	Heat a little oil in a pan. Dust watermelon lightly with spices and sauté on both sides. Remove and place on individual plates.
16 fresh scallops, cleaned	Clean out pan, add a little fresh oil and sear quickly over high heat. Place on top of watermelon.
vegetable oil wasabi flying fish roe (see page 49) 16 baby snowpeas, blanched	Place on top and drizzle with the vinaigrette.

Scallop Salad with Parmesan & Garlic Croutons

Serves 4

— as cooked on the foreshore at Napier

100 gm (3½ oz) unsalted butter 4 garlic cloves, crushed	Melt and then set aside for 10 minutes.
1 handful wild rocket (arugula) 1 head witloof, cleaned & sliced finely olive oil balsamic vinegar freshly ground salt & pepper	Toss leaves with oil, balsamic and seasoning to taste.
4 slices white toast bread, crusts removed & quartered freshly grated parmesan	Brush bread with garlic butter and pan-fry until golden. Toss with parmesan in a bowl.
16–20 scallops, cleaned olive oil spray	Preheat a grill plate. Spray scallops and sear quickly over high heat. Toss with salad and mound on plates. Arrange croutons around.

New Zealand: Hawke's Bay

According to the *Oxford Companion to Food*, Succotash is an ancient Southern American dish whose name derived from the Indian 'sukquttahash'. Originally it was corn and beans boiled together with the flesh of bear. But as there was no bear available when I cooked this in Canberra, I had to make do with some lovely fresh scallops.

Succotash with Scallops

Serves 4

– as cooked on the shores of Lake Burley Griffin

1 tbsp (½ fl oz) olive oil a knob of butter 3 small zucchini, finely diced	Heat oil and butter and sauté zucchini until fairly tender.
4 corn cobs (ears of corn), kernels removed	Add, toss and cook for 2 minutes.
60 ml (2 fl oz) cream a pinch of cayenne sea salt	Add, mix well, turn down heat and cook gently for another few minutes.
100 gm (3½ oz) canned cannelini beans, drained & rinsed 2 heaped tbsp chopped fresh basil 2 heaped tbsp chopped fresh parsley	Add and gently simmer for a few more minutes.
16 fresh scallops olive oil spray	Spray scallops and cook on a preheated grill plate for 1–2 minutes on each side. Place succotash in flat soup bowls and top with scallops.

'There is nothing worse than rubbery overcooked scallops so just sear them until lightly coloured over high heat.'

Australia: Canberra

The Great Barrier Feast on Hamilton Island off the coast of Queensland, is a celebration of the best in food and wine. Held every year during June, it is not unlike a bloody good party which just happens to last a little longer than usual (three days).

For example, can I tell you of the Grand Marque Champagne Tasting which was held on the first night – a tasting of Bollinger RD, Dom Perignon, Louis Roederer Cristal and Pol Roger 'Sir Winston Churchill'. Also, if you just happened to get thirsty in between (the tastings were exceedingly generous), copious quantities of Moet & Chandon were also being served.

And if you were in the mood for a bit of work, the stars were out in force to conduct the master classes. Len Evans, Jeffrey Grosset, Michael Hill-Smith, John Purbrick and many other leading winemakers were on hand to instruct you in their craft (and pour the odd drink). While leading chefs such as Peter Doyle from Est, Geoff Lindsay from Pearl, Gilbert Lau and Anthony Lui from the Flowerdrum, Allan Koh from Koko and Paul Wade from Little Nell in Aspen ensured that not only did you learn a cooking trick or two but you got fed to boot.

Steamed Scallops with Japanese Herb Vinaigrette

Serves 4

– as cooked by Allan Koh at the Great Barrier Feast

1 bunch shiso (or basil) leaves, finely chopped

100 ml (3 fl oz) mirin (Japanese rice wine)

100 ml (3 fl oz) champagne (or white wine) vinegar

100 ml (3 fl oz) fresh lime juice

100 gm (3½ oz) caster (superfine) sugar

1–2 chillies, finely chopped

grated zest of 1 lime

100 ml (3 fl oz) light soy sauce

50 ml (1½ fl oz) olive oil

Mix well and taste for seasoning.

12–16 fresh scallops in the half shell

Wash and clean and return to shell. Put a bamboo steamer basket over a wok of boiling water. Place scallops in, cover and steam for 2–3 minutes. Drain off any excess liquid from the scallops and dress with the vinaigrette.

'Shiso is a Japanese leaf that is available, normally in summer, in both green and red varieties. Can be sometimes found in Japanese or Asian markets.'

After the 2002 bombing in Kuta there was a marked collapse in the tourist market, particularly at the upper end, resulting in a huge decline in trade in the upper echelon restaurants such as Ku De Ta at Legian. Aimed fairly and squarely towards the well-heeled tourists, restaurants such as this offered the best of both local and imported ingredients, certainly with a touch of Bali, but with a definite Australian (if not European) bent. While I basically ate at the cheapies, I enjoyed a couple of excellent meals at both Ku De Ta and Mosiac in Ubud and would hope that they, and the few others of their standard, have ridden out the storm. Because, as we all know, whenever you travel overseas there always comes a time when you feel like eating something a little familiar (and that doesn't mean a visit to McDonald's).

Seared Scallops with Angel Hair Pasta, Parma Ham & Leeks
Serves 2

— as cooked by chef Toby Anderson at Ku De Ta

2 leeks, well washed & cut into lengths 125 ml (4 fl oz) chicken stock (bought or homemade, see page 280) 2 bay leaves 6 whole white peppercorns 1 tsp fresh thyme leaves 1 tsp butter freshly ground salt & pepper greaseproof (waxed) paper	Place in a small pot and bring to the boil. Cut greaseproof paper into a round to fit into pot and place on leeks. Turn heat down and gently simmer until just tender (about 10 minutes). Remove leeks and cut in half lengthways.
3 tbsp (1½ fl oz) olive oil 2–3 garlic cloves, finely chopped 2 red (French) shallots, finely sliced 4 thin slices prosciutto	At same time heat oil in a pan and sauté gently garlic and shallots until tender. Add prosciutto and sauté for a few minutes.
4 tbsp (2 fl oz) dry white wine 2 tbsp (1 fl oz) cream	Drain most of the oil from the pan, add the wine and the leeks. Bring to the boil and reduce a little. Then add the cream and once again reduce a little. Keep warm.
200 gm (6½ oz) angel hair pasta sea salt	Cook in plenty of lightly salted boiling water until al dente. Drain very well and add to the leek mix.
8 fresh scallops, cleaned freshly grated parmesan	Heat a non-stick pan, without oil, lightly coat scallops with parmesan and pan-fry until golden and just cooked.
freshly ground pepper	Place pasta on individual plates and top with scallops and a little pepper.

When we were driving along the Great Ocean Road on our way to Lorne, we saw a couple of divers at Skenes Creek fishing for abalone. We stopped and persuaded Paul Curtain and Troy Van Santen to snaffle us a few which I cooked right there and then.

Abalone with Shiitakes, Snowpeas & Garlic

Serves 4

— as cooked on the beach at Skenes Creek

8 large dried shiitake mushrooms	Soak in warm water for about 30 minutes until pliable. Then drain, cut off and discard stalks and slice caps.
2–3 large abalone, cleaned & washed in cold water juice of 1 lemon a good slurp of olive oil 2 garlic cloves, crushed	Slice abalone very finely then toss with lemon, oil and garlic. Marinate for 5–10 minutes.
1–2 tbsp (1–1½ fl oz) olive oil 8–12 snowpeas, shredded a good splash of low salt soy sauce	Heat oil in a wok until smoking. Toss in abalone and cook rapidly, tossing continually. Throw in snowpeas and soy and toss well. Remove from heat.
1 handful rocket (arugula)	Add, toss and mound on plates.

Australia: Great Ocean Road

Many people mistakenly believe that coconut milk is the water-like substance from the coconut's cavity. This is not the case. It is actually made from flesh from which the husk and brown skin have been removed. The flesh is then grated (or processed) and put in hot water. This is then strained through muslin and allowed to sit – the cream rises to the top and is then removed and the remainder is strained again to produce the coconut milk. And when making curries, Thais often boil the coconut cream first to 'crack' or split it. (With the canned product, you often need to add some oil to help achieve this.) The reason behind this process is to fry the curry paste rather than boil it as would happen if the oil had not separated – they feel this releases the paste's aromas and subsequently a better result is achieved.

Mussel & Pineapple Curry

Serves 4

– as cooked by the pool at Cape Panwa Hotel

200 ml (6½ fl oz) coconut cream 50 ml (1½ fl oz) vegetable oil	Boil to separate, stirring constantly to stop scorching.
2–3 tbsp yellow curry paste	Add and cook gently for a few more minutes.
2 tbsp (1 fl oz) Asian fish sauce 1 tbsp shaved palm sugar 1 tbsp (½ fl oz) tamarind water (see page 32)	Add and continue to cook until colour deepens.
500 ml (16 fl oz) coconut milk	Add and bring to boil.
1 kilo (2 lb) mussels, scrubbed & debearded (see page 9) ½ small pineapple, cubed (see page 37) 4 fresh kaffir lime leaves, shredded	Add and cook, covered, until mussels open, removing to bowls as they do so (and discarding any that don't).
2 long red chillies, seeded & sliced fresh coriander (cilantro) leaves	Pour curry over mussels and scatter over top.

Thailand: Phuket

'There are a number of mussel farms in the
Great Ocean Road region – these came from
Portarlington.'

Pasta with Mussels

Serves 4

– as cooked on the Geelong boardwalk

500 gm (1 lb) fettucine	Cook in plenty of lightly salted boiling water until al dente.
4 tbsp (2 fl oz) olive oil 2 garlic cloves, crushed a pinch of red pepper flakes	Heat oil in a wok and sauté gently.
150 ml (5 fl oz) dry white wine 600 gm (1¼ lb) mussels, cleaned & debearded (see page 9)	Add, cover and cook until opened removing as they do so. Shell, discarding any that don't open.
3 tbsp chopped fresh Italian (flat leaf) parsley	When pasta is ready, drain and add to wok along with the parsley and mussels. Toss well and serve.

Mussels with Roasted Red Capsicum & Anchovy Butter

Serves 4

– as cooked in a kitchen in Healesville

2 red capsicum (bell peppers)

Roast capsicums by preheating overhead grill and cutting tops and bottoms off capsicums and removing all seeds and membranes. Halve and place on tray, skin side up and cook under grill until blistered and brown-black. Cover with another tray and cool. Then peel.

2 anchovies
200 gm (6½ oz) soft, unsalted butter
½ tbsp chopped fresh parsley
freshly ground pepper

Process capsicum with anchovies and a little of the anchovy oil. Then mix into butter along with the parsley and pepper.

1 kilo (2 lb) mussels, scrubbed & debearded
   (see page 9)
60 ml (2 fl oz) white wine
a little chopped onion

Put in a large wok, cover and cook, removing the second they open. Remove and discard upper shell and, when cool, top mussels evenly with the butter. Then put in the fridge for at least 30 minutes before whacking under a preheated overhead grill until hot and bubbling.

Australia: Yarra Valley

A cook's tour

Our mates at New Zealand Tourism suggested we go on a couple of food tours. Having been on a number of such adventures around the world, I must admit I wasn't overly excited, feeling that it would be just more of the same – a visit to a local, touristy market, an ordinary meal in the guide's cousin's restaurant and, if lucky, maybe even a wine and cheese tasting with neither being of a standard to get one's heart racing.

Well, isn't it nice to be proven wrong? Admittedly, almost without exception, New Zealand Tourism's recommendations had been spot on, so I shouldn't have been surprised. But both the Zest and Farmer Dan's tours were special. To start off with, at Farmer Dan (aka Ian Thomas and Kent Baddeley), we tasted a terrific range of cured and smoked meats, visited a really good local produce market, imbibed in the odd glass of good wine (for which Hawke's Bay is famous) and, for the crowning glory, popped into a fascinating fish farming operation where they were not only farming seahorses for the Chinese and Hong Kong market and the most superb (and may I also say expensive) baby paua, but are also experimenting with New Zealand whitebait, which is to me one of the world's great delicacies. Then we enjoyed a terrific meal whipped up by Kent, a very talented chef. Obviously we were a group of happy campers.

On to Wellington, where Zest, who tailor their tours specifically to each individual group, also impressed. Picked up at our hotel in a 1958 Cadillac, we were first whisked off to Island Bay where Al Brown (co-owner and chef of the very highly-rated Logan Brown restaurant) gave us a lesson in the cooking of paua, the native abalone, which he had just pulled up from the ocean floor himself. Washed down with an excellent New

Zealand Riesling, we ate paua fritters, barbecued paua with lemon beurre blanc and my favourite, paua butties between thick slices of buttered bread. Then it was on to Kai in the Bay, where Te Huia Hamilton and Deseree Hildreth introduced us to Maori delicacies such as pikopiko, taewa, kawakawa, puha and the most delicious double-boiled mutton bird (titi). Next on the agenda was an old mate, Ruth Pretty, who joined us for a visit to Moore Wilson Fresh, a terrific one-stop shop for everything from sparkling fresh seafood and organic meat and poultry to smallgoods, vegetables and bread. Then, in their demonstration kitchen, Ruth cooked the most tender rack of Cervena venison wrapped in prosciutto and served with roasted tomatoes.

Unfortunately time defeated us and I didn't get a chance to prove my worth as a barista at the Mojo Coffee Cartel (where I could also have roasted my own beans) or visit the Martinborough wine region or even join Ruth Pretty in her Te Horo kitchens for some intensive training in the culinary arts. But I did make it to Logan Brown for dinner, so all in all a good day ended on a high note.

Wellington's highly regarded Logan Brown restaurant is the brainchild of owners Alister Brown and Steve Logan. It is set in a superbly restored bank chamber up the top of rather seedy Cuba St Mall. (Although on this last visit I did note some improvement to the mall, with new restaurants and bars springing up including a revitalised Matterhorn which, in my day, was a Swiss pastry shop, and the wonderful Good Luck Bar which serves Cambodian food in what is described as a 'retro Chinese opium den' – whatever that means.) But back to Logan Brown, this is a restaurant that with precise, sympathetic cooking showcases the terrific New Zealand ingredients perfectly.

Paua Fritters

Serves 4

– as caught and cooked by Al Brown at Island Bay

100 gm (3½ oz) plain (all-purpose) flour ½ tsp baking powder 2 eggs, beaten 1½ tbsp (¾ fl oz) milk	Sieve flour and baking powder into a bowl. Make a well in the centre. Add eggs and milk and whisk well.
500 gm (1 lb) minced (ground) paua (abalone) 25 gm (1 oz) finely diced red onion 2 tbsp chopped fresh coriander (cilantro) 1 tbsp (½ fl oz) sweet chilli sauce (bought) 1 tbsp (½ fl oz) fresh lime juice freshly ground salt & pepper	Add and fold in.
vegetable oil lemon wedges	Heat a thin layer of oil in a large pan and, without overcrowding, cook tablespoons of the mixture until golden. Drain well and serve with lemon.

'To mince the paua, Al used one of those wonderful old-fashioned mincers that did the job perfectly – you know, the ones that screw onto the table.'

New Zealand: Wellington

Paua Butties

— as cooked by Al Brown at Island Bay

2–3 whole paua (abalone), cleaned (see page 138) a good squeeze or two of fresh lemon juice	Slice very thinly and toss with lemon juice.
olive oil 1 large red onion, finely sliced 1–2 garlic cloves, crushed	Heat a little oil in a hot wok and sauté until tender. Add paua and toss briefly.
8 slices toast bread homemade mayonnaise (see page 281) a handful of baby rocket (arugula)	Place four slices of bread on a board. Smear generously with mayo, top with rocket then sautéed paua. Smear more mayo on the rest of the bread and press down firmly.

'I remember the butties of my youth — lots of chips between doorstops of buttered bread with plenty of tomato sauce. This version is a lot more classy (and healthier).'

As I have mentioned before I was blown out by the quality of the seafood being farmed by East Coast Aquaculture in Napier which is, need I say, on New Zealand's East Coast. Admittedly I didn't quite get into their main export, seahorses, but I made up for that by cooking (and eating) a significant number of baby paua. And the crew was pretty keen on the crab too.

Chilli Paua

Serves 4

— as cooked on the foreshore at Napier

16–120 baby paua (abalone), cleaned (or 2 large)	If baby keep whole, but if large pound lightly with a meat mallet, then cut into thin slices.
2 tbsp (1 fl oz) soy sauce 2 tbsp (1 fl oz) mirin (Japanese rice wine) 2 tbsp (1 fl oz) sake	Toss through and leave for 10 minutes.
4 green chillies, finely chopped 1 cm (³⁄₈ inch) piece fresh ginger, grated 2 garlic cloves, crushed	Pound in a mortar.
2 spring (green) onions, finely chopped 1 small bunch fresh coriander (cilantro), finely chopped	Add and pound more.
sesame oil	Heat a good splash in a wok. Quickly sauté paua then remove.
250 ml (8 fl oz) fish stock (bought or homemade, see page 280)	Add paste along with fish stock. Bring to boil and cook briefly adding more stock if necessary.
steamed rice	Return paua, toss well and serve on rice.

'To prepare paua, use your thumb to prise from the shell. Remove ring of gut and also push out the two small red teeth at the pointy end.'

Crab & Camembert Omelette

Serves 2

— as cooked on the foreshore at Napier

250 gm (8 oz) crabmeat	Pick over (see below) and put in bowl.
8 eggs a good splash of cream 1 camembert, rind removed & cubed 1–2 tbsp snipped fresh chives freshly ground salt & pepper	Whisk and mix in crab.
a good dollop of butter	Melt in large non-stick pan. Add egg mix and stir with wooden spoon, mixing in the outsides until soft curds form. Turn heat right down, cover and cook until centre just trembles when pan is shaken.

'Picking over crab means that you pick through it by hand to ensure that there is no shell left in it.'

The markets in Thailand, many of which are open day and night, are fantastic. My favourite was the bustling Night Bazaar in Bangkok, which was complete with a huge auditorium surrounded by food stalls of all shapes and sizes. Actually, this is about Thailand's oldest market site because it was situated on the original China-Southern Thailand route and, for centuries, it is where the various nationalities have traded their wares. It is also where I tasted some fabulous mussel cakes which I couldn't wait to attempt to recreate.

Thai Mussel Cakes with Stir-fried Beanshoots (Hawy Thawt)
Serves 4

– as enjoyed at the Night Bazaar Market

1 kg (2 lb) mussels, debearded (see page 9)	Cook, covered with a little water until opened, removing them as they do so. Discard those that don't open. Remove meat and chop coarsely.
50 gm (1¾ oz) plain (all-purpose) flour 40 gm (1½ oz) cornflour (cornstarch) 1 egg 1 tbsp (½ fl oz) Asian fish sauce 1 tsp shaved palm sugar 60 ml (2 fl oz) water	Whisk to make a smooth batter. Add chopped mussels.
vegetable oil	Heat a thin layer of oil in a large pan and drop tablespoons of the mussel mix in without overcrowding. Cook until golden on both sides then drain well on paper towels.
vegetable oil 2 handfuls beanshoots, washed & drained 6 spring (green) onions, shredded 1 garlic clove, crushed	While cakes are cooking, heat a little oil in a wok and quickly stir-fry until crisp-tender.
soy sauce 2 long chillies, seeded & sliced	Arrange cakes on plate, sprinkle with a little soy, mound with beanshoots and then sprinkle with chillies.

Thailand: Bangkok

The Flowerdrum in Melbourne is one of Australia's truly great restaurants. The reason for this – the consummate restaurateur, Gilbert Lau. He has sold, but to three of his long term staff, so he is still there on a regular basis as a consultant. Actually, it's interesting travelling around Australia and hearing about Gilbert. Whether it be the Asian vegetable grower just outside Darwin, the specialist fishmonger in Brisbane, the asparagus grower in Victoria or the pig farmer in Western Australia, they all seem to have a personal arrangement with Gilbert who they all say is a charming man but 'very particular'.

Sautéed Prawns with Pine Nuts & Shiitakes

Serves 4

— as cooked by Anthony Lui & Gilbert Lau at the Great Barrier Feast

3 cups dried shiitake mushrooms	Soak in warm water for 1½–2 hours. Then drain well, discard stalks and slice caps.
50 gm (1¾ oz) pine nuts	Preheat oven to 150°C (300°F). Put pine nuts on a baking tray and bake for 4–5 minutes until golden brown, shaking regularly.
16–20 green prawns (shrimps), shelled & veins removed	Wash under cold running water and dry well using paper towels.
40 gm (1½ oz) water chestnuts, halved 40 gm (1½ oz) bamboo shoots, diced ½ tsp sea salt	Place in a pot of boiling water along with shiitakes and cook for 2 minutes. Drain well.
½ tsp sugar ½ tsp potato flour 1 tsp sea salt 2½ tsp (½ fl oz) chicken stock or water	Mix until dissolved. Set aside.
400 ml (13 fl oz) peanut oil	Heat in a wok to about 110°C. Add prawns and sauté for 1 minute continually turning. Remove.
40 gm (1½ oz) asparagus, sliced on the diagonal 40 gm (1½ oz) red capsicum (bell peppers), cored, seeded & cut into 2 cm cubes 500 ml (16 fl oz) water	Pour off all but 1 tbsp (½ fl oz) of the oil then add shiitake mix and these vegies and toss for 30 seconds. Add water and the prawns and cook for another 30 seconds.
½ tbsp (¼ fl oz) Chinese rice wine	Add the flour mix and stir for a few seconds. Then add wine and briefly toss. Turn off heat add pine nuts and serve immediately.

Australia: Hamilton Island

One of the Great Ocean Road's true characters is Chris Talihmanidis from Chris's at Beacon Point which is just outside Apollo Bay. A true pioneer in this region, he has owned and operated cafes and restaurants in this area since the sixties when he first opened the Marine Cafe in the then sleepy little town of Lorne.

A hospitable man with sparkling eyes, Chris has mastered the art of presenting good fresh food in a style that reflects his Greek heritage. He has also, over the years, built up an enviable group of suppliers and if you want to eat super-fresh abalone, crayfish or even the local whiting (just as good as the South Australian King George whiting) then Chris's is the place for you. Add to that one of the best views in the world (true!) overlooking the Lorne coastline and a new dining room which takes even better advantage of this view (the old one burnt down a couple of years ago) and you may find it hard to leave and instead find yourself staying the night in one of the villas perched out over the hillside.

Lobster with a Brandy & Lemon Butter Sauce   Serves 2
– as cooked by Chris Talihmanidis at Beacon Point

1.2 k (2¼ lb) lobster, cut in half lengthways & cleaned olive oil spray	Preheat oiled grill or BBQ and cook lobster flesh side down first.
100 gm (3½ oz) unsalted butter juice of 1 lemon 30 ml (1 fl oz) brandy	While lobster is cooking melt butter in a pan, add lemon and brandy and reduce a little.
1 tsp chopped fresh thyme freshly ground salt & pepper	When lobster is cooked (to check make a small cut with a sharp knife) add thyme and seasonings to butter and pour over the top.

Ragout of Seafood with Creole Sauce

Serves 4

– as cooked on the beach at Pointe d'Esny

vegetable oil 2 large onions, finely chopped 1 leek, finely sliced 3 green chillies, finely chopped 2–3 garlic cloves, crushed 1 tbsp grated fresh ginger	Heat oil in a wok or deep-sided pan and sauté until tender.
4–5 ripe red tomatoes, cored & cut into wedges 250 ml (8 fl oz) fish or vegetable stock (bought or homemade, see page 281) freshly ground salt & pepper 2 tsp fresh thyme leaves	Add, mix well and cook fairly rapidly until tomatoes collapse (adding more stock if necessary).
1 tbsp fresh coriander (cilantro) leaves a splash of oyster sauce	Add and mix well.
4 x 80 gm (2¾ oz) pieces tuna fillet 4 x 80 gm (2¾ oz) pieces any steaky white fish (see page 4)	Add and bury in the sauce. Cook, gently for about 3–4 minutes.
2 calamari or squid tubes, cleaned & cut into rings 8 fresh scallops, cleaned	Put on top, cover and cook for a minute or two. Then share between individual bowls.
chopped fresh coriander (cilantro) 2 spring (green) onions, finely chopped	Scatter on the top.

Maurituis: Point d'Esny

Another one of Bali's most famous dishes, this satay demonstrates what I mean when I talk about recipes and food styles being assimilated into other cultures. This dish has obviously originated in the Middle East (or even India) where minced lamb is often fashioned into a sausage shape along a stick of one type or other. Here we find a similar process but in this case using seafood and instead of the original spices such as cumin and coriander, a mixture of flavours that is distinctly Balinese. As an added flavour boost, these satays are traditionally cooked over coconut husks and are moulded onto lemongrass stalks.

Grilled Spiced Minced Seafood on Lemongrass Stalks (Sate Lilit)

Serves 4

– as cooked by Mr Puto from the Waka Hotel Group

vegetable oil	Heat a little oil in a wok and sauté until just tender. Then pound in a mortar until a paste is formed (or process).
1 cm (³⁄₈ inch) piece fresh turmeric, finely sliced (or 1 tsp powdered)	
1 cm (³⁄₈ inch) piece fresh galangal (or ginger) finely sliced	
1 candle nut (kemiri nut), finely sliced	
2 small chillies, seeded & finely sliced	
1 garlic clove, finely sliced	
2 red (French) shallots, finely sliced (or ¼ small red onion)	
250 gm (8 oz) tuna, very finely chopped	Using your hands, mix together with 2 tbsp of the above paste (fry a little to check if more paste is needed).
10 small prawns (shrimp), peeled, cleaned & very finely chopped	
3 tbsp grated fresh coconut	
½ tsp finely chopped kaffir lime leaf	Add and mix in well.
juice of ½ lime	
freshly ground salt & pepper	
lemongrass stalks, white part only, cleaned & cut down to about 20 cm (8 inch) lengths	With wet hands, form 'sausages' on the upper half of each stalk and cook on a preheated lightly oiled grill or BBQ.
vegetable oil spray	

'It is important that you use fresh seafood as frozen may exude too much moisture. And the seafood can be whizzed up in a processor rather than finely chopped.

I remember when I was a young kid, I used to dig up pipis at our local beach with my best mate Michael O'Donnell and then eat them raw with a splash of vinegar. Obviously budding gourmets, we would then spoil the developing palates by visiting his parents' corner store where we would follow this treat up with meat pies with copious quantities of tomato sauce.

Pipis with Chilli, Coriander & Ginger

Serves 4–6

– as cooked at Mission Bay

vegetable oil 2 chillies, seeded & sliced 2 garlic cloves, crushed 2 cm (¾ inch) knob of ginger, peeled & grated	Heat a little oil in a wok and sauté quickly .
120 ml (4 fl oz) Chinese rice wine 120 ml (4 fl oz) fish or chicken stock (bought or homemade, see page 280) a good splash oyster sauce a good splash soy sauce	Add and bring to the boil.
1½ kilos (3 lb) pipis	Add, cover and cook removing as they open. Either remove top shell as you do so or just spread apart and leave intact. Put in bowls, discarding any that don't open.
brown sugar fresh lime juice 3 tbsp chopped fresh coriander (cilantro)	Add sugar and lime juice to taste. Then mix in coriander and pour over pipis

New Zealand: Auckland

Meat

I realise that New Zealand still has more sheep than it does humans. But it is interesting as you travel through the countryside (as we did with the *Skinny Cook* series) to note that not every paddock is now packed with sheep. Instead, grape vines, olive groves, deer farms and, in certain parts of the country, exotic vegies, abound.

Maybe that will mean that one day the humans will overtake our four-legged friends and Aussies will no longer feel the compunction to tell Kiwis every sheep joke known to mankind.

Minute Steak of Lamb with a Herb Sauce

Serves 4

— as cooked at the Walter Peak High Country Farm

2 backstraps of lamb (boned loin), trimmed of all fat & sinew	Cut in half crossways. Butterfly and batten out gently to an even thickness.
8–12 baby potatoes (chats), well scrubbed	Boil until tender. Drain and keep covered.
olive oil 1–2 lemons freshly ground salt & pepper	Heat a little oil in a heavy-bottomed pan and, in 2 lots, cook lamb over high heat to desired degree, squeezing lemon juice over as you do so and seasoning once sealed.
olive oil 1 lemon freshly ground salt & pepper	When lamb is almost ready, crush potatoes roughly with a potato masher or fork, adding oil, lemon juice and seasoning to taste.
3 tbsp chopped fresh basil 3 tbsp chopped fresh Italian (flat leaf) parsley 100 gm (3½ oz) unsalted butter	When lamb is ready, remove and add herbs and butter to pan. Place crushed potatoes on individual plates, top with lamb and, when foaming, pour pan juices over the top.

'To butterfly you cut the lamb lengthways down the middle almost right through.'

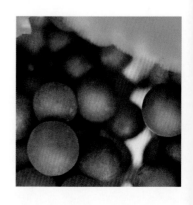

New Zealand: Queenstown

Lamb Pita Pockets

Serves 4

— as cooked on the balcony of Chris's at Beacon Point

3 lamb backstraps (boned loin), trimmed of all fat & sinew

3–4 spring (green) onions, finely chopped

juice of 1 lemon

2 garlic cloves, crushed

60 ml (2 fl oz) olive oil

Cut lamb into thin slices and toss with rest. Marinate for 15 minutes.

½ cup (4 oz) yoghurt

1 garlic clove, crushed

12 fresh mint leaves, sliced

a squeeze of lemon juice

3 tbsp diced continental (telegraph) cucumber

Combine and set aside.

4–8 pita breads

2 ripe tomatoes, cored & sliced

inner leaves of 1 cos (Romaine) lettuce

Heat a wok until very hot. Then throw in lamb and cook quickly tossing continually. Then grill pita and cut one edge off. Stuff with, lettuce, tomato, lamb and yoghurt mix.

Cumin Lamb Steaks with BBQ Kumara

Serves 4

— as cooked on Te Mata Peak

2–3 kumara (see below), scrubbed well sea salt	Cook in boiling, salted water until just tender when pierced with skewer. Drain.
2 tbsp cumin seeds 2 garlic cloves, crushed 1 tsp sea salt	Pound in a mortar (or process).
1 tbsp ground cumin juice of 1 lemon ½ cup (4 fl oz) olive oil	Add and mix well.
4–8 lamb steaks, cut from the leg	Pour marinade over and refrigerate for at least 1 hour. Cut kumara into thick slices and barbecue or grill along with lamb, brushing with marinade as you do so.

'Kumara is the New Zealand native sweet potato — any sweet potato can be substituted.'

New Zealand: Hawke's Bay

De Bortoli Vineyard Restaurant in the Yarra Valley conducts many successful cooking demonstrations. Coupled with a meal of what has just been demonstrated, the sessions are always quickly booked out.

And the chefs – they read like a Who's Who of world gastronomy. Nick Nairn, Antonio Carluccio, Diane Seed and Rick Stein spring to mind, as do many, many others from both Australia and around the world.

Noisettes of Lamb with Artichokes
Serves 4
– as cooked by Antonio Carluccio at De Bortoli

4 small fresh artichokes juice of 1 lemon	Wash and pull off the coarse outer leaves. Trim off the tops and, with a teaspoon remove the hairy chokes. Trim the stalks then quarter and place in a bowl of cold water with lemon juice.
4 tbsp (2 fl oz) olive oil 55 gm (1¾ oz) prosciutto, sliced 4 red (French) shallots, sliced 1 tbsp capers, rinsed & drained	Heat the oil in a pan, add along with drained artichokes and toss briefly.
60 ml (2 fl oz) chicken stock (bought or homemade, see page 280) freshly ground salt & pepper 2 tbsp chopped fresh Italian (flat leaf) parsley	Add stock, turn down heat and cook gently for about 15–20 minutes until artichokes are tender. Add seasonings and parsley and toss.
400 gm (13 oz) lamb backstrap (boned loin), trimmed of all fat & sinew	Cut into 2.5 cm (1 inch) cubes.
4 tbsp (2 fl oz) olive oil	Heat in a large pan and, over high heat, cook lamb to the desired degree. Serve on individual plates with the artichokes and any juices.

'When working with fresh artichokes always drop them into acidulated water immediately after preparation otherwise they will discolour.'

This is an old-fashioned favourite. Both my mother and grandmother regularly featured this on the menu. And delicious it is too. In fact I think Pumped Lamb deserves another fifteen minutes of fame. Prepared in a similar vein to corned or salted beef it is 'pumped' (injected) with a brine solution which gives it a delicate pink colour and a delicious slightly salty flavour. You may have to give your butcher 24 hours notice but any free standing butcher's shop can prepare it for you. As for the cooking, the only secret is to ensure that the water simmers very gently and that you keep it in the liquid until ready to serve, otherwise it may dry out. And the mash – another delicious classic from days gone by.

Pumped Lamb with Carrot & Parsnip Mash

Serves 6–8

– as cooked in a kitchen in New Zealand

1 leg of pumped lamb 2 bay leaves 10 whole black peppercorns 3 fresh parsley sprigs 1 large carrot, roughly chopped 1 medium onion, roughly chopped 2 celery stalks, roughly chopped	Place in a large pot and cover with water. Simmer gently for 1½ hours then leave in liquid until ready to serve.
1 tbsp (½ fl oz) olive oil 1 medium onion, finely chopped 1 garlic clove, crushed	At the same time, heat oil in another pot and sauté vegies until tender.
2 heaped tspn English mustard 2 x 400 gm (13 oz) cans diced tomatoes, drained a little 1½ litres (1⅕ quarts) beef stock (bought or homemade, see page 280) freshly ground salt & pepper	Add along with half of the stock. Whisk well and cook down to a sauce consistency adding the rest of the stock, little by little, as you do so. Check for seasoning.
4–6 medium carrots, cut in chunks 4–6 parsnips, cut in chunks	When lamb is almost ready, cook in lightly salted water until tender. Drain well.
2 good dollops of butter freshly ground salt & pepper	Add to vegies and mash coarsely. (This can be done in advance and reheated in the microwave.)
chopped fresh parsley	Slice the lamb and serve with a generous amount of sauce, a good spoonful of the mash and a sprinkling of parsley.

Prosciutto-wrapped Lamb with Tomato Chutney and Bashed Neeps

– as cooked in a New Zealand kitchen

12–16 thin slices prosciutto
2 lamb backstraps (boned loin),
   trimmed of all fat & sinew
freshly ground pepper
olive oil spray

Preheat oven to 210–220°C (410–425°C). Lay half the prosciutto on bench overlapping slightly. Place one backstrap on top, season with a little pepper and wrap up. Repeat process with other backstrap, spray oven tray lightly and place lamb seam side down. Cook for about 12 minutes until firmish when squeezed. Rest for 4–5 minutes before slicing.

3–4 swedes (rutabaga/yellow turnip), peeled & cubed
freshly ground salt & pepper
a good dollop of butter

While lamb is cooking, boil swedes until tender in lightly salted water. Drain and coarsely mash with butter and seasoning.

tomato relish or chutney

Put a mound of swede on individual plates. Top with lamb and serve with a dollop of chutney on the side.

'For some strange reason, in Scotland swedes (a very popular vegetable) are, when mashed, called bashed neeps which is the traditional accompaniment to haggis.'

New Zealand: Hawke's Bay

'Mini lamb roasts are cut from the leg and are also often known as lamb rumps.'

Mini Lamb Roasts with Greek Potatoes

Serves 4

— as cooked in the kitchens of Aubergine

2–3 mini lamb roasts, trimmed of all fat & sinew

3 garlic cloves, in slivers

18 fresh rosemary needles

Preheat oven to 220°C (425°F).

Cut about 6 slits in the top of each lamb roast and stud with garlic and rosemary, pushing well in.

---

10 baby waxy potatoes (kipfler or the like)

12–16 baby (pickling) onions, peeled

2 garlic cloves, unpeeled but crushed a little

olive oil

juice of 2 lemons

freshly ground salt & pepper

Place vegies in an ovenproof dish (over which you can fit a rack) and toss with olive oil, lemon juice and seasonings. Bake for about 30 minutes, tossing regularly until fairly tender and coloured (adding a little stock if sticking).

---

olive oil spray

freshly ground salt & pepper

Place rack on dish. Put lamb on top, spray with oil and season. Cook to desired degree (about 15 minutes for medium-rare).

---

chopped fresh parsley

Remove lamb and rest for 5 minutes then slice and serve on the potatoes with any meat juices and parsley over the top.

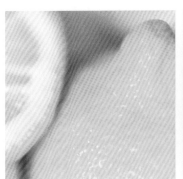

One of the most popular tourist destinations in Queenstown is the Walter Peak High Country Farm right on the shores of Lake Wakitipu. Still a working sheep station, if you want to know the ins and outs of sheep herding, shearing and the like, then this is the place for you. It is also one of the original New Zealand sheep stations which was first settled in 1860. Taken over in the 1880s by the McKenzie family who were pioneers in many of the principles of high country farming, during their 80-year reign it became one of New Zealand's most successful properties, with 170,000 acres, 40,000 sheep and 50 employees.

Lamb's Fry Persillade

Serves 4

— as cooked at Walter Peak High Country Farm

olive oil 8 thickish slices lamb's fry (liver), well trimmed plain (all-purpose) flour sea salt freshly ground pepper	Heat oil in a large pan. Flour and season lamb's fry (shaking off any excess flour) then pan-fry to seal on both sides. Remove.
½ red onion, finely chopped 1 garlic clove, crushed	Add along with more oil if necessary and sauté gently until tender.
250 ml (8 fl oz) chicken stock (bought or homemade, see page 280) a good squeeze of fresh lemon juice	Add and reduce.
3 tbsp chopped fresh parsley 2 good knobs of butter	Add along with lamb's fry and cook very gently until pink in the centre. Remove to individual plates. Pour pan juices over.
1–2 handfuls lettuce leaves olive oil balsamic vinegar freshly ground salt & pepper	Dress and season leaves and serve alongside.

New Zealand: Queenstown

For the last World Cup, I was asked to do a little promotional exercise for the New Zealand Rugby Union. I whipped up this Mixed Lamb Grill with Kiwi Fruit Chutney in Melbourne's Botanic Gardens with the explanation that I felt we needed a return to those days when 'real men' like Colin and Stan Meads, Brian Lochore, Kel Tremain and the like most probably ate lamb three times a day and subsequently had energy to match. Needless to say, the All Blacks beat South Africa that week but sadly I was not asked to repeat the dose and the next week they lost to the Wallabies (I sulked for a month).

And the chutney recipe – this comes from Digby Law, who was one of New Zealand's most loved food presenters (he sadly passed away in 1987). It can be premade and will keep for at least a month in the fridge – or put in sterilised preserving jars where it will last even longer.

Mixed Grill of Lamb with Kiwi Fruit Chutney Serves 4
– as cooked for the All Blacks

500 gm (1 lb) kiwi fruit, peeled & sliced

2 smallish onions, chopped

1 banana, diced

½ cup raisins

100 gm (3½ oz) soft brown sugar

1 tbsp chopped crystalised ginger

1 tsp salt

½ tsp ground ginger

good pinch cayenne

juice of 1 lemon

125 ml (4 fl oz) white wine vinegar

The day before, put in a heavy-bottomed pot and bring to the boil. Then simmer gently, stirring regularly until soft and thick. Cool, then refrigerate.

---

8 lamb cutlets (chops), well trimmed

8 lamb kidneys, cleaned, halved lengthways & cored

4 thick slices lamb's fry (liver)

4 large field mushrooms, peeled

olive oil spray

1 lemon

freshly ground salt & pepper

Heat an oiled ridged grill or BBQ. Spray everything with oil and starting with mushrooms, grill. Once mushies begin to collapse, add cutlets and kidneys and cook (keeping pink), squeezing lemon over the top and seasoning as they cook. Add lamb's fry towards the end then when everything is almost cooked. Put on individual plates along with a good dollop or two of the chutney.

As mentioned before, when you think of Queenstown in New Zealand's far south, bungee jumping and other extreme sports invariably spring to mind. Admittedly this is the bungee jumping capital of the world (the first commercial operation began here in 1988 from the Kawarau Suspension Bridge), but Queenstown is not just for adrenaline junkies. In winter, Coronet Peak and other ski fields are regarded amongst the best in the world; the bars, restaurants and cafes are plentiful and good; and for us wimps there is always a more sedate trip on the Lady of the Lake, *TSS Earnslaw* which has been traversing Lake Wakatipu since 1912 and which is one of the last remaining coal-fired passenger vessels in the world.

Lamb Cutlets with a Greek Cypriot Village Salad

Serves 4

— as cooked on the shores of Lake Wakatipu

3 racks of lamb	Trim off all fat and sinew and scrape bone. Then cut into cutlets.
120 ml (4 fl oz) olive oil juice of ½ lemon 1 garlic clove, crushed 2 tsp chopped fresh oregano	Whisk and pour half over the cutlets. Toss well and set the other half aside.
1 cos (Romaine) lettuce, small inner leaves only, washed & dried ½ small red onion, finely sliced ¼ continental (telegraph) cucumber, finely sliced 1 green capsicum (bell pepper), cored, seeded & finely sliced 10 pitted black olives, halved ½ punnet (tub) cherry tomatoes, halved 100 gm (3½ oz) feta, crumbled freshly ground pepper	After 30 minutes, toss in bowl along with reserved dressing to taste. Preheat grill or BBQ and cook lamb to desired degree, brushing with marinade as you do so. Mound salad on individual plates and top with cutlets.

It appears that New Zealand has almost built an industry out of the Lord of the Rings trilogy. So much so that when we visited the Kinloch Lodge on the upper reaches of Lake Wakatipu, we almost expected to see hobbits emerge from the mists just across the lake – the Westland National Park where Glenorchy, the so-called Gateway to Paradise, nestles in the centre of Lord of the Rings territory. That aside, this is a beautiful part of the world with snow-capped mountains, ancient beech forests, sheer rock faces and glacier-fed rivers, supplemented by some world famous walking tracks and great fishing and hunting.

Steak & Smothered Onion Sandwich

Serves 4

— as cooked at Kinloch Lodge

olive oil 2 large onions, finely sliced 1 garlic clove, crushed	Heat a good splash of oil in a pan and over moderate heat, cook until tender and well coloured.
150 ml (5 fl oz) tomato sauce 1 tbsp (½ fl oz) Worcestershire sauce 1 tbsp (½ fl oz) white vinegar ½ tbsp brown sugar ½ tbsp Dijon mustard ½ tbsp sambal oelek	Whisk, add and cook gently for about 10 minutes until thick and fragrant. Set aside in a warm spot.
2 x 200 gm (6½ oz) porterhouse, rump (sirloin), or fillet (tenderloin) steaks, trimmed of all fat & sinew olive oil spray freshly ground salt & pepper	Spray with oil and grill or BBQ to desired degree, seasoning after sealing. Rest for 5 minutes then slice.

1 French baguette, cut in 4 crossways then
  through middle lengthways
cos (Romaine) or iceberg lettuce leaves,
  either whole or shredded
	Grill or toast bread. Place bottoms on board then top with lettuce, steak and onions. Press top on firmly.

New Zealand: Queenstown

Taquitos of Porterhouse with Soft Goat Curd

Serves 4

— as cooked at Coolabine Farmstead

olive oil spray	Preheat grill or BBQ. Spray steaks with oil and cook to desired degree, sprinkling with lime juice as you do so and seasoning once sealed. Remove, rest for 5 minutes then slice on the diagonal.
2 x 180 gm (6 oz) porterhouse steaks, trimmed of all fat & sinew	
juice of 1 lime	
freshly ground salt & pepper	
8 cherry tomatoes, quartered	Put in bowl and gently toss.
½ continental (telegraph) cucumber, sliced & halved	
¼ cup fresh coriander (cilantro) leaves	
¼ cup fresh Italian (flat leaf) parsley	
juice of 1 lime	
a generous slurp of olive oil	
seasoning	
4–8 tortillas	Either heat on the grill or wrapped in foil in oven.
soft goat curd (or any fresh goat cheese)	Place tortillas on bench, spread with goat cheese then top with steak and salad, roll up and serve.

Waiheke Island is about a 30 minute ferry ride from Auckland's CBD. Once isolated farmland, in the sixties and seventies it became a haven for those seeking an alternative lifestyle (now isn't that more polite than saying it became over-run by hippies?). These days it is better known for its wines – in particular reds, with wineries such as Stonyridge and Goldwater producing some of New Zealand's finest (and most expensive). Unfortunately, I seem to have a bit of a problem with Waiheke. Whenever I visit, the weather is less than perfect. And this trip was no exception. After a morning trying to film on the various beaches and at the picturesque Te Whau Vineyard, the squalls and fierce winds forced us to retire to the covered balcony of Stonyridge where we whipped up a couple of recipes and then had a delightful lunch with the entertaining winemaker Stephen White, a former round-the-world yachtsman.

Steak with an Eggplant and Capsicum Peperonata

Serves 4

— as cooked on the balcony at Stonyridge Winery

1 cup (8 fl oz) olive oil 1 large eggplant, cut in 1 cm (⅜ inch) cubes	Heat oil in a wok or deep pot until almost smoking. Then in 3 or 4 lots fry eggplant until golden, reheating oil between each batch. Drain well on paper towels.
1 large onion, finely chopped 2 garlic cloves, crushed	Pour off most of the oil and sauté until lightly coloured.
2 celery stalks, diced 1 red capsicum (bell pepper), cored, seeded & diced 1 yellow capsicum (bell pepper), cored, seeded & diced	Add and toss for a few minutes.
2 x 400 gm (13 oz) cans diced tomatoes, drained a good splash of white wine a splash of balsamic vinegar 3 heaped tbsp chopped, pitted green olives 250 ml (8 fl oz) chicken stock (bought or homemade, see page 280) 2 tbsp chopped fresh parsley	Add and cook gently until thick and fragrant.
4 x 180 gm (6 oz) fillet (tenderloin), rump (sirloin) or porterhouse steaks, well trimmed olive oil freshly ground salt & pepper	Heat oiled grill or pan and cook steaks to desired degree, seasoning once sealed. When ready, rest steaks for a few minutes and then serve on a bed of the peperonata. The peperonata can be served either hot or cold.

This may seem like a heck of a lot of chillies and garlic (it is) but this is because the Thai's regard mince as needing lots of added flavour. I agree, and the result is delicious but, if you must, you can cut back on them a little. And because we were filming very early in the morning in Phuket to negate the heat, I actually had this on a piece of toast for brekkie – fantastic and nothing at all like my mum's mince on toast which was often a feature of the Hewitson household's breakfast. (After tasting this little Thai number, bland is a word that springs to mind about my mum's version.)

Minced Beef with Chilli, Garlic & Holy Basil (Phad Krapow Neua)
— as cooked in Phuket

Serves 4

vegetable oil 8 garlic cloves, crushed 6 red chillies, chopped	Heat oil in wok and stir-fry until they start to colour.
600–700 gm (1¼–1½ lb) lean minced (ground) beef	Add, stir and mash to break up and seal.
4 kaffir lime leaves, shredded 2 tbsp (1 fl oz) Asian fish sauce 1 tbsp (½ fl oz) oyster sauce a good splash of kecap manis 1 tbsp shaved palm sugar 250 ml (8 fl oz) chicken stock 　(bought or homemade, see page 280)	Add and cook, continuing to mash the meat, until thick and fragrant.
12–15 fresh holy basil leaves 2 long red chillies, sliced	Add and cook briefly. Place on platter.
2–3 spring (green) onions, finely sliced	Sprinkle over the top.

Fergusson's Vineyard at Yarra Glen is as well known for its spit roasts as it is for its big, bold reds. My mate Peter Fergusson is a larger-than-life host who carves the huge joints of beef that are cooked right in the middle of the dining room and then proceeds to plonk large slabs of the blessed stuff on everyone's plates. Over the years I have always eaten and, of course, drunk far too much when I have visited. Although at least I'm not the only one as the restaurant is a popular spot with tourists and locals alike (all of whom, seemingly, overimbibe in a similar vein).

Fillet of Beef 'Bourguignonne'

Serves 4

– as cooked amongst the vines at Fergusson's Vineyard

olive oil 4 x 180 gm (6 oz) fillet (tenderloin) steaks, trimmed of all fat & sinew freshly ground salt & pepper	Heat olive oil in a pan and sear steaks on all sides. Remove and season.
12 button mushrooms 12 baby (pickling) onions 1 x 2 cm (¾ inch) thick slice of bacon, cut into thick matchsticks 2 garlic cloves, crushed	Add and sauté for 3–4 minutes until lightly coloured.
1 heaped tbsp plain (all-purpose) flour	Add, mix well and cook over low heat for a few minutes.
250 ml (8 fl oz) chicken stock (bought or homemade, see page 280) 2 tsp tomato paste 500 ml (16 fl oz) red wine a few fresh thyme sprigs	Add, mix well and simmer for 12–15 minutes until onions are tender and liquid has reduced a little. Return steaks to pan along with any juices and cook to the desired degree, turning every now and then.
1 tbsp chopped fresh parsley a dollop of butter	Add, stir to melt butter, then serve in large flat soup bowls with the vegies around.

'The butter adds a gleam to the sauce but can be omitted if you like.'

Australia: Yarra Valley

Mauritius on a plate

The food of Mauritius is a fascinating mix. And no wonder. Discovered by the Portuguese, this uninhabited island was first settled by the Dutch in 1598. Their contribution to the island's food style was fairly negligible except for the fact that they ate all the dodos (a very large stupid bird which was a relative of the pigeon and, according to the Dutch, pretty tasteless – they called it Walghuogel which roughly means awful bird with tough flesh). They also discovered the palm heart, which is still a great local delicacy, and in doing so chopped down most of the palm trees (and they cut down all the ebony forests, but that's another story). At least there were a few positives during their period of occupancy – they introduced tobacco, sugar cane, wild boar and the red deer from Java which, to this day, remains in large numbers and which are eagerly hunted by the local sporting clubs.

The colony never really succeeded and they abandoned it in 1710. In 1715 the French arrived, renamed it Ile de France and within a short period the island was flourishing. They developed the sugar industry and introduced vegies such as pumpkins, sweet potatoes and zucchini, as well as cassava which became the basic food for the African slaves who had been first brought to the island by the Dutch. These slaves also played a role eventually introducing the flavours of their homelands.

Creole food (the Creoles are deemed to be persons of African–European descent and now make up 25 per cent of the population) is deemed to be the 'native' cuisine of Mauritius although much appears to have a strong Indian influence. Which brings me to the Indians. Brought to Mauritius as indentured labourers after slavery was abolished, they quickly added their flavours and spices to the melting pot of Mauritian cuisine. They also, to the joy of the Africans, introduced rice which soon replaced the revolting cassava as their basic food. At about the same time the Chinese also began to arrive. Many were indentured labourers too, but a fair number were traders and they are still, to this day, mainly involved in commerce. They also introduced new taste sensations and ingredients and although modern Mauritian Chinese food does involve many

'foreign' ingredients, many Creole dishes also involve a slurp of oyster sauce or the like.

Interestingly, the British who ruled the country for the longest period (from 1810 until independence in 1968) appear to have had the smallest influence. Seemingly they introduced little apart from curry powder and Worcestershire sauce, which are both still Mauritian staples, but which were both more Indian in origin than Anglo Saxon (curry powder, unfortunately, tended to replace the more traditional masalas – maybe it appealed more to the French palate). And on that note, the British had allowed the French to control the sugar plantations as well as continue with their own language, religion and legal system. Consequently they continued, as the moneyed class, to have an undue influence over all aspects of Mauritian life including the food (today they only make up 1 per cent of the population yet many local recipes still have French names – albeit a little bastardised).

All in all, it's a mix which works well. Sure some of the local French chefs are attempting a sort of fusion cuisine that doesn't quite come off. But in the main the mixture of French cooking techniques with Indian, Creole and Chinese flavours works although don't expect a dish like Chop Suey to be anything like what you would expect. And don't be surprised if the curry has a slurp or two of oyster sauce or the chicken fricassee has half a dozen vanilla beans poking out of it. But overall, even if some of the additions are surprising, the flavours are vibrant and the naturally occurring fusion of different cultures is fascinating.

Oyster Sauce Beef with Smothered Chinese Cabbage

Serves 4

— as cooked at Maison Eureka

60 ml (2 fl oz) peanut oil 3 tbsp (1½ fl oz) oyster sauce 2 tbsp (1 fl oz) soy sauce 3–4 garlic cloves, crushed juice of 2 limes a good pinch of sugar	Whisk.
4 x 180 gm (6 oz) porterhouse steaks, trimmed of all fat & sinew	Add, toss well and refrigerate for at least 30 minutes.
peanut oil 1 red onion, finely sliced ½–1 wonga bok (Chinese white cabbage), finely sliced 250 ml (8 fl oz) chicken stock (bought or homemade, see page 280) good splash of soy sauce freshly ground salt & pepper	While beef is marinating, heat a little oil in a wok and gently sauté onion. Add the rest of the ingredients and toss well. Cover and gently cook for 20–30 minutes tossing now and again.
cooking oil spray	Cook steak to the desired degree on a lightly oiled preheated ridged grill or BBQ, brushing with marinade as you do so.
2 tbsp chopped fresh coriander (cilantro) lime wedges	Mix coriander into the cabbage. Put on four plates, top with steaks and serve with lime on the side.

Another popular Mauritian dish is 'rougaille'. In similar vein to most classical dishes, (French cassoulet, Hungarian goulash) there are many different and varied versions. Sometimes it is simply a side dish (without meat, poultry or seafood) but is more likely to be served in the style of a sauté or even stew. But one thing that everyone seems to agree on is that its base is always onions, tomatoes, chillies and garlic. Hence its name which is said to come from a combination of the French 'rouge', which means red, and 'ail' which means garlic. Oh, and there also seems to be a number of spellings of which rougaille and rougail seem to be the most common.

Rougaille de Boeuf
— as cooked at Grand Baie

Serves 4–6

vegetable oil 600 gm (1¼ lb) well trimmed porterhouse or rump (sirloin) steak, sliced	Heat a little oil in a large pan until smoking. Toss in beef in 2 or 3 lots and sauté quickly until coloured. Remove and set aside.
2 large onions, finely sliced 2 tbsp finely grated ginger 4 garlic cloves, crushed 3–4 chillies, finely chopped	Add, along with more oil if necessary, and sauté until tender.
250 ml (8 fl oz) beef stock (bought or homemade, see page 280) 5–6 ripe red tomatoes, cored & cut in thin wedges a splash of soy sauce	And, stir and simmer fairly rapidly for about 10 minutes until tomatoes collapse.
3–4 tbsp mixed chopped fresh herbs such as coriander (cilantro), parsley, thyme 3 spring (green) onions, finely sliced	Add along with beef and any juices and toss for a minute or two.
steamed rice	Serve with rice.

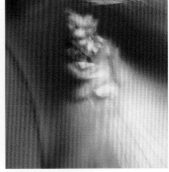

This is an interesting recipe. Originally from a Vietnamese restaurant in Bangkok (almost all of the world's cuisines are featured in this cosmopolitan city) I read about it in the *Bangkok Times* where it was a reprint from New York. Needless to say there has, seemingly, been a couple of variations along the way (for example, the fillet steak, butter and watercress) but the end result is definitely delicious and once again demonstrates my point about how recipes evolve.

Shakin' Beef
— as cooked outside the Sukothai Hotel

Serves 6

750 gm (1½ lb) fillet (tenderloin) steak, trimmed of all fat & sinew 2 tbsp chopped garlic 1 tbsp (½ fl oz) vegetable oil 1 tbsp sugar freshly ground salt & pepper	Cut steak into 2.5 cm (1 inch) cubes. Toss well with the garlic, oil and sugar and seasonings. Cover and refrigerate for 2 hours.
60 ml (2 fl oz) rice wine vinegar 60 ml (2 fl oz) Chinese wine 1 tbsp (½ fl oz) Asian fish sauce 1 tbsp sugar 3 tbsp (1½ fl oz) soy sauce	Whisk in a bowl.
vegetable oil	Heat a little in a large pan until smoking. Then, in 2 or 3 lots, and without overcrowding, add meat in one layer. When crust forms, turn over and continue to cook until crusty on all sides but rare within. Remove beef and put on plate, once again in one layer. Repeat process.
1 large red onion, finely sliced 3 spring (green) onions, cut into lengths 4 baby carrots, peeled & sliced 4 green beans, finely chopped	Add, along with more oil as necessary and toss for a few minutes. Add vinegar–wine mix and bubble until reduced a little.
3 tbsp butter a handful of watercress, well washed & dried & torn into pieces	Add along with beef and cook, tossing continually until warmed through.
steamed rice	Place on a platter or individual plates and top with beef and sauce.

Thailand: Bangkok

The food of Thailand could be said to be one of the original 'fusion' cuisines, because, like sponges, Thai chefs have for centuries been soaking up cooking methods and ingredients from around the world. One of the most significant 'new' ingredients was the chilli, introduced from South America by Portuguese traders in the 16th Century. But the Chinese also played a significant role by introducing, amongst other things, pigs, cattle, and poultry as well as a number of different cooking methods. And the Indians also contributed by introducing the Thais to a whole new range of spices.

Neighbours have also played a role. In the north around Chiang Mai, we see a strong Burmese influence. (The north was under Burmese rule between the 16th and 18th centuries and, as well, many Burmese labourers came to the region to work the teak plantations.) Whilst in the north-east, because of its isolation from the rest of Thailand, the food has many similarities to that of neighbouring Laos. In the south we see a similar thing happening with Malaysia and Indonesia.

And last, just to prove my point, let us look at some of Thailand's modern classics – satays, spring rolls, money bags, the famous Mussaman Curries (which originated in Persia) and of course the many noodle dishes. None of these are Thai in origin but, with a twist or two, have become ingrained in this country's cuisine.

Beef with Thai Sweet Basil (Neua Phat Bai Hohrapha)
— as cooked in Chiang Mai

Serves 4

2 x 180 gm (6 oz) rump (sirloin), porterhouse or fillet (tenderloin) steaks, trimmed of all fat & sinew Asian fish sauce	Toss steaks in a little fish sauce and marinate for 10–15 minutes. Then grill or pan fry to just under desired degree. Set aside to rest for about 10 minutes then slice.
125 ml (4 fl oz) chicken stock (bought or homemade, see page 280) 3 tbsp (1½ fl oz) kecap manis 1½ (¾ fl oz) tbsp Asian fish sauce	Whisk.
vegetable oil 3 garlic cloves, finely sliced 4 small red chillies, finely sliced	Heat a little oil in a wok and toss briefly.
¼ wonga bok (Chinese white cabbage), shredded 6 spring (green) onions, shredded	Add, toss well and then add sauce. Cook to wilt vegies, tossing regularly. Turn off.
1 large handful fresh Thai sweet basil leaves 1 long red chilli, finely sliced on the diagonal	Add beef and basil, toss well and mound in bowls with chilli on top.

Beef Teriyaki with Cucumber Pickles

Serves 4

– as cooked at the Healesville Hotel

250 ml (8 fl oz) teriyaki marinade (bought) 1 tsp freshly grated ginger 4 x 180 gm (6 oz) porterhouse steaks, trimmed of all fat & sinew	Combine marinade and ginger and pour over the steaks. Leave for 30–40 minutes turning every now and then.
1 tbsp (½ fl oz) vegetable oil 1 heaped tsp mustard seeds	Heat oil in a heavy-bottomed pot. Add mustard seeds and cook until they begin to crackle.
1 tsp turmeric 2 tsp salt 2 tsp sambal oelek	Add and mix to toast the spices for a minute or so.
170 ml (6 fl oz) red wine vinegar 140 gm (4½ oz) sugar	Add and bring to the boil, continually stirring.
2 continental (telegraph) cucumbers, halved lengthways & sliced	Add, bring back to the boil then transfer to a bowl.
cooking oil spray	Preheat ridged grill. Spray, and cook steaks to desired degree. While cooking put marinade in a pot and reduce to a sauce consistency. To serve, place steaks on plate, drizzle with a little sauce and place pickles down the centre of the steak.

'The pickles can, of course, be made in advance.'

Australia: Yarra Valley

Pork is far more popular in the north than in other regions of Thailand and to this day, it is still considered to be a sign of wealth and prosperity to kill a pig for any occasion such as a feast or wedding.

There are also a number of pork sausages served in the north, particularly by the street vendors. The most popular is the 'Pot Sausage' (Naem Maw), which is a fermented sausage made from minced pork, pork rind, sticky rice and various spices. A fairly acquired taste (and one that I didn't acquire), the mix is then put into a pot and left for three days – the 'fermenting' cooks them. Far more suited to my palate was Sai Ka, which are delicious bright red little numbers made from pork and chillies.

Burmese Style Pork Curry (Kaeng Hangleh Muu)
– as cooked in Chiang Mai

Serves 6–8

3 tbsp tamarind paste 250 ml (8 fl oz) warm water	Mix together and set aside for 10–15 minutes. Push through a fine sieve, discarding solids.
2 dried long chillies	In another bowl, soak in warm water for about 10 minutes until pliable then chop and remove seeds.
1 tbsp cumin seeds 1 tbsp coriander seeds	Dry roast in a pan until fragrant then put in a processor along with chillies.
¼ red onion, chopped 4 garlic cloves, crushed 1 tbsp grated fresh galangal (or ginger) 1 tsp grated fresh turmeric (or ½ tsp powdered) ½ tsp shrimp paste ½ tsp sea salt 2–3 tbsp (1–1½ fl oz) vegetable oil	Add to processor and blend until smooth (adding a little more oil if necessary).
1 lemongrass stalk, white part only, smashed & finely sliced 750 gm (1½ lb) lean pork, cut into 2 cm cubes	Fry paste in a wok along with the lemongrass until fragrant. Then add pork and cook for 5 minutes until well coated.
750 ml (25 fl oz) chicken stock (bought or homemade, see page 280) 4 tbsp pan-roasted peanuts (see page 50) 3 tbsp (1½ fl oz) Asian fish sauce 3 tbsp shaved palm sugar ½ cup pea eggplants	Add, along with 4 tbsp (2 fl oz) tamarind water and mix well. Simmer gently for 1¼ –1½ hours, until meat is very tender (adding more stock if necessary).
steamed rice	Serve on rice.

Another popular pork preparation is the Deep-fried Pork Rind. With the large amount of pork meat being consumed in the north (and keeping in mind that the Thais like to use everything including the squeak), pork rind is their equivalent of potato crisps. Every market appears to have stalls that are devoted to nothing else and, not only is the rind eaten as a snack, but it is used in soups, salads and curries, as a dipping medium with various relishes and is often sprinkled over dishes such as this stir-fried ground pork.

Stir-fried Ground Pork with Thai Sweet Basil (Moo Phad Kapaw)

Serves 6

— as cooked by chef Vira Sanguanwong from the Hotel Sukothai

15 small green chillies, chopped 5 small red chillies, chopped 2 garlic cloves, crushed	Pound in a mortar (or process).
1 tbsp (½ fl oz) vegetable oil	Heat oil in a wok and stir-fry chilli mix for one minute.
600 gm (1¼ lb) minced (ground) pork	Add and cook, mashing for 1 to 2 minutes until sealed.
2 tbsp (1 fl oz) soy sauce 2 tbsp (1 fl oz) oyster sauce 1 tbsp caster (superfine) sugar 1 tsp ground white pepper	Add and toss for another couple of minutes.
6 Kaffir lime leaves, shredded 4 long (snake) beans, chopped small handful fresh Thai sweet basil leaves 2 long red chillies, sliced lengthways	Add and stir to heat through, then put in bowls.
crispy fried fresh Thai sweet basil leaves steamed rice	Sprinkle basil over the top and serve with rice.

'To fry basil leaves, wash and pat dry before frying in two cups of hot oil until crispy — drain well.'

A jungle curry is traditionally hot, salty and spicy. Made with stock rather than coconut milk, its name came from the fact that this is a curry that was made using whatever ingredients were available in the surrounding jungle by people travelling through Thailand's central plains. And to this day people living outside the major towns still whip up jungle curries harvesting the wild ingredients themselves. It is also a more time effective dish than a normal curry because a premium cut of meat, which requires a briefer cooking period, is often used.

Pork Jungle Curry (Gaeng Pak Prik Muu)

Serves 4

— as cooked in Chiang Mai

1 tbsp (½ fl oz) vegetable oil	Heat oil in a wok and sauté paste for a few minutes.
3 tbsp (1½ fl oz) Thai red curry paste	Add fish sauce and cook one more minute.
1 tbsp (½ fl oz) Asian fish sauce	
2–3 pork fillets, trimmed of all fat & sinew & sliced	Add and toss to seal.
500–750 ml (16–25 fl oz) chicken stock (bought or homemade, see page 280)	Add and toss very well. Simmer briefly until pork is just cooked.
3 kaffir lime leaves, shredded	
12 fresh holy basil leaves, torn	
4–5 long/snake beans, in lengths	
½ cup pea eggplants	
1 stem fresh green peppercorns, rinsed	
1 tbsp (½ fl oz) Mekhong Whiskey	
steamed rice	Serve on rice in bowls with chilli sprinkled over the top.
2 long red chillies, seeded & sliced	

'Canned green peppercorns can be substituted for the fresh ones (rinse them well) and any whiskey can be used. Pea eggplants are often found in specialist Asian markets.'

178 NEVER TRUST A SKINNY COOK

Thailand: Chiang Mai

Grilled Pork Fillet with Sage, Lemon & Prosciutto

Serves 4

— as cooked at Eastwind Farm

3 tbsp chopped fresh sage leaves grated zest of 2 lemons 4 slices prosciutto, chopped	Pound to a paste with a mortar.
juice of 2 lemons	Add and mix well.
4 pork fillets, trimmed of all fat & sinew	Cut down the centre lengthways and flatten out a little. Make three slashes in each crossways and massage paste into them well. Leave for 30 minutes.
8 chat (baby) potatoes, scrubbed well freshly ground salt	Cook until tender in lightly salted water then drain well and leave covered.
olive oil spray freshly ground pepper 1 lemon	When pork is ready, cook on a preheated, lightly oiled BBQ or ridged grill, paste side down first. Season once sealed and squeeze lemon juice over the top.
freshly ground salt & pepper olive oil 150 gm (5 oz) butter 10 fresh sage leaves	When almost ready crush potatoes with a fork adding seasonings and a little oil. At the same time melt butter in a pan with sage and cook until lightly brown. Place crushed potatoes on individual plates, top with pork and pour butter over the top.

'The Eastwind Rare Breeds Farm is an interesting spot because, apart from producing the most wonderful pork, they also train animals for movies, TV ads and the like.'

A couple of leading Melbourne chefs had mentioned a passionate pig farmer in the Yarra Valley – Christine Young from the Eastwind Rare Breeds Farm. Of course I had to visit and was pretty excited to discover that the pigs in question were the rare Large Blacks. A very tasty breed originally from Cornwell, they are, according to Christine, highly endangered with only 50 breeding sows left in Australia. But with local chefs raving about the sheer quality of the meat, one would presume that this will change in the near future.

And, on a slightly different note, when I got out into the paddock to cook a few pork chops, I found myself in the middle of a rather fierce hail storm. Still, I finished the dish and although the sauce was maybe a little watery (from the heavens that is) the pork was certainly tender and delicious.

Pork Cutlets with Smoked Paprika & Sherry Vinegar

Serves 4

— as cooked during a hailstorm at Eastwind Farm

smoked paprika freshly ground salt	Put a generous amount of paprika on a plate, add a little salt and mix well.
4 pork loin cutlets (chops)	Dip into the mix and coat reasonably well.
olive oil	Heat a thin layer in a heavy-bottomed pan, add pork and seal on both sides. Remove.
60 ml (2 fl oz) sherry vinegar	Pour oil from pan and add. Reduce by one third.
2 x 400 gm (13 oz) cans diced tomatoes, drained well 250 ml (8 fl oz) chicken stock (bought or homemade, see page 280)	Add, mix and bring to the boil. Turn down to a simmer, return pork and any juices and any leftover paprika mix. Cook gently until tender adding more stock as necessary.

'Crisp green beans are a perfect accompaniment.'

Australia: Yarra Valley

During Daylesford's Swiss–Italian Festival, the Lake House held a pasta sauce competition. The judges were *Age* and *Gourmet Traveller* restaurant reviewer, John Lethlean and the esteemed Florentino chef, Guy Grossi. I didn't envy their task. There were tons of entries which they manfully tasted. I helped out for about ten minutes and then, sadly, had to go and do something important, like have a drink, but I did eventually taste the winning little number which, if my memory serves me right, contained rabbit (I do remember that it was delicious). Actually, jokes aside, the standard was very high, the judging was very professional and the entrants included everyone from local apprentice chefs to housewives.

Orrechetti con Broccoli

Serves 4

— as cooked by Guy Grossi at Daylesford's Swiss-Italian Festival

4 kipfler (waxy) potatoes, skin on sea salt	Boil in lightly salted water until tender. Drain, peel and cut into 1 cm (⅜ inch) dice.
500 gm (16 oz) orrechetti 300 gm (10 oz) broccoli, in florets	Cook pasta until al dente adding the broccoli for the last 5 minutes.
olive oil 100 gm (3½ oz) finely sliced smoked pig's cheek (or pancetta) 10 gm (½ oz) chopped fresh basil mixed with a little oil 2 red (French) shallots, finely chopped 2 garlic cloves, finely sliced 1 chilli, seeded & finely chopped	Heat a little oil in a large pan and sauté. When tender add pasta and broccoli.
freshly grated pecorino or parmesan 3 tbsp chopped fresh Italian (flat leaf) parsley olive oil	Add with a little more olive oil if needed and toss well.

'Guy actually made his own orrechetti (small ear-shaped pasta) but there are many good commercial ones available.'

Australia: Daylesford

While little pork is consumed in Indonesia itself because it is mainly Muslim, in Bali, where the majority are Hindu, it is a different story. Spit roasted suckling pig (Babi Guling), as I have mentioned elsewhere, is probably Bali's most famous festival offering but pork is offered in many other guises from blood pudding and sausages to glazed pork chops (Iga Babi Panggang) and fragrant sautés. But it is still a relatively expensive meat so it doesn't often feature as an everyday offering. (But do remember, that in similar vein to the eating habits of the Thais, rice is the predominant ingredient and only very small portions of meat, poultry or seafood are served.)

Fragrant Pork Stew (Be Celeng Base Manis)

Serves 4

— as cooked while dodging mad scooter drivers

2 tbsp (1 fl oz) vegetable oil 4 red (French) shallots, sliced (or ½ red onion) 5–6 garlic cloves, crushed	Heat oil in a wok and sauté gently.
1 heaped tsp grated fresh galangal (or ginger) 600 gm (1¼ lb) cubed lean shoulder pork	Add and toss until the meat is sealed.
250–375 ml (8–12 fl oz) chicken stock (bought or homemade, see page 280) 4 tbsp (2 fl oz) kecap manis 2 tbsp (1 fl oz) soy sauce 2 cinnamon sticks 2 star anise 8 whole small chillies	Add, mix well and gently simmer (about 1¼ hours) until tender, stirring every now and then and adding more stock if necessary.
8 long (snake) beans, cut in lengths steamed rice	When ready, blanch beans briefly in boiling water. Add to stew and serve on steamed rice.

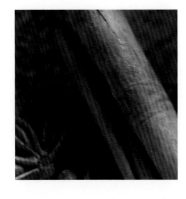

Fernleigh Farm is an organic farm just outside Daylesford which supplies organic vegetables such as carrots and a large range of potatoes and various salad ingredients to many of Australia's major retailers. In 1995 they also began breeding the rare Wessex Saddleback pig, once again using organic principles. In a similar vein to the Eastwind Rare Breed's Farm, chefs have discovered this delicious pork and local restaurants often feature it on their menu. The rillettes at Cliffy's in Daylesford are made using this pork and are absolutely delicious.

Pork San Choi Bao

Serves 6–8

– as cooked at Fernleigh Farm

6–8 dried shiitake mushrooms	Soak in warm water for 30 minutes or so. Then drain, discard stalks and slice caps.
1 tbsp (½ fl oz) peanut oil 1 tsp freshly grated ginger 1 garlic clove, crushed 1 chilli, seeded & finely sliced	Heat oil in a wok and cook until soft.
500 gm (1 lb) minced (ground) pork (not too lean)	Add and stir-fry for a few minutes mashing as you do so.
2 Chinese sausages, diced	Add along with the shiitakes and cook for a minute.
2 tbsp (1 fl oz) Chinese rice wine 1 heaped tbsp oyster sauce 1 tbsp (½ fl oz) soy sauce a pinch of caster (superfine) sugar 1 scant tsp sesame oil chicken stock (bought or homemade, see page 280)	Add, along with a splash of chicken stock, and cook until pork is tender, mashing every now and then and adding more stock when necessary (mix should be dryish).
1 small–medium carrot, julienned 2 spring (green) onions, chopped ¼ wonga bok (Chinese white cabbage), finely sliced a small handful of beanshoots	Add, mix well and cook until vegies are slightly wilted. Taste and adjust flavours if necessary i.e. add more soy or oyster sauce.
inner leaves of iceberg lettuce, separated & trimmed into cups	Serve in a bowl with a pile of lettuce cups alongside.

'To eat, you spoon the mix into the lettuce cups, fold up and, carefully, eat the lot.'

Australia: Daylesford

As the owner of a classic motor car (1969 Ford Mustang) I was pretty thrilled to be cooking on the foreshore at Napier right next to a Classic Car Show. Although I didn't notice any Mustangs which were quite up to my standards, there were some ripper cars with my favourite being a 1950s Chevy complete with fins as long as a city block. But back to cooking, for the most flavour, scrub beetroot well and wrap individually in foil and then roast in a pre-heated 200°C (400°F) oven until tender when pierced with a knife. Unwrap and peel when cool enough to handle (with rubber gloves on, if you like).

Venison with Beetroot & Pepper Sauce
Serves 4
– as cooked on the foreshore at Napier

olive oil 1 red capsicum (bell pepper), cored, seeded & chopped ½ onion, chopped	Heat a little oil in a pot and toss briefly.
60 ml (2 fl oz) red wine 60 ml (2 fl oz) port 60 ml (2 fl oz) red wine vinegar	Add and reduce by half.
1 litre (32 fl oz) beef stock (bought or homemade, see page 280) 1 heaped tsp juniper berries 1 heaped tbsp cranberry jelly	Add and whisk.
2 tbsp whole black peppercorns	Grind coarsely in mortar and add. Boil until of a sauce consistency, then strain.
2–3 beetroot (beets), cooked, peeled & cut into wedges	Add to strained sauce and put over gentle heat.
4 x 180 gm (6 oz) venison loin steaks, trimmed of all fat & sinew freshly ground salt	Either pan-fry or grill to desired degree (no more than medium), seasoning once sealed. Place on individual plates then ladle over sauce and serve beetroot on the side.

Veal Scaloppine with Lemon & Sage

Serves 4

— as cooked on the boardwalk at Geelong

olive oil a knob of butter	Heat in a large pan until foaming.
8–12 fresh sage leaves 4 veal scaloppine, trimmed of all fat & sinew plain (all-purpose) flour freshly ground salt & pepper	Add sage and lightly floured scaloppine. Season and cook, briefly, until coloured on both sides.
125 ml dry white wine	Add and reduce quite heavily. Remove veal and set aside.
juice of 1 lemon 60–125 ml cream 125 ml chicken stock (bought or homemade, see page 280)	Add, mix well and reduce to a sauce consistency. Check seasoning, return veal and gently heat.
20 green beans or asparagus spears sea salt	At same time blanch in lots of rapidly boiling, lightly salted water until crisp-tender. Drain well, place on individual plates and top with veal and the sauce.

Australia: Great Ocean Road

In similar fashion to the appellation system for champagne, cervena is the appellation for premium farmed venison in New Zealand. This certification guarantees that both the production and the processing of the deer has been done in accordance with a series of quality controls. The name itself comes from a combination of the Latin 'cervidae', which means deer and venison which originally meant hunting and a for premium quality. But that aside, cervena is the most tender, delicious venison I have ever tasted and this recipe prepared by Ruth Pretty, the caterer to the stars, was terrific.

Ruth Pretty's Rack of Cervena wrapped in Prosciutto with Roasted Tomatoes

Serves 4–8

— as cooked in the kitchens of Moore Wilson Fresh

olive oil	Preheat oven to 220°C (425°F).
1 tbsp finely grated lemon zest	
2 garlic cloves, crushed	Combine ingredients well.
2 tbsp chopped fresh Italian (flat leaf) parsley	
1 tsp sea salt	
½ tsp freshly ground black pepper	

olive oil	Brush roasting tray with oil. Rub above mix over the
1 x 8 cutlet (chop) rack of venison, trimmed of all sinew	venison then wrap a slice of prosciutto around each
10 slices prosciutto	cutlet passing it through the rack bones.

600–700 gm (1¼–1½ lb) ripe tomatoes	Put tomatoes in roasting tray and sprinkle with oil,
2 tbsp (1 fl oz) extra virgin olive oil	balsamic and seasonings. Place venison in centre and
2 tbsp (1 fl oz) balsamic vinegar	cook for 15–20 minutes until medium-rare. Rest,
freshly ground salt & pepper	covered for 10 minutes. Then carve into cutlets and serve with roasted tomatoes.

Lemony Veal Cutlets with Red Capsicum Relish   Serves 4
— as cooked at the Great Barrier Feast

125 ml (4 fl oz) extra virgin olive oil grated zest & juice of 2 lemons freshly ground salt & pepper	Mix.
4–8 veal cutlets (chops)	Add, mix well and leave for at least 30 minutes turning every now and then.
1 bottle chargrilled capsicums (bell peppers) preserved in oil, or 6 pieces roasted red capsicum (bell peppers) cut in chunks 1 medium onion, finely chopped 1 garlic clove, crushed	Heat 2 tablespoons of the capsicum oil in a pot and sauté onion and garlic until tender.
4 tbsp chopped fresh herbs (basil, thyme & parsley) freshly ground salt & pepper	Add along with the drained capsicums and cook briefly until combined.
125 ml (4 fl oz) chicken stock (bought or homemade, see page 280)	Heat some of the marinade in a heavy-bottomed pan and seal veal on both sides until well coloured. Then add stock and more marinade and cook gently until veal is cooked and a glaze is formed (adding more marinade if necessary). Mound relish on plates, top with veal and pour glaze over.

Australia: Hamilton Island

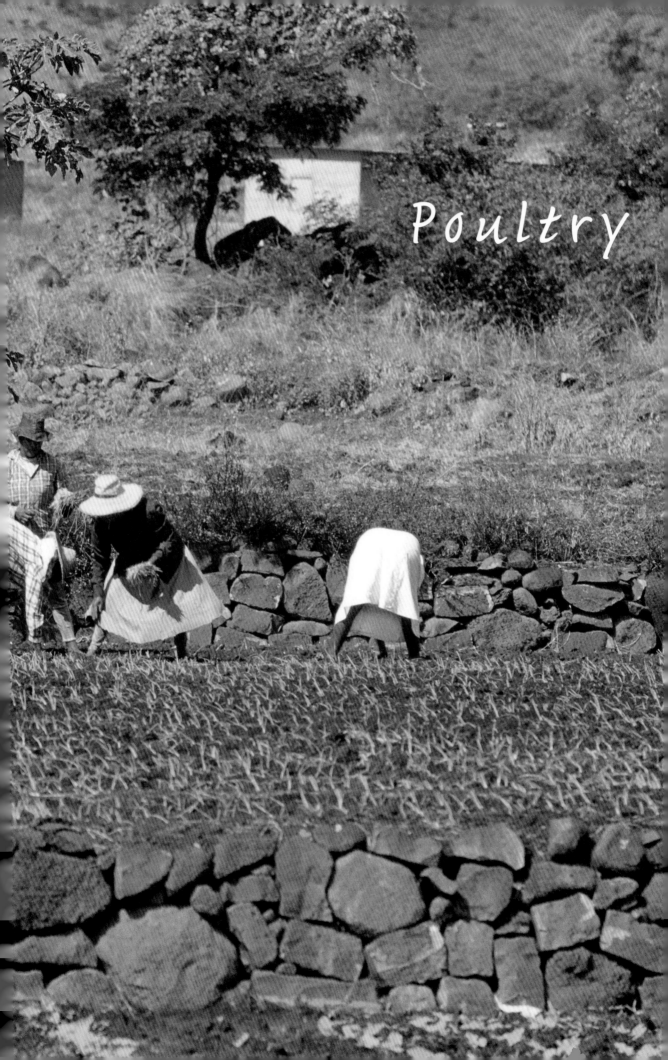

Poultry

Roast Chicken Carbonara

– as cooked in a kitchen in Daylesford

4 chicken marylands (joined leg & thigh), skin on (see page 196) olive oil spray sea salt flakes freshly ground pepper	Preheat oven to 220°C (425°F). Place chicken in a baking dish, skin side up and spray with oil. Season and bake for about 20 minutes until the juices run clear when pricked with a fork and the skin is crispy.
400 gm (13 oz) any pasta sea salt	When chicken has been cooking for 10 minutes, cook pasta in plenty of lightly salted boiling water until al dente. Then drain well.
olive oil ½ red onion, finely chopped 2–3 rindless bacon rashers, diced	At same time heat a little oil in a pan and sauté until tender. Put in a bowl.
3 egg yolks 3 tbsp (1½ fl oz) cream 100 gm (3½ oz) freshly grated parmesan 1–2 tbsp chopped fresh parsley freshly ground salt & pepper	Add to bowl and whisk until frothy. Then add hot pasta and toss well. Place in four individual bowls and top with chicken (either whole or taken off the bone and cut into pieces).

Australia: Daylesford

Eumundi, which is just down the road from Noosa, has a couple of claims to fame. Firstly the Saturday market which attracts thousands of visitors and where you can buy everything from Auntie Flora's homemade jams to the latest in kitsch jewellery. The food isn't bad either and you can wash it down with this small town's other claim to fame – a Eumundi Lager (which used to be brewed in the local pub but now, I'm sad to report, is being made on the Gold Coast).

Glazed Honey & Soy Chicken

Serves 4

– as cooked at Eumundi

60 ml (2 fl oz) vegetable oil	Whisk in a bowl.
60 ml (2 fl oz) soy sauce	
2 good tbsp honey	
2 tbsp (1 fl oz) Chinese rice wine	
1 heaped tsp sambal oelek	
1 tbsp freshly grated ginger	
2 garlic cloves, crushed	
freshly ground pepper	

1 whole large chicken, portioned into 4, skin on	Add, toss well and marinate for at least 1 hour turning every now and then.

vegetable oil	Heat a little oil in a large pan and add chicken, skin side down. Cover and cook for 20–25 minutes until ready, adding marinade and stock little by little as it does so. Remove chicken from pan and reduce juices to a glaze.
chicken stock (bought or homemade, see page 280)	

3 dozen snowpeas, topped & tailed	When ready, toss snowpeas briefly in a hot wok, place on plates, top with chicken and pour sauce over the top. Garnish with spring onions.
2 spring (green) onions, shredded	

'Ask your butcher or poulterer to portion chicken into two breasts and two marylands (and give you the bones and wings etc. for stock).'

Fast Roast Chicken with Herby Juices

Serves 4

— as cooked in a Daylesford kitchen

1 tbsp chopped fresh rosemary
1 tbsp chopped fresh parsley
1 tbsp chopped fresh thyme
2 garlic cloves, crushed
3 tbsp (1½ fl oz) olive oil
2 tbsp Dijon mustard
juice of 1 lemon

Preheat oven to its highest degree.
Whisk in a bowl.

---

1 whole large chicken
sea salt

Using kitchen scissors, cut along each side of the backbone and remove. Turn chicken skin side up and flatten breast with some blows from the palm of your hand. Tuck wings under. Place in an oven tray and rub the herb mix in thoroughly. Sprinkle with salt and cook for about 30–35 minutes until the juices from the thigh run clear when pricked with a fork. Baste every now and again.

---

2 good knobs of butter
2 handfuls watercress, washed & dried

Remove chicken to board and then joint. Add butter to tray and swirl to combine. Place a mound of watercress on individual plates, top with a piece of chicken and pour juices over the top.

Australia: Daylesford

Asian fish sauce or naam plaa is one of the basics of Thai food. Often acting as the salt component in many classics, it is made from an anchovy-like fish, which is salted and left to ferment naturally in the heat. The resulting liquid is then strained and pasteurised. And while it really does smell in its natural form, thankfully once cooked, the stink dissipates.

Green Chicken Curry (Kaeng Khiaw-Waan Kai)

Serves 4–6

– as cooked at the Sukothai Hotel

1 tbsp grated galangal (or ginger)	Whisk.
2 garlic cloves, crushed	
60 ml (2 fl oz) coconut cream	
a good pinch of sea salt	
2–3 skinless chicken breasts, cubed	Add, toss well, cover and refrigerate overnight.
125 ml (4 fl oz) coconut cream	Put in wok and simmer to thicken.
25 ml (¾ fl oz) vegetable oil	
2 heaped tbsp Thai green curry paste	Add and simmer gently for another 5 minutes.
2 tbsp (1 fl oz) Asian fish sauce	Add along with chook and simmer for 5 minutes.
2 tbsp grated galangal (or ginger)	
1 tbsp shaved palm sugar	
375 ml (12 fl oz) coconut milk	
4 small round eggplants, quartered	Add and cook for a further 10 minutes, stirring every now and then.
12 pea eggplants	
6 Kaffir lime leaves, shredded	
12 fresh Thai holy basil leaves, torn	Add basil and mix in. Put in bowl and scatter chillies over the top, serve with rice on the side.
1 long red chilli, seeded & finely sliced	
1 long green chilli, seeded & finely sliced	
steamed rice	

'One of the true Thai classics, often badly presented because little more than green curry paste and coconut milk is used.'

Noodles are popular all over Thailand, but it is in the north (due to the large number of Chinese and Burmese people who live there) that they are at their very best. In Chiang Mai, Khao Sawy is most probably the best known. It is a delicious mix of noodles with chicken or beef curry and is often served with a variety of condiments and a mound of fried noodles on top. Originally a Yunnanese Muslim dish, it is to this day sold by street vendors particularly around the mosques.

Chiang Mai Chicken Noodles (Khao Sawy)   Serves 4
— as cooked overlooking the rice paddies of Chiang Mai

500 ml (16 fl oz) coconut cream 25 ml (¾ fl oz) vegetable oil	Place in a wok and boil over a medium heat until thickish.
2 heaped tbsp Thai red curry paste 2 garlic cloves, crushed 2 tsp grated fresh turmeric (1 tsp ground)	Add and cook for a few minutes, stirring continually.
2 small chicken marylands, halved 500 ml (16 fl oz) chicken stock (bought or homemade, see page 280) 2 tbsp (1 fl oz) dark soy sauce 1 tbsp grated palm sugar	Add chicken and toss until well coated. Add the rest and simmer gently for 15 minutes, turning regularly and adding more stock if necessary.
1 tbsp (½ fl oz) Asian fish sauce juice of ½ lime	Add, mix well and taste for seasoning.
1 litre (32 fl oz) vegetable oil 100 gm (3½ oz) fresh egg noodles 1 large onion, finely sliced	While chicken is cooking, heat oil in a pot and fry noodles in small batches until crisp and golden. Drain well on kitchen towels, then fry onion until light brown and crispy and drain well too.
400 gm (13 oz) fresh egg noodles	Boil until tender and put in four large bowls.
2–3 spring (green) onions, sliced finely 1 long red chilli, finely sliced a good handful of fresh coriander (cilantro) leaves	Toss fried noodles and onion with these. Top boiled noodles with chicken and sauce and then garnish with the fried noodle mix.

'A maryland of chicken is the piece that combines both leg and thigh. And we used one of the local organic free range little numbers — wonderful.'

Thai Table Manners

Traditionally, Thai food was eaten with the fingers (and this still happens in certain areas). But in most cases now, except in Chinese restaurants where you will be given chopsticks, you will eat using a spoon and fork. They first appeared in the early 1900s when Bangkok restaurateurs began setting the table in imitation of the royal palaces with what was known as the 'Royal Table Setting'. The idea quickly caught on in Bangkok and then through most parts of Thailand.

The fork should never be put completely into the mouth. In similar vein to Western disdain for putting a knife in your mouth, it is regarded the height of bad manners.
The fork is instead used to steer or place food on the spoon.

When dining, do keep in mind that rice is regarded as the most important part of the meal and the ratio should be one to one of rice and other food. The food itself is mainly served all at once on platters or in bowls, rather than in separate courses. It is also considered bad manners to begin until all the food has arrived. (It is not regarded as important that the food be piping hot. In fact, it is considered quite rude to take very hot food, as it implies that you can't wait to dive in.) With serving itself, there are a few rules. Don't put more than a couple of spoonfuls of food on your plate at any one time, rice first. And never pick up the platter or bowl, but instead reach over with your spoon (even if this means that you are leaning across the table). If the most delectable food just happens to be out of reach, pass your plate to the nearest person. Although, in most cases the very hospitable Thais will have noticed this and already offered to serve you or, as is common, simply plopped a spoonful on your plate.

And very importantly, always leave some food on both the serving plate and your own plate, because by cleaning either, you are implying that the host didn't offer enough food.

Enjoy!

In recent years I have tended to be a little critical of many of our non-Asian chefs who are attempting to incorporate Thai flavours into their food. Of course there are exceptions such as Neil Perry and Geoff Lindsay but in many cases others appear to get the balance wrong, particularly in the case of palm sugar which often appears to overwhelm the whole dish. Because Thai cooking is all about balance (sweet – salty – tart – spicy) none of which overpowers (presuming of course, that you have a Thai-like tolerance for chillies).

But just to shoot my whole argument in the foot about balance being the backbone of Thai cooking, here is a northern Thai dish which I enjoyed in a local cafe where the sweetness definitely dominates but which I suspect leans more to Laos or Vietnam than it does to Thailand (well, that's my excuse anyway).

Chicken with a Galangal & Palm Sugar Caramel   Serves 4
– as enjoyed in a Raan Aahaan in Chiang Mai

3 tbsp shaved palm sugar 2 tbsp (1 fl oz) water	Put in a small heavy-bottomed pot and cook over medium heat until it begins to bubble and turns golden brown.
125 ml (4 fl oz) water	Add carefully and cook until richly coloured and reduced, stirring frequently.
vegetable oil 8 boneless, skinless chicken thighs, halved lengthways	At same time, heat a thin layer of oil in a sauté pan and cook chicken, covered, until crisp and golden on both sides. Remove.
6–8 red (French) shallots, finely sliced (or 1 red onion) 2 tsp grated fresh galangal (or ginger) 3 tbsp (1½ fl oz) Asian fish sauce 125 ml (4 fl oz) chicken stock (bought or homemade, see page 280) 1 heaped tsp sambal oelek	Pour off most of the oil and sauté shallots and galangal until tender. Add the rest along with the caramel to taste. Mix well and cook for 2 minutes. Return chicken to pan and gently cook for 10 minutes adding more stock if needed.
6 long (snake) beans, cut in lengths 6 spring (green) onions, cut in lengths	When chicken is almost ready, add and cook until beans are crisp-tender. Check sauce for balance.
steamed rice	Serve on steamed rice.

'This was served with the more traditional sticky rice but plain steamed is fine.'

The French plantation owners in Mauritius certainly lived well. While the slaves ate cassava root three times a day, they dined on truffles, goose liver and the best cheeses, all imported from France. The wine and champagne were also imported while whole suckling pigs and various birds were roasted in the large woodfired ovens. But in David Burton's excellent book *French Colonial Cooking* he notes that the famous 19th Century caterer Flore Mauricienne 'did not regard it as beneath its dignity to provide blistering Indian curries and pickles at special occasions even serving Mulligatawny Soup at the official banquet in Port Louis for the Duke of Edinburgh on his visit in 1870'.

Chicken Mulligatawny
Serves 4–6
– as cooked at Le Saint Aubin

250 gm (8 oz) dholl (yellow split peas)	Put in a pot, just cover with water and gently cook for about 15 minutes until tender. Drain well.
1 tbsp (½ fl oz) vegetable oil 1 large onion, finely chopped 1 medium carrot, diced 1 large celery stalk, diced 3 garlic cloves, crushed 2 tsp grated fresh ginger	Heat oil in a large heavy-bottomed pot and sauté until tender.
2 skinless chicken breasts, cubed	Add (along with more oil if necessary) and toss to seal.
2 heaped tsp curry powder 1 tsp ground cumin ½ tsp cayenne 1 tsp turmeric	Add and toss well.
1½ litres (1⅕ quarts) chicken stock (bought or homemade, see page 280) freshly ground salt & pepper	Then add dholl together with stock to cover. Season and gently simmer for about 15 minutes until very tender adding more stock if necessary.
plain yoghurt chopped fresh coriander (cilantro)	Serve in individual bowls with a sprinkling of yoghurt and coriander.

'The Mauritian Mulligatawny is more of a stew than a soup.'

Maurituis: Saint Aubin

We stayed at the Sugar Beach Resort in Mauritius. It was the perfect holiday resort – a number of bars for Dad, numerous pools and a wonderful beach for Mum and, best of all, a fantastic kids' club for Charlotte. She had a ball. Lots of swings and slides and games plus all the normal activities such as finger painting, dressing up etc. But what I loved was the wood fired pizza oven where the kids often helped cook their own lunch. Complete with chef's hats and aprons they whipped up their very own pizzas and the like and then, impatiently, waited for them to emerge from the oven (which was, of course, securely situated away from little fingers). And to crown it all off, the staff, in typical Mauritian style, were friendly and helpful and seemed to be having just as much fun as the kids.

Chicken Chop Suey
Serves 4

– Charlotte's favourite from Mauritius

1 packet hokkien noodles	Soak in hot water until separated then drain.
2–3 Chinese sausages	At the same time, blanch in boiling water for 1–2 minutes then slice on the diagonal.
2 skinless chicken breasts	Slice into long strips and also blanch in boiling water for 30 seconds. Drain.
125 ml (4 fl oz) pineapple juice, canned or bottled 60 ml (2 fl oz) cup chicken stock (bought or homemade, see page 280) 2–3 tbsp (1–1½ fl oz) honey 4 tbsp (2 fl oz) soy sauce 1 tbsp cornflour (cornstarch)	Put in a bowl and whisk.
vegetable oil 4 baby carrots, peeled & sliced on the diagonal 1 red capsicum (bell pepper), cored, seeded & finely sliced 2 celery stalks, sliced on the diagonal	Heat a little oil in a wok and sauté for a few minutes. Then add chicken and noodles and toss for a minute or so.
¼ wonga bok (Chinese white cabbage), shredded 3 spring (green) onions, shredded	Add along with liquid and sausage and cook, tossing until vegies wilt a little.

As I have mentioned time and time again, I am rather keen on markets and the Central Market in Port Louis in Mauritius is pretty good. Maybe not as impressive as the markets of Thailand or Bali but interesting none the less. And if you've been over-imbibing, make for the stalls selling traditional Indian herbal medicines. In most cases you make a tea out of these leaves and they are guaranteed to cure everything from gout and obesity to flatulence. Mauritius is also famous for its textiles. The clothes for many major companies such as Ralph Lauren, Hugo Boss and Calvin Klein are manufactured here so a section of the market is dedicated to such things. But be a little careful – I did notice a Hugo Bass and a Kevin Klein (I thought he was an actor) amongst the labels. I don't think they were terribly authentic.

Chicken Fricassee Mauritian Style

Serves 4

– as cooked at the Central Market in Port Louis

12–16 dried shiitake mushrooms	Soak in warm water for 30 minutes or so. Then drain, cut off stalks and discard and cut caps in four.
vegetable oil 1 large chicken, jointed into 4 (see page 193), skin on	Heat oil in a large pan and cook chicken, skin side down first and covered for about 8–9 minutes, turning 2 or 3 times. Remove.
1 large onion, sliced 1 tsp freshly grated ginger 2 chillies, seeded & finely sliced 3–4 garlic cloves, crushed	Add and sauté until lightly coloured.
6 ripe red tomatoes, cut in wedges ½ tsp cinnamon freshly ground salt & pepper a splash of soy sauce a splash of oyster sauce 1 tsp fresh thyme leaves 250 ml (8 fl oz) chicken stock (bought or homemade, see page 280)	Add and cook until thickish and fragrant. Then return chicken, add shiitakes and cook very gently for another 10–15 minutes adding more stock as necessary.

'Tomatoes are a basic in Mauritian cooking – they are also beautiful, red and ripe. So please search out the best but if not at the height of their season then maybe canned should be substituted.'

'As mushrooms are very porous never wash them.
Instead just wipe them with a damp cloth.'

Old-fashioned Chicken Casserole

Serves 4

– in similar vein to one enjoyed at Cliffy's

olive oil

1 medium carrot, sliced

2 celery stalks, sliced

1 large onion, chopped

2–3 rashers pancetta (or bacon), chopped

Heat a little oil in a deep pan or pot and sauté vegies and pancetta until tender.

---

2 tbsp plain (all-purpose) flour

Add, mix well and cook gently for 2–3 minutes.

6–8 boneless, skinless chicken thighs, cubed

500 ml (16 fl oz) chicken stock
   (bought or homemade, see page 280)

a splash of Worcestershire sauce

6 small kipfler (or any waxy) potatoes, peeled
   & cut in chunks

12 button mushrooms, stalks removed

Add, mix well then simmer gently for about 15–20 minutes until the potatoes are tender, adding more stock if necessary.

---

2 cups broccoli florets

1 tbsp chopped fresh parsley

freshly ground salt & pepper

When ready, briefly blanch broccoli in lots of boiling water. Then add to casserole along with the parsley and seasoning to taste.

Australia: Daylesford

The minute you arrive in Hawke's Bay, you realise that you are in serious wine territory. Signs everywhere welcome you to 'Wine Country' and vineyards appear to be on every second block. And serious money too. Amongst others we visited Craggy Range, which is an amazing multi-million dollar set up owned (I am told) by a Canadian who lives in Queensland. I also had a chance to catch up with an old mate John Buck, one of the pioneers in the region. His vineyard, Te Mata Estate, is New Zealand's oldest, dating back to 1890 and his wines have an amazing reputation overseas and are difficult to source, even in New Zealand. And the secret to their success – all wine produced is from their own Hawke's Bay vineyards, ten in all.

New Wave Coq Au Vin

Serves 4

– as cooked amongst the vines at Te Mata Estate

olive oil 4 chicken breasts, skin on freshly ground salt & pepper	Heat oil in a heavy-bottomed pan and cook seasoned chicken, skin side down first, until well browned. Remove.
16 small (pickling) onions 16 small button mushrooms 1 garlic clove, crushed	Add, along with a little more oil if necessary, and toss until lightly coloured.
1 heaped tbsp plain (all-purpose) flour	Add, turn down heat and cook for a few minutes mixing well.
250 ml (8 fl oz) red wine 250 ml (8 fl oz) beef stock (bought or homemade, see page 280) 1 x 400 gm (13 oz) can diced tomatoes, drained a few sprigs fresh thyme 2 bay leaves freshly ground salt & pepper	Add and bring to boil. Mix well to combine, turn heat down and return chicken. Simmer gently turning once or twice until cooked.
chopped fresh parsley	Serve sprinkled with parsley and, if you like, some plain boiled spuds on the side.

'I sometimes add another splash of red wine at the end to give a little "freshness" to the sauce.'

Wellington's bar and restaurant scene is alive and kicking. Supposedly with more establishments per capita than New York, I had a great time attempting to visit them all.

I particularly enjoyed Zibibbo (in the old Taranaki St Police Station, which fortunately I had never visited in its previous incarnation), Kai in the Bay, Citron, the Boulcott St Bistro, a terrific casual Malaysian cafe, Kopi and Logan Brown, which rates many mentions in this book. In the bar stakes there are far too many to mention, although seemingly every one in either Courtenay Place or Cuba St was pretty damned good.

Tuscan Chicken Livers with Pesto Mash
Serves 4

— as enjoyed in a Wellington cafe whose name I have completely forgotten

4–6 large potatoes, peeled sea salt	Boil until tender in salted water. Drain, return to pot and cover.
olive oil 600 gm (1¼ lb) chicken livers, cleaned	Heat oil to smoking in a pan then toss in livers in 2 or 3 lots. Seal livers on both sides. Remove.
1 medium onion, chopped 2 garlic cloves, crushed	Add and sauté until tender.
6 tbsp (3 fl oz) balsamic vinegar	Add and reduce by one third.
250 ml (8 fl oz) chicken stock (bought or homemade, see page 280) 2 tbsp chopped fresh parsley a good knob of butter	Add, bring back to boil then add livers and gently cook (keep pink).
60 ml (2 fl oz) milk a good knob of butter	While livers are cooking, turn heat back on under potatoes to dry out and then add milk and butter and mash over heat.
3–4 tbsp pesto (bought or homemade, see page 281)	Add to mash, mix in well and mound on individual plates. Top with livers and sauce.

There are times when it just seems right to cook a particular dish. In Daylesford, where ingredients thrive, I was given a couple of beautiful local organic chickens plus a basketful of super-fresh vegies, once again organically grown. So such produce demanded a rather special dish – something that didn't obscure the quality and flavour of the ingredients but highlighted them nonetheless.

Bourride is a Flemish dish which is basically their version of poached chicken. In similar vein to France's Chicken in Half Mourning (Poularde Demi-Deuil) it is often poached whole with fresh truffles stuffed under the skin. But because I was in a backyard in Daylesford where truffles were noticeable by their absence and my cooking equipment was rather limited I just cooked the breasts, reserving the legs for another use (see page 192).

Bourride of Chicken
Serves 4

– as cooked in a backyard in Daylesford

1 tbsp (½ fl oz) olive oil	Heat oil in a large sauté pan and sauté until tender.
1 onion, chopped	
2 small leeks, well washed & sliced	
1 celery stalk, sliced	
4 baby carrots, peeled & sliced	
2 garlic cloves, crushed	
125 ml (4 fl oz) cup dry white wine	Add, mix well and cook for 5 minutes.
250 ml (8 fl oz) chicken stock (bought or homemade, see page 280)	
1 x 400 gm (13 oz) can diced tomatoes, drained a little	
2 pieces orange peel	
2 bay leaves	
3 fresh thyme sprigs	
sea salt flakes	
freshly ground pepper	
4 skinless chicken breasts	Put on top, tightly cover and cook very gently for 15 minutes turning once and adding more stock if necessary.
¼ cup aioli (garlic mayonnaise, see page 281)	Remove chicken and set aside. Taste sauce for seasoning then, off the heat, add the aioli, little by little, mixing well between each addition. Add parsley. Place vegies in flat soup bowls (keeping some of the liquid behind) place chicken on top and pour over the sauce.
chopped fresh parsley	

'I have made this once or twice where I whizzed up the vegie-sauce mix along with the aioli. This also worked well.'

I will always remember The Jetty at Boreen Point, just outside Noosa, when it was owned by the charming, affable Eddie Brunetti. It reminded me of the decadent Sunday lunches at my establishment, Clichy, where people would arrive for lunch at 1 pm and the earliest anyone would leave would be 8 pm (the record was set by one particular group from Donlevy's restaurant, including the master himself, who decided to pull up stumps at 4 am the next morning). Well, The Jetty was similar except it happened in that vein almost every day. Lots and lots of wonderful country food, great hospitality, a good wine list and afterwards, almost best of all, either the Jetty's own bus or a water taxi to deposit you right at your hotel door – always with a traveller in hand, of course.

Pot-roasted Chicken with Lemon and Harissa Broth

Serves 4

— as cooked at Garnisha Spices at Boreen Point

1 whole large chicken, skin on	Wash and dry. Tuck wings under the body and put a bamboo skewer through the legs and point of breast (break off if too long).
olive oil	Heat a little oil in a heavy-bottomed pot or casserole and brown chicken all over. Remove.
2 large onions, finely sliced 2 garlic cloves, crushed 1 heaped tbsp harissa paste, bought	Add along with a little more oil if necessary and sauté until tender. Pour off any excess oil.

500 ml (16 fl oz) chicken stock
  (bought or homemade, see page 280)
4 pieces preserved lemon, flesh discarded & rind
  finely sliced (or 1 whole lemon finely sliced)
16 pitted green olives
1 tsp saffron threads soaked in 3 tbsp (1½ fl oz) water
8–12 baby (chat) potatoes, peeled
freshly ground salt & pepper
	Add to pot along with the chicken, breast side up. Tightly cover and simmer very gently for 40 minutes.

1 x 400 gm (13 oz) can chickpeas, drained & rinsed	Add, along with more stock if necessary, cover and simmer for another 15 minutes. Carefully remove chicken.
2 tbsp chopped fresh coriander (cilantro)	Add to liquid and reduce until syrupy. Portion chicken and place on individual plates along with sauce and the various goodies.

'Couscous would go well with this.'

Ubud is about 90 minutes drive from Bali's capital Denpasar. It is perched on gentle slopes on the way to the central mountains and is regarded as the cultural capital of Bali. It is surrounded by picturesque rice paddies that emphasise that rice is Ubud's major crop and, in the background there are many ancient temples and palaces. It is also renowned for its hand-woven silks and fabrics and many bargains are available. And while the bars and nightlife are pretty limited, some of Bali's best food, whether it be Balinese or from other parts of Asia, is to be found here.

Chicken in Red Sauce (Ayam Panggang Bumbu Merah)

Serves 4

— as cooked in the main street of Ubud

vegetable oil 1 large chicken, portioned into 4 or 8 pieces rice flour freshly ground salt & pepper	Heat oil in a large sauté pan. Flour and season chicken and gently cook, covered, until golden brown, skin side down first.
6 chillies, finely sliced 4 garlic cloves, finely sliced	In another pan, sauté in a little oil until tender.
4 large ripe tomatoes, diced 250 ml (8 fl oz) cup chicken stock (bought or homemade, see page 280) juice of 2 limes grated zest of 1 lime 1/2 tbsp shaved palm sugar good splash of soy sauce 1/2 tsp tamarind paste 1 tsp shrimp paste 1 tsp kecap manis	Add along with ¾ cup of chicken stock and cook until thick and fragrant, adding more stock as necessary. Taste to check balance. Drain chicken and add to sauce. Cook until ready, turning once or twice.
steamed rice	Serve in individual bowls on rice.

'I like the Balinese idea of cooking the chicken until crispy before adding to the sauce — gives a terrific contrast of both flavours and textures. And the rice flour also gives it a lighter, crispier finish.'

Ayam Goreng is a very popular Warung or street dish in Bali. In its simplest form the chicken is marinated in a spicy mix before being barbecued and served with a spicy sambal. There is a slightly more up-market version which involves a 'green' sauce which is why this recipe is also sometimes known as green chicken. In my version I use stock but coconut milk is most probably more traditional (I think I had just got to the stage where I was tired of putting coconut milk in everything).

Balinese Fried Chicken (Ayam Goreng)
– as cooked at the Waka di Ume in Ubud

Serves 4

5 red (French) shallots, chopped (or 1 red onion) 10 green chillies, chopped good pinch of sea salt	Make the sambal by pounding in a mortar until coarse paste is formed.
2 tsp shrimp paste 2 tbsp shaved palm sugar	Add and continue to pound.
1 good tsp tamarind paste 2 tbsp (1 fl oz) vegetable oil	Add, mix well and set aside (taste for balance).
vegetable oil 1 large chicken, portioned into eight rice flour freshly ground salt & pepper	Heat a thin layer of oil in a pan. Lightly flour and season chicken and cook, covered, until golden brown. Remove.
2 green chillies, finely sliced 2 garlic cloves, finely sliced 2 kaffir lime leaves, finely sliced 1 lemongrass stalk, white part only, smashed & finely sliced	Pour off most of the oil and sauté gently for 5 minutes.
3 green tomatoes, chopped 125 ml (4 fl oz) chicken stock (bought or homemade, see page 280) grated zest of 1 lime juice of 1½ limes	Add, mix well and simmer for 5–10 minutes adding more stock if necessary (the dish should be fairly dry).
2–3 spring (green) onions, finely sliced 6–8 long (snake) beans (or normal beans) cut into lengths	Add along with chicken and cook (covered) for another few minutes until beans are crisp-tender.
steamed rice	Serve on rice with sauce and the sambal on the side (or on the top).

Chicken Curry with Young Jackfruit (Gudeq)

Serves 4

— as cooked at the Klungkung Farmer's Market

vegetable oil 1 large chicken, portioned in 4 rice flour	Heat a thin layer of oil in a sauté pan and cook floured chicken, covered, until golden brown, skin side down first.
5 red (French) shallots, finely chopped 5 chillies, finely sliced 5 garlic cloves, finely chopped	While chicken is cooking, heat a little more oil in another pan and sauté gently.
1 heaped tsp grated fresh galangal (or ginger) 1 tsp grated fresh turmeric (or ½ tsp powdered) 5 candle nuts (kemiri nuts), grated	Add and toss briefly.
500 ml (16 fl oz) coconut cream 250 ml (8 fl oz) chicken stock (bought or homemade, see page 280) 250 ml (8 fl oz) coconut water (from a fresh coconut) or coconut milk 1 tsp shrimp paste 1 heaped tsp shaved palm sugar 1 tsp sambal oelek a good splash of soy sauce	Add, whisk well and bring to the boil. Simmer for about 10 minutes (adding a little more stock and coconut water if it gets too thick).
½–1 young (green) jackfruit (peeled & cubed) or 2 sweet potatoes 2 salam leaves (if available) finely sliced	Add along with drained chicken and cook until jackfruit is tender, adding more liquid if necessary.

'The young jackfruit is unripe and therefore used as a vegetable rather than a fruit. And although my books say that salam leaves are similar to bay leaves, I could see no similarity whatsoever so if they are unavailable, leave them out.'

As mentioned before, the chilli, which tends to feature in almost every Thai recipe, is not a native of this country. It was introduced by the Portuguese in the sixteenth century but is now so ingrained that even a man who is faithful to his wife is said to eat his chilli paste from one bowl: 'kin naam phrik thuay diaw'.

And remember when using chillies avoid touching your eyes or other delicate parts of the body, as the volatile oils released can cause major irritation (particularly in the case of the eyes, where a major flood tends to occur as well as pain).

Grilled Chicken with Sweet Chilli Sauce (Kai Yaang)

Serves 4

— as cooked on the beach at Cape Panwa

1 lemongrass stalk, white part only, smashed & finely sliced 5 garlic cloves, chopped 2 coriander roots, scraped & chopped 1 tsp sea salt	Pound in a mortar (or blend in a processor).
2 tbsp (1 fl oz) Asian fish sauce 1 tsp shaved palm sugar	Add and pound a little more to incorporate.
4 chicken breasts or 8 thighs, skin on	Smear above mix all over and set aside for 15–20 minutes, then grill or barbecue over moderate heat.
4 chillies, finely chopped 1 tbsp (½ fl oz) rice wine vinegar 1 heaped tsp shaved palm sugar 1 garlic clove, crushed 2 tbsp (1 fl oz) Asian fish sauce 3 tbsp (1½ fl oz) vegetable oil juice of 2–3 limes 2 tbsp chopped fresh coriander (cilantro)	While the chicken is cooking, whisk and taste for seasoning.
fresh coriander (cilantro) sprigs	Serve chicken on plates garnished with coriander with bowls of sauce alongside.

Thailand: Phuket

Noodles with Chicken & Vegies (Mie Jawa)

Serves 4

– as cooked on the beach at Nusa Dua

400 gm (13 oz) lomein or Singapore noodles	Put in a bowl, pour hot water over them and leave until separated. Drain and set aside.
1 tbsp (½ fl oz) vegetable oil 2 small red chillies, sliced 2 large green chillies, sliced 1 lemongrass stalk, white part only, smashed & finely sliced 2 garlic cloves, crushed	Heat oil in a wok and sauté until tender.
2 leeks, well washed & finely sliced ¼–½ small wonga bok (Chinese white cabbage), shredded a good handful of bean shoots a small handful of Chinese or normal celery leaves	Add and toss briefly.
125–250 ml (4–8 fl oz) chicken stock (bought or homemade, see page 280) 1–2 tbsp (½–1 fl oz) kecap manis	Add and bring to the boil.
1 cup shredded poached chicken	Add along with noodles and toss to heat through.
fried red (French) shallots, bought or homemade (see page 52)	Serve in deep bowls with shallots sprinkled on the top.

'I originally made this using coconut or palm oil which I thought had a very distinctive flavour – it was only later that I found out that most is reused, filtered oil that has been used to fry dried fish first. So maybe vegetable oil is a better bet.'

The Daylesford region is renowned for its wild mushrooms. In season, slippery jacks and pine mushrooms abound and I have even seen the odd morel which is a real treat. But just one word of warning – picking wild mushrooms can be a bit of a hazard unless you know what you are doing. Don't get carried away and experiment with new varieties or even try to identify them from a book. Instead, you need the help of an experienced forager who will not only take you to the best spots as then Frangos and Frangos chef Andrew Bates did, but who will also steer you well clear of those that may cause you grief.

Fricassee of Squab & Wild Forest Mushrooms Serves 4
– as cooked by Andrew Bates in Daylesford's main street

2 tbsp (1 fl oz) olive oil 25 gm (¾ oz) butter plain (all-purpose) flour freshly ground salt & pepper 4 squab (pigeon) breasts, skin on	Heat oil and butter in a large heavy-bottomed pan. Dust squab with seasoned flour. Then seal, skin side down first. Remove from pan.
50 gm (1¾ oz) butter 200 gm (6½ oz) wild mushrooms, cleaned & sliced or quartered 1 garlic clove, finely sliced freshly ground salt & pepper	Add to pan, toss well and cook for 1 minute.
100 ml (3 fl oz) dry white wine 200 ml (6½ fl oz) chicken stock (bought or homemade, see page 280)	Add and cook gently until liquid is reduced by half.
100 ml (3 fl oz) cream ¼ bunch spring (green) onions, cut in lengths 1 tbsp chopped fresh Italian (flat leaf) parsley	Add and reduce a little. Then return squab and gently cook to desired degree (a little pink is best).
200–300 gm (6½–10 oz) pappardelle pasta sea salt	While squab is cooking, cook in a large pot of rapidly boiling, lightly salted water until al dente. Drain and mound on individual plates, top with squab and spoon sauce over.

The Cookery School at the Four Season's Chiang Mai Resort is overseen by chef Pitak Srichon. It includes in its curriculum most of the regional classics such as Kaeng Phet Pet Yaang (red duck curry), Kaow Soi Kon (curried noodle soup) and Kaeng Hung Lay (dry spiced pork curry with pickled garlic). It also offers fruit and vegetable carving classes, visits to local markets and has its own garden where the ingredients such as lemongrass, galangal and turmeric are grown for the resort's (and cooking school's) use. The classes are conducted in English in a purpose built pavilion with individual cooking stations.

Red Duck Curry (Kaeng Phet Pet Yaang)

Serves 4

— as cooked at the Four Seasons Cookery School

3 tbsp (1½ fl oz) vegetable oil 2 tbsp red curry paste 500 ml (16 fl oz) coconut milk 2 fresh kaffir lime leaves, shredded	Heat oil in wok, add the rest of the ingredients and bring to boil. Simmer for 5 minutes.
½ Chinese roasted duck, boned & cut into chunks 2 tbsp (1 fl oz) Asian fish sauce 2 tbsp shaved palm sugar 8 cherry tomatoes 2 thick slices fresh pineapple, each cut in 8	Add and simmer gently for a few minutes. Put in a bowl.
1 red chilli, seeded & sliced 1 green chilli, seeded & sliced 8 fresh Thai basil leaves, torn	Scatter over the top.
steamed rice	Serve with rice.

Thailand: Chiang Mai

As I mention elsewhere in this book, about the first decent restaurant meal I ever had was at The Coachman in Wellington. For my main course, I ordered Duck a l'Orange, a dish which these days is out of fashion but which when cooked carefully can still be delicious. (Actually, Simon Humble, who was for many years chef at Melbourne's Scusia Mi and who these days has the terrific Tutto Benne, has for years continued with an orange duckling of sorts with a sweet and sour orange sauce flavoured – if I remember correctly – with Aperol).

But I digress. Here is a modern version of Duck a l'Orange using one of the trendy new ingredients, pomegranate molasses, which is available in Middle Eastern or good continental delis or markets.

Duck Breasts with Pomegranate Molasses & Orange

Serves 4

— as cooked at Moore Wilson Fresh

125 ml (4 fl oz) pomegranate molasses 125 ml (4 fl oz) red wine vinegar 3 tbsp (1½ fl oz) honey	Preheat oven to 210°C (410°F). Place in a pot and simmer gently until reduced by half.
750 ml (24 fl oz) salt-reduced chicken stock (bought or homemade, see page 280)	Add, whisk well and reduce to a light sauce consistency.
4 duck breasts, trimmed olive oil	Heat oil in a pan which can go into the oven and sear duck, skin side down, for 5 minutes. Then turn over, put in the oven and cook for about 8 minutes until firmish when pressed with your finger. Rest in a warm spot for 5 minutes.
2–3 oranges, segmented juice of 1 orange a good knob of butter	Add to sauce and gently heat.
a bunch of watercress, cleaned, washed & dried	Place duck breast on individual plates (sliced if you prefer), spoon sauce over and serve with watercress alongside.

Vegetarian

Father Des Britten, Wellington City Missioner

When I began working in kitchens in Wellington during the sixties, about the only thing that I learnt was how bad restaurant food could be, mainly because the chefs I worked with were either down-on-their-luck gamblers, ships' cooks who had jumped ship, or alcoholics – or in many cases all three.

Not that it mattered much to me. Masquerading as a musician (New Zealand Battle of the Bands winners – 'Sebastian's Floral Array' and 'Cellophane') I felt that I was just passing through and it didn't really concern me overly much.

Fate then took a hand. Lack of talent won out (musically that is) and a life in kitchens beckoned. Fortunately at about this time my brother Don, who was working at the Coachman Restaurant in Courteney Place, shouted me dinner at same for a birthday treat. It was a revelation. I still remember what I ate – Chicken Liver Pâté, Duckling a l'Orange and Chocolate Soufflé. Now in this day and age this may seem pretty mundane stuff, but do remember this was the sixties and a typical meal tended to revolve around bad seafood cocktails, Chicken Maryland deep-fried within an inch of its life and Peach Melba made with canned peaches and bottled raspberry sauce (and that's talking about the better establishments). So, it was pretty exciting stuff for a young Huey. And I must also mention the Coachman's vegies – cooked perfectly and full of flavour. I feel some of today's superstars could learn a thing or two from the obvious care that the Coachman's chef took when cooking them.

Which brings me to chef-proprietor, Des Britten. In a previous life he had been one of New Zealand's leading DJs who had successfully turned an interest in food into a career. Many years ahead of his time, I feel that he single-handedly turned New Zealand's restaurant industry on its ear. He inspired, cajoled, and taught a whole generation of Kiwis about good food and the joy of eating, and, at the same time, forced other restaurateurs to lift their game in an attempt to emulate his success. Few succeeded in doing so, but much of New Zealand's later restaurant success stories owe a debt to this pioneer. Not just because he showed his customers the way, but also because he shared his passion for ingredients with growers and suppliers.

These days, Des is still helping people to find their way in his position as Wellington's City Missioner. But food still plays a part in his life. He reviews restaurants for one of the leading newspapers and, when I interviewed him for *Never Trust a Skinny Cook*, he was very excited about the successful processing plant he (in his role as City Missioner) had set up to produce meals for the less fortunate, which was now supplying many other charitable organisations. Obviously, there is still a little bit of the entrepreneur left in him.

When I interviewed Des he mentioned his visits to the market in search of potatoes that were suitable for his Pommes Dauphine. Those were the days when potatoes were just potatoes and the only really successful way to find out their characteristics was to cook the blessed things. So because this dish was so dependent on dry, floury potatoes, he would grab a few from different sacks, run around to the restaurant to cook them and then would purchase the suitable ones from the grower (hoping, of course that they hadn't sold them all in the meantime).

If you don't have a deep-frying thermometer, just use a cube of bread to check the temperature. If it sinks to the bottom it is not hot enough. And if it cooks instantly it is too hot (to drop temperature quickly add a bit more oil). But if it sizzles gently and turns golden around the edges in a minute or so then it's perfect and you're ready for action.

Des Britten's Pommes Dauphine

Serves 8–12

— as cooked at the Coachman Restaurant circa 1968

1 kg (2 lb) floury potatoes, peeled 2 tbsp salt	Cook in boiling, salted water until just tender. Drain very well and then mash.
340 ml (11½ fl oz) water 100 gm (3½ oz) unsalted butter 1 tbsp salt	Put in a heavy-bottomed pot over a high heat.
365 gm (11¾ oz) plain (all-purpose) flour	When butter melts, add flour all at once and beat vigorously with a wooden spoon until mixture comes away from the sides and forms a light crust on the bottom. Remove from heat and set aside for a few minutes.
4 eggs	Add one at a time stirring vigorously between each addition.
freshly ground pepper a little ground nutmeg 1½ litres (1⅕ quarts) vegetable oil for deep-frying	Add pepper and nutmeg. Heat oil to 180°–190°C (350°–375°F). Then without crowding, drop spoonfuls of the mix into the oil and cook until golden brown. Drain well on paper towels.

'When I prepared this on Skinny Cook I served it with prosciutto – not because this was how the Coachman served it, but because you can buy the real stuff (imported from Italy) in New Zealand and I couldn't resist using it with something.'

Mushrooms à la Grecque

Serves 6–8

– as also on the Coachman's menu circa 1968

425 ml (12¼ fl oz) water 75 ml (2½ fl oz) olive oil juice of 1 large lemon ½ teaspoon sea salt 12 whole black peppercorns 12 whole fennel seeds 6 whole coriander (cilantro) seeds 6 sprigs fresh parsley ¼ red onion, finely chopped 1 celery stalk, finely diced	Bring to the boil and simmer for 10 minutes.
450 gm (14¼ oz) button mushrooms, wiped with a damp cloth	Add and simmer for another 10 minutes. Remove mushrooms. Boil liquid to reduce by about one third then strain over mushies. Chill.
chopped fresh Italian (flat leaf) parsley crusty bread	Serve sprinkled with parsley with bread on the side.

New Zealand: Wellington

Scrumptious Mushrooms on Toast

Serves 4

— as cooked at the Great Barrier Feast

100 gm (3½ oz) unsalted butter, soft
1 heaped tsp Dijon mustard
1 heaped tsp chopped fresh thyme
1 large garlic clove, crushed
a squeeze of fresh lemon juice

Preheat oven to 190°C (375°F)

Mix together.

---

12 medium flat mushrooms, peeled & stalks removed
sea salt
freshly ground pepper
fresh lemon juice

Put mushrooms on an oven tray, season and top with dobs of the butter and a little lemon juice. Bake until mushrooms collapse and are very tender.

---

4 thick slices country-style bread

When mushrooms are almost ready, smear bread generously with the butter and bake in the bottom shelf of the oven until golden.

---

chopped fresh parsley

Place bread on individual plates, top with mushrooms and sprinkle with parsley.

I love cabbage rolls – Greek, Italian, Jewish, Middle Eastern – I don't care. As long as they've got plenty of flavour I will devour them. Actually, I think the best I've eaten were at a little Greek cafe in Lonsdale Street in Melbourne (long gone) where Mama was out the back and, in a similar vein to many of the Chinese restaurants of that period, didn't offer the true peasant cooking to us Aussies. Obviously we wouldn't understand or appreciate the real stuff so our lot was moussaka that had been sitting in the bain marie for days and, if we were lucky, a skewer or two of tough lamb. Fortunately Mama took pity on a poor local and because I obviously enjoyed my food (I was fat) I was allowed the house specialties, one of which was the aforementioned cabbage rolls. Of course Mama's version involved minced lamb but I think this vegetarian version is just as delicious.

Cabbage Rolls with Cheese Stuffing & a Fresh Tomato Sauce

Serves 6

– as cooked in George Biron's kitchen at Birregurra

1 tbsp (½ fl oz) olive oil 1 large onion, chopped 2 garlic cloves, crushed	Preheat oven to 190°C (375°F). Heat oil in a large, heavy-bottomed pot and sauté vegies.
3 x 400 gm (13 oz) cans diced tomatoes, drained a little 250 ml (8 fl oz) vegetable stock (bought or homemade, see page 281) a good pinch of sugar a splash of balsamic vinegar ½ tsp sambal oelek 3 anchovies, chopped freshly ground salt & pepper	Add and cook gently until thick and fragrant.
1 savoy cabbage, cleaned & cored	Put the whole cabbage in a pot of boiling water. Leave for a few minutes, remove and peel off leaves carefully. Drain well and cut out stalks (this process may need to be repeated to get the required number of leaves).
400 gm (13 oz) mascarpone 250 gm (8 oz) sour cream 4 tbsp chopped fresh dill freshly ground salt & pepper	Whiz up in a processor until well mixed. Lay 8–12 cabbage leaves on a board, mound stuffing on top and roll up like an envelope.
freshly ground salt & pepper grated tasty cheese freshly grated parmesan	Spoon layer of sauce in oven dish. Top with rolls, seam side down, in one layer. Season, pour the rest of the sauce over the top and sprinkle generously with both cheeses. Bake for 15–20 minutes.

White Restaurant in Auckland's Hilton Hotel is one of the new breed of hotel restaurants. Geared to succeed in its own right and not just depend on hotel guests as its customers, this is a smart operation right on the water with a fabulous view over the harbour.

For the first year or so of its life, Sydney superchef Luke Mangan was a consultant and the menu still reflects a little of that Mangan magic, although subsequent chefs such as Geoff Scott certainly haven't been slouches either.

Curried Eggplant & Potato Pie

Serves 4–6

— as cooked by me at the Hilton Hotel

1 kilo (2 lb) baby potatoes, scrubbed well sea salt	Preheat oven to 200°C (400°F). Cook in lightly salted water until tender. Drain, cover and set aside.
olive oil 1 large onion, finely chopped 2 garlic cloves, crushed	While potatoes are cooking, heat a little oil in a large pot and sauté vegies until tender.
1 tbsp mild curry paste	Add and cook briefly.
2 large eggplants, cut into chunks	Add and cook for 5 minutes tossing regularly.
2 x 400 gm (13 oz) cans diced tomatoes, drained a little 250 ml (8 fl oz) vegetable stock (bought or homemade, see page 281) freshly ground salt & pepper	Add, mix and cook gently for about 15 minutes until tender, stirring regularly.
1 x 400 gm (13 oz) can chickpeas, drained & rinsed	Add, mix and put in a deep gratin dish.
olive oil freshly ground salt & pepper grated tasty cheese	Mash potatoes roughly along with seasoning and olive oil to taste. Put on top of eggplant, sprinkle with plenty of grated cheese and bake until golden and bubbling.

'As a classy accompaniment to a roast or grill, cook in individual dishes or ramekins.'

*'Showing the multicultural influences, we have the
raisins of the English curries, the oyster sauce
from the Chinese and a mish mash of a name.'*

Dry Curry de Legumes

Serves 6–8

— as cooked on the beach in Mauritius

2 tbsp (1 fl oz) vegetable oil 2 red onions, cut in wedges 1 garlic clove, crushed 2 cooking apples, cored, peeled & cut in wedges	Heat oil in a wok and sauté gently.
2 tbsp mild Indian curry paste (or 1 heaped tbsp curry powder)	Add and stir for a minute or two to release aromas.

6–8 ripe red tomatoes, cored & cut in 8
500 ml (16 fl oz) vegetable stock
  (bought or homemade, see page 281)
½ small cauliflower, cut in florets
¼ smallish pumpkin (butternut squash), peeled,
  seeded & cut in wedges
2 medium carrots, thickly sliced
3 tbsp raisins, soaked in rum
a slurp of oyster sauce (the vegetarian version if you like)
freshly ground salt & pepper
	Add, mix well and season. Cover and simmer very gently for 45 minutes or until vegies are very tender (it should be fairly dry but add more stock if needed).

3 tbsp chopped fresh coriander (cilantro) steamed rice	Add coriander and mix in. Serve with rice.

Mauritius: Flic en Flac

As a man who basically has two brown thumbs, I was pretty impressed by the Canberra Floriade. Staged yearly from mid September to mid October, this is the largest spring festival in the southern hemisphere. More than one million flowers are planted, over 300,000 people visit and every year there is a different theme (our year it was Heavens in Bloom, a celebration of the solar systems). But to make up for my lack of gardening skills, I cooked this bright, colourful vegie burger which, I think, reflected the colours of the rainbow that surrounded me.'

Italian BBQ Vegie Burger

Serves 4

– as prepared at Floriade Festival

olive oil spray

½ eggplant, sliced

2 zucchini, sliced

1 red capsicum (bell pepper), cored, seeded & cut in pieces

1 green capsicum (bell pepper), cored, seeded
  & cut in pieces

freshly ground salt & pepper

Preheat BBQ or grill.

Spray and season vegies and cook until blistered and tender, spraying with more oil as necessary.

¼ cup mayonnaise (bought or homemade,
  see page 281)

2 tbsp (1 fl oz) sour cream

2–3 tbsp pesto (bought or homemade, see page 281)

1 garlic clove, crushed

a squeeze of fresh lemon juice

Mix together. Taste for seasoning.

---

4 large burger buns, halved

2–3 ripe, red tomatoes, thickly sliced

4 cos (Romaine) lettuce leaves

shavings of parmesan

When vegies are ready, remove and then grill buns and tomatoes. Place bun bottoms on board, smear generously with mayo. Then top with tomato, lettuce, vegies, more mayo and the parmesan. Press tops on firmly.

Parmesan Crumbed Mushroom Steaks with a Coriander & Lime Tartare

Serves 4

— as cooked at the National Museum

½ cup mayonnaise (bought or homemade, see page 281) 3 tbsp (1½ fl oz) sour cream 1 tbsp chopped capers 1 tbsp chopped gherkins juice of 1 lime 2 heaped tbsp chopped fresh coriander (cilantro)	Combine.
plain (all-purpose) flour freshly ground salt & pepper 2 eggs 125 ml (4 fl oz) milk 1–2 cups packet breadcrumbs 3 tbsp freshly grated parmesan 8–12 large flat field mushrooms, peeled & stalks discarded	Place flour and seasonings in one bowl, beaten eggs and milk in another, then crumbs and parmesan in a third. Dust mushrooms well with flour then dip in eggwash before pressing firmly into breadcrumbs.
olive oil	Heat a thin layer of oil in a large non-stick pan and, without overcrowding, gently fry mushrooms until golden all over. Drain well on paper towels. Arrange on a platter with a bowl of tartare on the side.

'You may need to cut the mushrooms down a little (if the edges curl upwards) to make into even steaks.'

Australia: Canberra

'Serve as a main course with a green salad simply tossed with a good slurp each of balsamic vinegar and extra virgin olive oil.'

Eggplant 'Lasagne'

Serves 6–8

– as cooked in my room on Hamilton Island

olive oil spray
3 large eggplant, thinly sliced lengthways

Preheat oven to 180°C (350°F). Also preheat ridged grill.
Spray eggplant with oil and grill
until tender.

pesto (bought or homemade, see page 281)
2 x 400 gm (13 oz) cans diced tomatoes, drained a little
250 ml (8 fl oz) tomato-based pasta sauce
400 gm (13 oz) grated tasty cheese
freshly grated parmesan
125–250 ml (4–8 fl oz) cream
freshly ground salt & pepper

Layer an ovenproof dish in this order – one third of the eggplant, half the tomatoes and pasta sauce, a drizzle of pesto, then half the tasty cheese along with some parmesan, a good sprinkling of cream and seasoning. Repeat process finishing with cheese and cream. Bake in oven for about 30–40 minutes until golden and bubbling.

Everyone has the perfect recipe for cooking pasta. Some insist that adding a little oil to the pot will stop it sticking; others insist that it is the salt in the water that achieves this. I've even read somewhere that you should put the pasta in one piece at a time (ridiculous). And what about the cook who insists that a little prayer over the boiling water doesn't hurt (she was joking – I hope).

Well here is my perfect method. First of all you need *lots* of rapidly boiling, lightly salted water. Throw the pasta in, mix it up, cover and bring it back to the boil as fast as possible. Remove the lid once it comes back to the boil and, every now and then, separate it with your tongs. And if the packet instructions say it will take about 12 minutes to cook, start checking at about 10 minutes.

Spaghetti with Zucchini Flowers

Serves 4

– as cooked outside the Lake House

500 gm (1 lb) spaghetti sea salt	Cook in plenty of rapidly boiling, lightly salted water until al dente. Drain well.
12 zucchini flowers (female preferably)	Cut flowers from the baby zucchini. Cut the flowers in half lengthways, then slice the zucchini itself.
60–125 ml (2–4 fl oz) extra virgin olive oil 3 garlic cloves, crushed 1–2 chillies, seeded & finely sliced 1 medium onion, chopped	While pasta is cooking, heat oil in a large pan or wok. Then add vegies along with the sliced zucchini and cook until just tender.
1 tbsp fresh thyme leaves 4 anchovies, chopped (optional) freshly ground pepper 75 ml (2½ fl oz) fresh lemon juice	Add, mix well and cook for a minute or two. Add pasta and zucchini flowers and toss well just to wilt flowers slightly.
freshly grated parmesan (optional)	Put in bowls and sprinkle with parmesan.

'Zucchini flowers are often available at specialist greengrocers. There are two types – the male which is on the stalk and the female which comes attached to a small zucchini. And for this recipe, if you can only find the male ones buy a couple of small zucchini as well.'

Australia: Daylesford

Vegetable Fritto Misto

Serves 6–8

— as cooked overlooking Noosa Heads

125 ml (4 fl oz) cold water
250 ml (8 fl oz) freshly opened lager (beer),
    at room temperature
a pinch of sea salt
self raising flour
1 tsp baking powder

Whisk water, beer and salt together. Then, whisking continually, add flour and baking powder gradually until the batter coats your finger lightly.

---

2 litres (1¾ quarts) vegetable oil

Heat in a large deep sided pot to 180°C (350°F).

¼ butternut pumpkin (squash), peeled,
    seeded & finely sliced
1 yellow capsicum (bell pepper), cored,
    seeded & sliced into 1 cm (³⁄₈ inch) strips
1 red capsicum (bell pepper), cored, seeded
    & sliced into 1 cm (³⁄₈ inch) strips
1 red onion, sliced into thickish rings
6–8 small flat field mushrooms, peeled & stalks removed
2 small zucchini, sliced on the diagonal
2 Japanese eggplants, sliced on the diagonal

Without overcrowding, dip the vegies in the batter and fry until golden and crisp. Drain well on paper towels. Pile on individual plates or on a platter.

24–30 fresh basil leaves, washed & dried
sea salt
lemon wedges

Fry the basil until crispy. Season the vegies, top with basil and serve with lemon on the side.

'For a light, crispy batter I use freshly opened lager (never cold) which has natural yeasts that interact with the other ingredients.'

Polenta Pasticciata

— as cooked at De Bortoli Vineyard

1 tbsp (½ fl oz) olive oil 1 large onion, chopped 2 green capsicums (bell peppers), cored, seeded & diced 3 garlic cloves, crushed	Preheat oven to 200°C (400°F). Heat oil and sauté vegies, gently, until tender.
3 x 400 gm (13 oz) cans diced tomatoes, drained a little 250 ml (8 fl oz) vegetable stock (bought or homemade, see page 281) sea salt flakes freshly ground pepper a good pinch of brown sugar	Add, mix well and cook for 15–20 minutes until thick and fragrant.
10 fresh basil leaves, shredded	Mix in and turn off.
750 ml (24 fl oz) water 200 gm (6½ oz) polenta 1 heaped tsp sea salt	While sauce is cooking, place in a microwave-proof bowl. Mix well and microwave, uncovered, at 100% for 6 minutes. Stir well, loosely cover with greaseproof paper and cook for a further 6 minutes.
50 gm (1¾ oz) freshly grated parmesan 2 dollops of butter freshly ground pepper	Add and mix well. Pour into a deep gratin dish and spread out evenly.
1 cup cubed mozzarella	Mix into tomato sauce and pour on top of polenta.
freshly grated parmesan	Sprinkle over the top and bake for 15–20 minutes until bubbling.

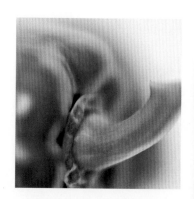

Australia: Yarra Valley

Garlic Eggplant with Chinese Celery Noodles

– as cooked on the beach at Kuta

125 ml (4 fl oz) soy sauce 125 ml (4 fl oz) mirin (Japanese rice wine) 125 ml (4 fl oz) sake a good splash of kecap manis 4 garlic cloves, finely chopped	Put in a pot and simmer to thicken and develop flavours.
60 ml (2 fl oz) vegetable oil 1 cup Chinese celery leaves or fresh coriander (cilantro) 1 large knob of fresh ginger, grated a splash of sesame oil 1 tsp sambal oelek 1 garlic clove, crushed sea salt flakes freshly ground pepper	Whiz up in a blender or processor. Set aside.
1–2 packets hokkien noodles	Blanch in boiling water as per instructions until just tender. Drain and plunge into cold water. Drain again and toss with celery dressing and taste for balance of flavours. Set aside.
1 egg yolk 125 ml (4 fl oz) iced water 1 cup rice flour	Make batter by combining egg and water in a bowl. Add flour and combine lightly (should still be lumpy). Refrigerate until needed.
1.5 litres (1⅕ quarts) vegetable oil	Preheat oil for frying to 180°–190°C (350°–375°F) in a wok or deep sided pot.
2–3 eggplants, sliced lengthways & then halved crossways rice flour	When ready to serve, spread flour out on a tray. Dust eggplant lightly then dip in batter and deep-fry in 3 or 4 lots until golden. Drain well on paper towels. Mound noodles on individual plates, top with eggplant and then with the garlic-soy mix.

'Chinese celery is not to be confused with normal celery. It has a very pronounced celery flavour, is used as a herb rather than a vegetable and coriander, in this case, would be a good substitute.'

The Daylesford region has always been renowned for its mineral springs and spas. And the Hepburn Spa is still a popular tourist attraction. It has also, in past years, been a bit of a hippys' paradise, known for its alternative lifestyle.

But these days, it has also developed into a retreat from the hustle and bustle of city life. The alternative lifestyle sector has seen organics flourishing and good, friendly country cafes and restaurants springing up using these ingredients, while the refugees from city life have brought with them a degree of sophistication in both food tastes and culture. No longer the backwater it once was, particularly on the weekends, this is a bustling busy town with lots to offer even the most discerning of visitors. Restaurants such as The Lake House and Frangos and Frangos are wonderful. As is Iseta Harris's Food Gallery and a great country pub, the Farmer's Arms. And then there is Cliffy's – about the best food store in Australia. Many of the slow-cooked dishes, available either to take away or eat in the rather eclectic dining room, are cooked in an Aga stove. If available, you must try the Pork Rillettes made from local organic pork.

Pumpkin Rosemary Fritters with a Yoghurt Coriander Sauce

Serves 6–8

— as cooked by Iseta Harris at the Food Gallery

6 cups grated pumpkin (butternut squash)	Put in a large bowl and mix well.
½ onion, finely chopped	
200 gm (6½ oz) plain (all-purpose) flour	
1 egg	
50 gm (1¾ oz) freshly grated parmesan	
1 tsp Cajun spice	
2 tsp chopped fresh rosemary	
freshly ground salt & pepper	
2 cups packet breadcrumbs	Add breadcrumbs gradually along with egg if too firm. Form into patties.
1 egg	
vegetable oil	Heat a thin layer in a large pan. Add patties and fry until golden brown on both sides. Drain well on paper towels.
¾ cup yoghurt	Mix together and serve with patties.
3 tbsp chopped fresh coriander (cilantro)	
juice of ½–1 lemon	
freshly ground salt & pepper	

In New Zealand at the terrific Moore Wilson Fresh market in Wellington, I came across some fantastic tiny fennel which was so delicious you could almost eat it like an apple (I said almost).

I can never understand why fennel isn't more popular. Even the people at Moore Wilson said that it hardly walked out the door. It's the same in Australia – except for the Greeks and Italians, few cook with it. Maybe it's not a trendy little number but fennel can be delicious if even cooked with a modicum of care. I like it braised in stock with some of the chopped frond to finish. It's also terrific simply oiled and seasoned and bunged on the barbie, or just shaved finely and thrown into a salad.

But I was faced with something special in these baby versions and, at the risk of patting myself on the back, I also achieved something a little special in the recipe stakes.

Herb Crumbed Fennel with Red Capsicum Rouille

Serves 4

— as cooked in the kitchens of Moore Wilson Fresh

6–8 baby fennel bulbs, cleaned sea salt	Simmer in lightly salted water until almost tender. Cool and then carefully slice lengthways.
2 whole eggs 2 egg yolks 1 heaped tsp mustard 2 pinches sea salt flakes 1 garlic clove, crushed	While fennel is cooking, make rouille by whizzing up in a food processor for 2 minutes.
500 ml (16 fl oz) vegetable oil	Add, little by little, through feeder tube.
a squeeze of fresh lemon juice 3–4 pieces roasted red capsicum (bell pepper), chopped (see page 133) freshly ground pepper 1 tsp sambal oelek	Add and process for another minute or so until well blended.
1 egg 60 ml (2 fl oz) milk plain (all-purpose) flour 2 cups packet breadcrumbs 3 tbsp chopped fresh herbs (parsley, basil & mint)	Set up three bowls. Put egg and milk in one and beat. Put flour in the second and in the third, mix the crumbs, and herbs. Lightly flour the fennel, dip into the eggwash and coat well with the crumbs.
vegetable oil	Heat a layer of oil in a large pan and, without overcrowding, fry the fennel until golden brown. Drain well and arrange on individual plates with a good spoonful of rouille.

Fennel Tarte Tatin

— as cooked in a kitchen in Canberra

Serves 2–4

3–4 fennel bulbs, cleaned & hard core cut out ½ tbsp (¼ oz) butter	Preheat oven to 200°C (400°F). Cut fennel into wedges, melt butter in a round, flattish ovenproof dish (or omelette pan). Then tightly pack in fennel, in one layer, cut side up.
1 heaped tsp brown sugar a good splash of balsamic vinegar a good splash of red wine 1 tbsp (½ oz) butter	Sprinkle sugar, balsamic and wine over the top and dot with butter. Cook in oven for about 30 minutes until tender.
1 frozen puff pastry sheet	Cut into a round slightly larger than the dish and place on top. Tuck in the sides and cook for about 8–10 minutes until pastry is golden.
chopped fresh Italian (flat leaf) parsley	Turn out onto a large plate (fennel upwards) and sprinkle with parsley.

'I used a tarte tatin dish from Le Creuset – worked perfectly.'

Asparagus with Mushrooms & Sherry Vinegar

Serves 4

– as cooked overlooking Wellington Harbour

20–24 thickish spears of asparagus	Bend until the spears snap. Discard bottom and lightly peel 2 centimetres or so from the spear.
olive oil 12–16 button mushrooms, halved or quartered	Heat a little oil and sauté mushrooms until almost tender.
2–3 tbsp (1–½ fl oz) sherry vinegar	Add and reduce by one third.
250 ml (8 fl oz) vegetable stock (bought or homemade, see page 281) a good knob of butter 2–3 tbsp fresh tarragon leaves	Add and cook until syrupy.
sea salt	When you add the stock, blanch the asparagus in lots of rapidly boiling salted water until crisp-tender. Drain well and place on plates or platter.
6 snowpeas, shredded finely	Toss with mushrooms for a few seconds to warm then spoon over the asparagus.

On the nose

It's amazing how quickly you get used to the smell of Rotorua. The first whiff of its sulphuric aroma leaves you wondering how anyone could possibly live here, but although it doesn't ever completely disappear, within hours you find yourself wondering whether the odour has dissipated (it hasn't).

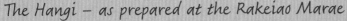

Anyway, that aside, Rotorua is a virtual wonderland of volcanic activity – sort of like a real life Disneyland. Full of geysers, boiling mud pools, volcanic crater lakes and mineral springs, it is a reminder of the region's tumultuous geological past. It is also the spiritual home to the Maori of Te Arawa (one third of the population is Maori, New Zealand's largest concentration of Maoris) and as such, the perfect place to visit a Marae (sacred meeting place) and experience a Hangi, the traditional Maori feast.

The Hangi – as prepared at the Rakeiao Marae

First of all you dig a pit in the ground (the size depends on the number of rocks and the amount of food to be cooked). Next you crumble up some newspaper and put it in the pit. Add plenty of kindling and then build a frame on top of the pit by placing a layer of hard wood side by side, resting on the edges of the pit with about a 1 centimetre gap between each piece. When covered, repeat the process with another layer of wood at right angles to the first. Then another layer, once again at right angles. Top with plenty of either river or volcanic stones. Light the newspaper. When the wood burns down, the by now white hot rocks will fall into the pit (about two hours). Rake the rocks to one side and with a long-handled shovel remove all the unburned pieces of wood. Then make a flat bed of the rocks.

Throw a couple of handfuls of cold water on to them to get rid of the ash. Traditionally, the meat and vegies were then placed in the pit in woven flax baskets, but these days metal cages are used with cabbage leaves covering the bottom. The food (chickens, pork joints, sweet potato, corn, etc.) is placed on this and then a few litres of water is thrown over the lot to produce steam. Quickly cover with a wet white sheet or the like, in layers. Now add a layer of wet sacks, sprinkling more water as you do so. Then cover in a mound shape with soil, watching for any cracks where steam can escape. Leave to cook for 2 – 3 hours.

Desserts

Whilst on Phuket we stayed in the Cape Panwa Hotel on the South Eastern tip. Thankfully away from the more touristy parts of the island, the hotel has its own private beach, many excellent restaurants and bars and even its own pub. And while I didn't quite get around to enrolling in any of them, classes in everything from ice and vegetable carving and Thai cookery to traditional painting and basic Thai language lessons were conducted. It is also one of the friendliest hotels I've stayed in, with both management and staff keen to cater to every whim. (No wonder everyone from Elizabeth Taylor to Pierce Brosnan and Leonardo DiCaprio have been in residence at one time or other.)

We dined one night at their traditional Thai restaurant, Panwa House, which is situated in and around an old plantation house. (The architecture of this period was deemed to be Sino–Portuguese because of the strong influence of the Portuguese traders.) The banquet prepared by chef Phudon Prachum and his team was brilliant and, with a little persuasion, Phudon recreated the steamed pumpkin custards for the cameras the next day.

Steamed Pumpkin Custard (Sangkaya Fuk-Thong)

Serves 4–6

– as cooked by chef Phudon Prachum

1 small round pumpkin (butternut squash)	Cut a small slice off the top and carefully remove seeds with a spoon without piercing body.
4 eggs, well beaten 100 gm (3½ oz) shaved palm sugar, lightly heated to dissolve 100 gm (3½ oz) white sugar 200 ml (6½ fl oz) coconut milk ½ tsp sea salt	Whisk together then strain through a sieve into the pumpkin. Place lid on and steam, covered, over gently simmering water for about 90 minutes until custard is set.
vanilla ice cream, bought or homemade (see page 270)	Serve hot or cold cut into wedges with ice cream on the side.

Thailand: Phuket

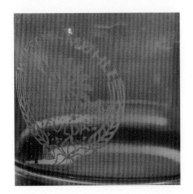

Pear, Goat Cheese & Honey Tart

Serves 4

— as cooked in the Yarra Valley

3–4 ripe pears, peeled, cored & cut into thin wedges 1 tbsp (½ fl oz) fresh lemon juice	Preheat oven to 200°C (400°F). Place pears in a bowl and toss with lemon juice.
1 sheet frozen puff pastry cooking oil spray	Place on a lightly oiled baking sheet and lightly score a border around all edges with a sharp knife.
1–2 logs fresh goat cheese, lightly mashed	Spread over the base inside the border.
caster (superfine) sugar 1 egg 2 tbsp (1 fl oz) milk	Lay the pears on top and sprinkle generously with the sugar. Mix egg and milk together and brush around edges. Bake for about 12–15 minutes until pastry is golden and risen.
melted honey thickened cream	Brush with honey and serve with cream on the side.

Whilst my mother did tend to overcook the vegies and meat (although maybe not to the extent of other mothers) when it came to anything sweet she was a whiz. I remember she used to make cakes and puddings for the local grocer – that was until the Health Department found out and demanded that she build a completely separate kitchen for the ten or so that she sold every week – isn't it good to see that some things haven't changed. But I digress, this is my slightly updated version of one of her classics, the main variation being the addition of Grand Marnier which was maybe not to be found in the Hewitson pantry.

Golden Syrup & Orange Parfait

Serves 4–6

– as cooked by Sybil Hewitson circa 1960

200 gm (6½ oz) caster (superfine) sugar 175 ml (6 fl oz) water 1 vanilla bean, split grated zest of 1 orange	Put in a pot, bring to boil then turn off and leave to infuse for 15 minutes. Remove vanilla bean and boil for a few minutes.
3 egg whites a pinch of cream of tartar	Beat with a hand mixer until soft peaks form. Then, continue beating while adding hot syrup little by little. Continue until mix is shiny and firm.
300 ml (10 fl oz) thickened cream 4 tbsp (2 fl oz) Grand Marnier	Whip until fairly thick then gently fold into above.
3–4 tbsp golden syrup	Line a bowl with kitchen wrap and spoon in the mix. Drizzle the golden syrup on top and using a plastic spatula, gently swirl into the mix (don't over mix).
a mixture of fresh berries	Freeze overnight and serve topped with a mixture of berries.

New Zealand: Levin

Ice Cream Stuffed Brioche with Chocolate Sauce

Serves 6

— as cooked in a Noosa kitchen

6 mini brioches	Preheat oven to 190°C (375°F). Heat in the oven.
200 gm (6½ oz) dark cooking chocolate	At same time, melt in a pan over simmering water.
150 ml (5 fl oz) milk 30 gm (1 oz) caster (superfine) sugar 2 tbsp (1 fl oz) cream	Bring to the boil in a pot, regularly whisking. Then pour into chocolate and whisk well.
30 gm (1 oz) soft unsalted butter, diced	Add little by little, whisking continually.
6 scoops vanilla ice cream, bought or homemade (see page 270) icing (confectioners') sugar	Cut brioches in half, place bottom in serving dishes and place a scoop of ice cream on top. Spoon a little chocolate sauce over the top, place brioche lids on and spoon more chocolate sauce over the lot. Sprinkle with icing sugar.

It's funny that although we are both based in Melbourne, Geoff Lindsay from the highly rated Pearl Restaurant had never appeared on any of my shows. It may have had something to do with the fact that I just hadn't got around to asking him (rather than him telling me to clear off). But I grabbed the chance when he was appearing at Hamilton Island's Great Barrier Feast.

A popular guest chef and master class presenter, he is one of the few Anglo Saxon Australian chefs who can produce Asian-influenced food that actually has an authentic ring rather than feeling contrived. In fact when *Gourmet Traveller* magazine last year named its fifty top restaurant dishes, Pearl's Red Curry of Duck with Crisp Fried Egg was right up there. I also loved a dish he presented at the Great Barrier Feast – Raw Tuna with Shredded Apple, Ponzu and Wasabi Flavoured Roe (see page 49). And as a man who doesn't really have much of a sweet tooth, I must admit that there is one dessert I do love, another Lindsay classic – Sticky Rice Pudding from his book *Chow Down*.

Sticky Rice Pudding with Palm Sugar Syrup & Grilled Bananas

Serves 4

— as cooked in Chiang Mai

250 gm (8 oz) jasmine rice	Wash well and drain.
600 ml (20 fl oz) coconut milk 1 tsp salt 2½ tbsp caster (superfine) sugar aluminium foil	Put in a heavy-bottomed pot along with the rice. Cover tightly with the foil then a lid and simmer gently for 10 minutes. Remove from heat and leave, covered, for another 10 minutes. DON'T PEEK.
100 gm (3½ oz) palm sugar 2 tbsp (1 fl oz) fresh orange juice	Simmer to form a thick syrup.
2 bananas, skin on	Cut in half lengthways and then grill flesh side down until lightly caramelised. Put on plates with a good spoon of rice and a drizzle of syrup. Serve hot or warm.

A Foodie's Feast

The Great Ocan Road is one of Victoria's most popular tourist destinations and it's worth the ride just for the scenery (a helicopter ride over the rock formation, the Twelve Apostles, is breathtaking). But these days the region is also a foodie's paradise. From the award winning wineries around Geelong (actually, during the mid-1800s Geelong was Victoria's premium wine region – it was also the first region to be attacked by phylloxera) and cheesemakers such as Timboon, Mount Emu Creek, Meredith and the like, to smallgood producers such as the Cobden Smokehouse and Angel Cardoso (see page 28) at Lara. And let us not forget the traditional fisherfolk and beef, sheep and vegetable farmers who these days talk endlessly of 'value-added' and do everything from farm eels to produce organic ice cream right next to the milking sheds. Abalone and crayfish is also big business. A huge export market has developed but, if lucky, you may snare some at the local co-op (or in the case of abalone, dive for them yourself – you can legally harvest ten per person per day which when you consider that an abalone diver's permit changes hands for over one million bucks, is maybe a cheaper way to go).

Vegetables also play a major role in the Great Ocean Road region. The rich, fertile soil of the area has always produced large amounts of spuds and the like for the Melbourne market. But these days growers are spreading their wings, many of them following organic principles. I can still taste the superb strawberries from Hanlon's at Irrewarra, which were ripe red all the way through and tasted emphatically of the sun. And the most beautiful tomatoes from Organix, which were so delicious I ate them like apples (once again red right through and with that sweet-acid balance so essential in a decent tomato). Another bonus is the fact that scattered throughout the countryside you will find roadside stalls selling local produce. I bought some strawberry jam as well as some tiny new potatoes which were both delicious but which, I must say, I didn't cook together.

All in all a terrific journey. Taking into account the still country friendly charms of the seaside resorts of Lorne and Apollo Bay, the wonderful scenery and the super fresh produce, we enjoyed ourselves greatly.

BBQ Berry Puddings

— as prepared at the Split Point Lighthouse

aluminium foil
cooking oil spray
4 blueberry muffins
1 punnet (tub) strawberries, hulled & quartered
Muscat, Tokay or any fortified wine

Cut 4 squares of foil. Lightly oil one side. Cut muffins from top to bottom almost completely through and place on foil. Place strawberries in centre, sprinkle generously with fortified wine, wrap up and cook on BBQ for 8–10 minutes.

150 gm (5 oz) mascarpone
grated zest & juice of 1 orange
2 tbsp (1 fl oz) honey

Combine.

icing (confectioners') sugar
fresh mint sprigs

Unwrap muffins, place on plates and pour any cooking juices over the top. Add a good dollop of the mascarpone and sprinkle with icing sugar. Garnish with mint.

Strawberry Bruschetta

– as cooked at Airey's Inlet

a good knob of unsalted butter
1 punnet (tub) strawberries, hulled & quartered
a good slurp of Muscat, Tokay or any fortified wine
1 tbsp (½ fl oz) honey

Melt butter in a non-stick pan. Add strawberries, fortified wine and honey and gently cook for 2 minutes stirring now and again.

4 thick slices fruit loaf
orange mascarpone (see page 253)
icing (confectioners') sugar

Grill or toast fruit loaf, place on plates and top with berries and juices and then with a dollop of the mascarpone. Sprinkle with icing sugar.

'You, of course, could use a mixture of berries, and the wonderful fruit bread I used came from the Irrewarra Sourdough Bakery who continue to make all their breads using the old-fashioned methods.'

Eton Mess

Serves 4

– as cooked amongst the strawberry fields of Irrewarra

250 ml (8 fl oz) thickened cream

Whip until thick and set aside.

1 punnet (tub) strawberries, quartered
a good slurp of Grand Marnier
½ tsp caster (superfine) sugar

Combine in a bowl and mash a little.

4 medium–large bought meringues, broken into pieces

Gently mix all together and put in serving glasses.

'A simple yet delicious dessert for which you can use any fruit (I often make it with stewed rhubarb but in that case I add Framboise rather than Grand Marnier).'

I remember gazing into the local sweet shop as a young child. I was never much of a fan of liquorice so the piles of that didn't interest me (although I quite enjoyed the odd liquorice allsort). But what I did like was Rocky Road – and obviously I wasn't the only one because, seemingly, half the window was piled high with the blessed stuff. Chockful of brazil nuts, marshmallows and lots of other goodies it seemed so exotic – and the quantity I got for one penny, well that's another story.

Rocky Road Sundae
Serves 4

– as cooked in a Napier kitchen

125 gm (4 oz) dark cooking chocolate, chopped	Place over a double boiler and gently stir until combined. Allow to cool a little.
125 ml (4 fl oz) thickened cream	
125 ml (4 fl oz) milk	
1 tsp honey	
chocolate ice cream	Layer sundae glasses with the ice cream, cherries, marshmallows, sauce, nuts and Flake.
glacé (candied) cherries	
mini marshmallows	
toasted brazil nuts	
1 Flake bar, broken in pieces	
whipped cream	Mound cream on top and sprinkle with hundreds and thousands.
hundreds & thousands (sprinkles)	

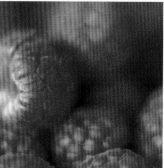

Impossible Pie

Serves 4–6

— as cooked on Hamilton Island

100 gm (2½ oz) plain (all purpose) flour, sifted	Preheat oven to 190°C (375°F).
90 gm (3 oz) desiccated (unsweetened/shredded) coconut	Using a wooden spoon mix together.
125 gm (4 oz) melted butter	
280 gm (9 oz) caster (superfine) sugar	
2 tsp vanilla essence	
500 ml (16 fl oz) milk	
4 eggs, lightly beaten	

melted butter	Grease a pudding or gratin dish, pour in mix and cook in the oven for about 45 minutes until golden brown and set.

mixed berries	Cool a little then serve with the berries and ice cream or cream on top.
whipped cream or vanilla ice cream, bought or homemade (see page 270)	

'If my memory serves me correctly this is an old recipe from the Women's Weekly and the 'impossible' refers to the fact that, as it cooks, it forms separate layers and also because it is so bloody simple to prepare.'

Elizabeth David is regarded by many as the doyen of food writers. She had a great enthusiasm for the subject and had the ability to emphasise the class in even the simplest of meals. I remember when I first started cooking, reading her story about a visit to a French country inn – the kitchen was closed but the owner, taking pity on a hungry traveller, seated her in the garden, picked some tomatoes straight from the vine and served them along with a good loaf of bread, some sea salt and the best butter from Normandy. I could almost taste the feast. And feast it was too because what David was demonstrating was that the best ingredients, served simply in a way which enhances their natural attributes, are hard to beat.

In such a manner, through her books and articles, Elizabeth David introduced a whole generation of English to the joys of not just eating but dining. And in doing so is credited with shaping the tastes of a nation, post war, when olive oil was something to be found in the chemists shop right next to cod liver oil and the food of France, Italy and the Mediterranean was regarded as 'foreign muck'.

And just a couple of points concerning her recipe. Firstly, when melting chocolate make sure that the bowl doesn't touch the water otherwise the chocolate may seize. And secondly, when beating egg whites always ensure that everything is bone dry as even a drop of water will stop the whites from expanding.

Elizabeth David's Chocolate & Orange Mousse Serves 4–6
– as cooked in a kitchen in Rotorua

125 gm (4 oz) dark cooking chocolate	Melt over simmering water.
4 egg yolks	Beat with a hand mixer until thick. Remove chocolate from heat and mix in with a wooden spoon.
30 gm (1 oz) soft unsalted butter juice of 1 large orange 1 tbsp (½ fl oz) Grand Marnier	Add butter and stir well. Then add orange juice and, with a whisk, beat well. Last of all mix in liqueur.
4 egg whites	Beat, with hand mixer, until stiff peaks form. Then add to chocolate mix, little by little, using a spatula. Put into a large bowl, small glasses or even coffee cups and refrigerate for at least 3 hours.

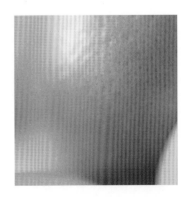

One of the best things about getting out into a wine area and whipping up a dish or two is that the very hospitable winemakers are always offering the odd glass of wine. At De Bortoli it was no exception. Except in this case it was a bottle of their exquisite Noble One dessert wine which inspired me to cook up some fresh peaches to accompany it.

Poached Peaches in a Vanilla Bean & Cinnamon Syrup

Serves 6

– as cooked overlooking the vines at De Bortoli

1 litre (32 fl oz) water 50 gm (1¾ oz) caster (superfine) sugar 2 cinnamon sticks 1 vanilla bean, cut in 4	Bring water to the boil and add the rest.
6 ripe peaches, unpeeled	Add, weigh down with a plate and simmer for 5–8 minutes (depending on ripeness of peaches). Turn heat off and leave in the pot to cool.
cream	Skin and stone peaches and serve with cream and a glass of dessert wine.

Australia: Yarra Valley

The clafoutis originated in Limousin in France, which is a cherry growing area, and was traditionally made with the first cherries of the season. It can be made with almost any fruit and, in fact, at my restaurant Fleurie we used to make a pear tart clafoutis (baked in a shortcrust tart shell) which was fabulous. But I have also seen the dish made with everything from apples to figs, strawberries and peaches, and most fruit in between. With this version, depending on how tart the rhubarb is, you may sometimes need to up the quantity of sugar although I do tend to steer clear of the mature fruit and go for the smaller, younger numbers.

Rhubarb Clafoutis

Serves 4–6

– as cooked in a kitchen in Hawke's Bay

500 gm (1 lb) rhubarb, washed well & cut into 3 cm (1¼ inch) pieces	Preheat oven to 200°C (400°F). Blanch rhubarb in boiling water for 2 minutes. Drain well.
4 eggs 100 gm (3½ oz) white (granulated) sugar 1 vanilla bean, split & cut into 3 pieces a splash of Framboise (or any other berry liqueur) a pinch of salt 100 gm (3½ oz) plain (all-purpose) flour	Whisk eggs and sugar until foaming. Then add rest and whisk until smooth.
150 ml (5 fl oz) cream 200 ml (6½ fl oz) milk	Add and whisk well. Place rhubarb in ovenproof dish, pour over batter and bake for about 45 min until golden and risen.
icing (confectioners') sugar vanilla ice cream, bought or homemade (see page 270)	Dust with icing sugar and serve with ice cream on the side.

In similar vein to Wellington I was very impressed by the restaurants in Auckland. Good fresh food with lots of flair. Of course one of my favourites is Antoines in Parnell which is owned by my great mates Tony and Beth Astle (see pages 124). But I also ate extremely well at White, Mikano, The French Cafe, Vinnies and the super popular Soul at Viaduct Harbour. And because another great mate Don Fletcher (head of the Restaurant and Caterers' Association) lives just around the corner, I regularly dined in Ponsenby Road which has a great and varied choice of places to eat. Which brings me to the reason for the story. Although I had sworn off desserts I was persuaded to try these terrific Spanish doughnuts at Rocco, one of Ponsenby's most popular establishments. I must admit my diet immediately went out the window because they were so moreish I ordered another portion. Then just in case I had a craving for them when I returned home the chef kindly gave me the recipe.

Churros with Chocolate Sauce

Serves 4

— as cooked at Rocco Restaurant in Ponsenby Road

200 ml (4 fl oz) cream	Bring to the boil in a small heavy-bottomed pot.
150 gm (5 oz) dark cooking chocolate, chopped ½ tsp vanilla extract	Remove pot from heat, add chocolate and when dissolved whisk well and add vanilla. Set aside in a warm spot.
100 gm (3½ oz) caster (superfine) sugar ½ tsp ground cinnamon	Mix together and also set aside.
250 gm (8 oz) flour a pinch of sea salt	Sieve into a bowl.
400 ml (12½ oz) boiling water	Make a well in the flour, pour in and stir with a wooden spoon until just combined.
1.5 litres (1⅕ quarts) vegetable oil	In a wok or large pot, heat to 180°–190°C (350°–375°F). Put batter in a piping bag with a 2 cm (¾ inch) star nozzle, then pipe lengths of the batter directly into the oil. Fry until golden brown then drain well and toss in the sugar mix. Serve with chocolate sauce for dunking.

'Traditionally churros are served with a mug of rich hot chocolate.'

Tipsy Berry Trifle

Serves 6–8

— as cooked at Birregurra

170 gm (5½ oz) red jelly crystals 440 ml (14 fl oz) boiling water	Place in a bowl and stir to dissolve. Then pour into a shallow dish and refrigerate until *just* set but not solid.
250 gm (8 oz) mascarpone 2 tsp caster (superfine) sugar 1 tbsp (½ fl oz) Frangelico 1 cup whipped cream	When jelly is ready put mascarpone, sugar and liqueur in another bowl and mix. Then fold into cream.
250 ml (8 fl oz) brandy 250 ml (8 fl oz) milk 500 gm (1 lb) Savoiardi (sponge finger biscuits) 500 gm (1 lb) mixed berries Framboise (or any berry liqueur) brown sugar	Mix brandy and milk together. Dip half of the biscuits in this and lay on the bottom of a large bowl or dish. Spoon half the jelly on top and then sprinkle the berries generously with the Framboise and put half on top of jelly then half the mascarpone mix. Repeat the process finishing with the mascarpone. Sprinkle brown sugar over that and refrigerate for a few hours.

Australia: Great Ocean Road

When I first began cooking on TV I must admit to being swayed by the idea of all the glamorous places in which I would be setting up my stove. And whilst I have certainly cooked up a storm in some pretty swish destinations I must also say I have had my fair share of less-than-perfect experiences including cooking in the middle of a hailstorm (see page 180), on main streets with drivers seemingly intent on knocking me flying and, on more than one occasion, in the middle of paddocks surrounded by various leftovers.

Fruit 'Pizza'

Serves 6–8

– as assembled in a cow paddock in the Yarra Valley

1 small panettone (see page 271)	Cut into 6–8 rounds to form pizza bases.
2 passionfruit, pulp removed 3 kiwi fruit, peeled & sliced 1 punnet (tub) strawberries, halved 1 large banana, peeled & sliced 4 slices pineapple, peeled, cored & diced Grand Marnier	Put fruit in a bowl and gently toss with a good splash of Grand Marnier. Set aside.
250–375 gm (8–12 oz) mascarpone grated zest & juice of 1 large orange a good splash of Grand Marnier	Gently mix together and smear over 'pizza' bases. Arrange fruit salad on top.
350 gm (11¾ oz) raspberries, fresh or frozen 2 tbsp (1 fl oz) Framboise (or any fruit liqueur) 1 tsp icing (confectioners') sugar	Whiz up in a blender and flick over the top (taste for sweetness first; add extra sugar if necessary).
icing (confectioners') sugar	Sprinkle over the top.

I have owned and operated (in partnership with Ruth Allen) Tolarno Bistro in St Kilda for fourteen years. One of the Melbourne originals, it was opened by the Mora family in 1965 in what was then the Tolarno Hotel. It had originally been a beach house, built sometime around the end of the nineteenth century by a family that owned and operated a cattle station on the Darling River also named Tolarno. In the 1920s it was turned into a private hotel whose main claim to fame was that it was the first hotel to install an electric bell system between the guest rooms and service areas. In the 1950s the present facade was added but it was not until Georges and Mirka Mora took charge that the present bohemian atmosphere was created. Mirka, a world renowned artist (and St Kilda identity), transformed the restaurant walls with images of colourful plump cherubs and other angelic and mystical creatures while Georges, a perfect host, charmingly looked after the artists, politicians and writers who soon made it their home. It was the first restaurant I visited when I arrived in Melbourne thirty years ago and I will always remember feeling that I was back in Paris. Consummate restaurateur Leon Massoni took over the reins in the mid-seventies and, in similar vein to us, regarded himself as the custodian, rather than owner, of a very special place. We have continued that tradition.

Kahlua Poached Dates in Crisp Filo

Serves 4

— as cooked at Tolarno Bistro

8 dates	Soak in boiling water for 1 minute. Drain well and remove skin and pits.
250 ml (8 fl oz) Kahlua 140 gm (4½ oz) caster (superfine) sugar	Put in pot, stir well and bring to boil. Turn heat down to very low, add dates and gently poach for 5 minutes. Remove dates and set aside to cool a little.
5 filo pastry sheets 250 gm (8 oz) unsalted butter, melted	Lay pastry sheets on top of each other brushing each with melted butter as you do so (leaving the top sheet unbuttered). Cut into 8 rectangles. Place a date at top of pastry layers and fold up as you would an envelope.
vegetable oil a dollop of unsalted butter	Heat oil and butter in a pan and, without over-crowding, fry seam side down first until golden brown all over. At same time reduce Kahlua mix to a glaze.
vanilla ice cream, bought or homemade (see page 270)	Serve with ice cream on the side and the glaze sprinkled over the top.

'A dessert from Tolarno's pastry chef Cameron Cox,
who often appears on Huey's Cooking Adventures.'

Australia: Melbourne

'If you haven't got deep pastry cutters take the top and bottom off a tuna can or similar, wash and dry it well and use as a substitute.'

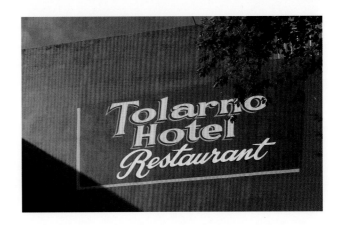

Banana Split revisited

Serves 4

– as cooked in the Tolarno kitchen

200 ml (6½ fl oz) thickened cream 150 gm (5 oz) dark cooking chocolate, chopped ½ tsp vanilla extract	Preheat overhead grill. Heat over simmering water until just melted, stirring regularly.
4 large ripe bananas soft brown sugar	Cut bananas in half crossways then in half lengthways. Put in ovenproof dish cut side up sprinkle generously with sugar and grill until caramelised.
vanilla ice cream, bought or homemade (see page 270) 8 large strawberries, hulled & sliced	With a medium large deep pastry cutter, cut 4 1 cm (⅜ inch) thick rounds from ice cream. Then put cutter on plate, place one quarter of strawberries on bottom, top with one ice cream round and then with 4 pieces of banana. Repeat process on other 3 plates.
whipped cream fresh mint sprigs icing (confectioners') sugar	Drizzle chocolate sauce around, place a dollop of cream on top along with a mint sprig and then sprinkle the lot with icing sugar.

Australia: Melbourne

About three hours drive from Denpasar is Semarapura which was once the centre of Bali's most important kingdom. More commonly known by its ancient name of Klungkung, it is also home to Bali's most famous open air market. But one word of warning – you need to be there when the market opens at 6 am because later in the day the humidity (and the flies) makes it rather uncomfortable.

It's like stepping back in time as you watch villagers from all over the region converging on this old-fashioned farmer's market. The quality and variety of ingredients is terrific and the noise level rises dramatically as the locals heckle and bargain with the stall keepers.

Our guide for the day was then Ku De Ta chef, Toby Anderson, who had spent the past four years both experimenting with some of the more unusual ingredients and guiding tourists through the market. So we quickly found our feet and not only discovered the best of the best but ate the odd snack along the way (served on banana leaves and eaten with the fingers of the right hand – the fingers of the left are reserved for another purpose – I wonder what happens if you're left handed?).

Fried Bananas with Lime, Honey & Coconut Serves 4
– as cooked at the Klungkung market

4 firm but ripe bananas	Peel and cut in half lengthways and then in half crossways.
100 gm (3½ oz) unsalted butter	Melt in pan, add bananas and fry until lightly browned.
4 tbsp honey 2 tbsp (1 fl oz) fresh lime juice grated zest of 1 lime	Add and cook briefly. Put bananas on individual plates and pour syrup over top.
toasted, desiccated (unsweetened shredded) coconut	Sprinkle over.

'To toast coconut, spread out on a tray and put in preheated 200°C (400°F) oven. Cook until coloured around the edges.'

Bali: Semarapura

Middle Eastern Fruit Compote with Banana Bread

— as cooked in a kitchen in Noosa

420 gm (14 oz) caster (superfine) sugar 250 gm (8 oz) soft unsalted butter	Preheat oven to 190°C (375°F). Cream with a hand mixer until well combined.
2 eggs	Add one at a time beating after each addition.
150 gm (5 oz) plain (all-purpose) flour 150 gm (5 oz) wholemeal flour	Combine and add to above. Mix well with a wooden spoon.
2 cups walnut halves 325 gm (10½ oz) raisins 6 ripe bananas, chopped 2 Granny Smith apples, peeled, cored & sliced 1 tsp bicarb of soda (baking soda) 2 tsp ground nutmeg 1 tsp ground cinnamon 500 ml (16 fl oz) boiling water oil spray	Add and mix until well combined. Then lightly spray a springform cake or bread tin and line the bottom with baking paper. Pour in mix, give it a good tap and bake for about 1¼ hours until a skewer comes out clean.
280 gm (9 oz) white (granulated) sugar 250 ml (8 fl oz) water	Put in a pot and boil, stirring until sugar dissolves
500 ml (16 fl oz) red wine grated zest of 1 lemon 1 cinnamon stick 50 gm (1¾ oz) ginger, peeled & finely sliced	Add, bring to the boil and boil for 3 minutes.
100 gm (3½ oz) dried pears, halved 100 gm (3½ oz) dried figs 125 gm (4 oz) dried apricots 250 gm (8 oz) pitted prunes	Add, toss and once again bring back to the boil. Immediately turn off and set aside.
thickened cream or plain yoghurt	When bread is ready allow to cool a little and then cut into slices or wedges. Place on individual plates, top with fruit and some of the syrup along with a dollop of cream or yoghurt.

'This was one of the most popular desserts at one of my restaurants, 'Memories of the Mediterranean'. It was a creation of pastry chef Lucinda McCook.'

Gingerbread Cake with Caramel Sauce

Serves 6–8

– as cooked on Huey's Cooking Adventures

500 gm (16 oz) plain (all purpose) flour ½ tsp baking powder 3 tsp bicarb of soda (baking soda) 2 tsp ground ginger 1½ tsp ground cinnamon ½ tsp ground nutmeg ¼ tsp ground cloves	Preheat oven to 175°C (330°F). Sift into a bowl and make a well in the centre.
150 gm (5 oz) packed brown sugar 3 eggs, lightly beaten 180 gm (6 oz) melted, unsalted butter 150 gm (5 oz) golden syrup	Put in another bowl and mix well using a rubber spatula.
250 ml (8 fl oz) boiling water cooking oil spray	Pour wet mix into the centre of the flour. Stir with spatula, add water and mix well. Pour into a lightly oiled, lined springform cake tin and bake for about 30 minutes until a skewer comes out clean. Cool a little on a cake rack.
200 gm (6½ oz) white (granulated) sugar a few drops of fresh lemon juice 3 tbsp water	Place in a heavy-bottomed pot and cook until it is a rich caramel colour, swirling but not stirring.
300 ml (10 fl oz) cream	Add to caramel and stir until smooth.
icing (confectioners') sugar clotted or whipped cream	Cut the cake into wedges and serve warm with the sauce spooned over, a sprinkling of icing sugar and the cream on the side.

'This recipe comes from Mark Armstrong, a very talented New Zealand-born chef who owned a number of restaurants in Sydney, including Pegrums, The Macleay St Bistro and Armstrong's.'

Australia: Melbourne

Hokey Pokey Ice Cream is a true New Zealand classic. Basically it is vanilla ice cream to which chunks of honeycomb are added. And if you happen to have an ice cream machine you can easily produce your very own. But I have also made it by allowing some good bought vanilla ice cream to soften and then folding in the honeycomb (a story which I'm only sharing with you, so I'd prefer it if you didn't tell anyone about my cheat's version).

Also, I mustn't forget, there is one other secret – don't crush the honeycomb too much as it should be in small chunks not slivers.

Hokey Pokey Ice Cream
– as cooked in Auckland

Serves 8

12 egg yolks 500 gm (1 lb) caster (superfine) sugar	To make the vanilla ice cream, whisk with a hand mixer until pale and thick.
500 ml (16 fl oz) milk seeds of 2 vanilla beans	Bring to just below the boil. Add to yolk mix and cook, whisking, over simmering water until it coats your finger (or a wooden spoon). Remove and cool over ice.
500 ml (16 fl oz) thickened cream	Add and churn in an ice cream machine.
4 heaped tbsp white (granulated) sugar 3 heaped tbsp golden syrup	To make honeycomb slowly dissolve in a heavy-bottomed pan, continually stirring until golden brown.
1 level tsp bicarb of soda (baking soda) cooking oil spray	Remove from heat, add and stir until it begins to froth. Pour into an oiled shallow pan and set aside to cool. Then put in a zip-top bag and break up with a steak hammer. Add crushed honeycomb to ice cream and mix well. Freeze.

It doesn't seem that long ago that eating in the country in either New Zealand or Australia was akin to taking one's life into ones own hands. The country pubs, which had been famous for old fashioned comfort food and juicy, tender steaks which hung over either side of the plate, had lost their way and were concentrating on poorly executed stir fries, curries and the like.

Thankfully that has all changed. Every country town, no matter how small, seemingly has at least one establishment serving interesting food. And what is even better (at least to me) is that many are not attempting to mimic their big city counterparts but are presenting updated versions of some of the good old classics of yesteryear.

Whiskey & Panettone Butter Pudding

Serves 6

– as enjoyed in a country cafe in New Zealand

1 cup dried apricots, chopped ½ cup pitted prunes, chopped a good slug of whiskey	Preheat oven to 160°C (320°F). Combine and set aside for 15 minutes. Drain, reserving liquid.
125 gm (4 oz) caster (superfine) sugar 3 large eggs	Put in a mixer and cream.
250 ml (8 fl oz) thickened cream 250 ml (8 fl oz) milk 1 vanilla bean, split	Place in a pot and bring to the boil. Then add little by little to sugar mix, whisking continually on low. Add 3–4 tbsp of the fruit liquid at the end.
soft unsalted butter 200–300 gm (6½–10 oz) panettone, sliced	Generously grease an ovenproof dish with butter. Butter the slices of panettone and layer in the dish, sprinkling each layer with the marinated fruit. Press down firmly and then pour the custard over. Place a couple of sheets of newspaper in a large deep-sided baking sheet, put the pudding in and pour in boiling water to come halfway up the sides of the dish. Bake for 40–45 minutes until risen and golden but still a little wobbly in the centre.
150 gm (5 oz) apricot jam icing (confectioners') sugar vanilla ice cream, bought or homemade (see page 270)	When ready, melt jam and brush over the top. Sprinkle with icing sugar and serve with ice cream on the side.

'Panettone is a rich yeast cake which is a specialty of Milan. Traditionally eaten at Christmas or Easter, these days it is available year round at most good delis.'

When we went to Mauritius our producer Michael 'Mosh' Dickinson had somehow forgotten to take any shoes (don't ask, it's a long story). Anyway all the Oberoi Resort shop had was a pair of fluorescent yellow and blue ones which were at least three sizes too large and were designed for walking on coral reefs. Imagine the surprise of the General Manager when Mr Dickinson arrived to introduce himself complete with clown shoes – I presume his subsequent phone call to Australia went something like 'who the f... have you sent me?'.

Speaking of Mauritius, while the sugar industry is not quite as successful as it once was it still produces one of the great sugar varieties of the world – muscovado, which is almost caramel-like in its intensity. And a by-product of the sugar cane – rum – is also popular although you couldn't say the local variety is renowned for its subtlety. Interestingly, when I cooked this dish I ended up using canned New Zealand butter, something I had never seen before. Maybe, instead, I should have used ghee which is definitely the local 'butter' of choice.

Pineapple with a Muscovado, Rum & Orange Sauce

Serves 4

– as cooked amongst the sugar canes of Mauritius

2 large knobs of butter 1 tbsp Muscovado sugar	Heat in a large non-stick pan until lightly caramelised.
¼ cup (2 fl oz) dark rum juice of 3–4 oranges	Add and cook down a little.
8–12 fresh pineapple rings, cored (see page 37)	Add and cook until a light glaze is formed (adding more orange juice if necessary). Place pineapple on individual plates. Reduce sauce if needed and pour over top.
vanilla ice cream, bought or homemade (see page 270) or whipped cream	Serve on the side.

Mauritius: Saint Aubin

'I had a dessert very similar to this in Mauritius.'

Vermicelli Kheer

Serves 4–6

— as cooked by Davinder Bedi on Huey's Cooking Adventures

20 ml (¾ fl oz) vegetable oil 100 gm (3½ oz) vermicelli (sewain) broken up a little	Heat oil in a large saucepan and cook vermicelli until light brown, continually stirring.
1 litre (32 fl oz) milk 10 sultanas (golden raisins) 3 green cardamom pods, crushed	Gradually add, bring to the boil and cook for about 5 minutes until thick, stirring every now and then.
2 tbsp white (granulated) sugar	Add and stir until well combined. Serve hot or cold.

When I first began working in kitchens, both Bombe Alaska and Crepes Suzette were huge hits. Both flamed at the table, I presume their popularity had a lot to do with strong recommendations from the waiters who, I think, were all pyromaniacs at heart and saw this as a 'legal' opportunity to fulfill their hidden fantasies.

Rudy Loenen, my business partner from Christchurch's Galleon Restaurant, was a perfect example. A gentle giant, his main aim in life appeared to be to reach the ceiling with the flames, a feat he achieved on a number of occasions. And although his crepes were always delicious I feel today's breathalysers would have a problem with the amount of liqueur imbibed from the crepes alone.

Then there was Tiger Johnson, a young waiter of Wellington's Plaza restaurant, who almost burnt the place down with an overly enthusiastic application of brandy to the Bombe. Sadly a more experienced waiter threw a full ice bucket over the lot which quickly doused the flames (I say sadly because if there was ever a restaurant that deserved to be burnt down it was the bloody awful Plaza).

And while I can never understand why you would want to pour flaming brandy over a Bombe Alaska, in its purest form I think it's a pretty great, and impressive-looking, dessert.

Bombe Alaska

Serves 4

— nothing like the one served at the Plaza

4 egg whites 180 gm (6 oz) caster (superfine) sugar	Preheat oven to 230°C (450°F). Beat whites with a mixer until soft peaks form. Add sugar and continue to beat until stiff and shiny. Put in piping bag with a star nozzle.
4 thick slices Swiss (jelly) Roll 2 mangoes peeled & thinly sliced vanilla ice cream, bought or homemade (see page 270) Framboise (or any berry) liqueur	Lay Swiss Roll on baking sheet. Top with mango, scoops of ice cream and a sprinkling of Framboise. Pipe meringue all over and cook in oven for 2–3 minutes until lightly browned.

Lemon Cheesecake Between Leaves of Pastry

— as cooked in the Yarra Valley

2 sheets bought puff pastry plain (all purpose) flour	Preheat oven to 200°C (400°F). Roll out pastry on a floured surface until it fits over your springform cake tin. Cut out two rounds using the inner rim of the tin as a measure. Prick all over with a fork and freeze until firm.
1 egg 60 ml (2 fl oz) milk	Beat together, brush over pastry and bake until puffed and golden. Press down gently with a clean towel and cool on a rack.
400 gm (13 oz) soft cream cheese 800 gm (26 oz) condensed milk juice & grated zest of 6 lemons 300 ml (10 fl oz) cream	Put in a bowl and, with a wooden spoon, mix well. Then, using a whisk, beat until smooth. Place one round of pastry in baking tin, trimming as necessary, and top with cheesecake mix. Top with other pastry round and refrigerate until set. Cut into wedges to serve (with a berry sauce of you like).

Australia: Yarra Valley

Crepes Suzette

— as cooked by Rudy Loenen at the Galleon Restaurant

180 ml (6 fl oz) milk 2 large eggs a pinch of sugar a pinch of salt 145 gm(4½ oz) flour	Whisk eggs, milk, sugar and salt. Then add flour and whisk until smooth (should be the consistency of heavy cream). Set aside for 30 minutes.
a good knob of butter	When ready, melt butter in a crepe pan and whisk into batter. Then spoon a thin layer of the batter into the pan and cook until lightly browned on both sides. Continue until all batter is used. Cover crepes and set aside.
200 gm (6½ oz) butter 80 gm (2¾ oz) caster (superfine) sugar	Put in a large pan and melt.
grated zest & juice of 4 oranges 4 tbsp (2 fl oz) Grand Marnier	Add and bring to the boil. Add one crepe at a time, carefully fold in half then in half again and push to the side of the pan. Repeat process until all crepes are used (adding more orange juice if needed).
1 heaped tbsp caster (superfine) sugar 3 tbsp (1½ fl oz) Grand Marnier 3 tbsp (1½ fl oz) brandy	Spread out crepes and sprinkle with sugar and then liquor. Flame, and when flames subside, place on individual plates.
vanilla ice cream, bought or homemade (see page 270) or whipped cream	Spoon juices over the top and serve with ice cream or whipped cream.

'Crepes Suzette, when correctly cooked, are superb (after all they were created by the king of chefs, Escoffier).'

Basics

Chicken Stock

(makes 3-4 litres)

1 boiling fowl
2 kg (4 lb 6 oz) chicken carcasses
2 onions, chopped
2 carrots, washed & chopped
2 leeks, washed & chopped
1 celery stalk, washed & chopped
5 litres (8 pints) cold water
3 fresh thyme sprigs
1 slice of fresh lemon
1 bay leaf
4 whole black peppercorns

Section the fowl and chop the carcasses. Put in a stockpot along with everything else. Bring to the boil and simmer very, very gently for 3 hours, skimming frequently and topping up with more water if chicken becomes exposed. DO NOT STIR. Then strain, cool and refrigerate overnight.

Next day, remove fat from the surface.

Fish Stock

(makes 2 litres)
2 kg (4 lb 6 oz) fish bones, including heads
2 onions, roughly chopped
1 celery stalk, chopped
1 medium carrot, chopped
2 leeks, well washed & chopped
2 tbsp (1 fl oz) olive oil
2 garlic cloves, chopped
10 black peppercorns
2 bay leaves
4 parsley stalks
2.5 litres (4 pints) of water
500 ml (16 fl oz) dry white wine

Thoroughly wash bones, removing all traces of blood. Then take out eyes and gills and also wash heads well. Chop bones into 10 cm (4 in) lengths.

Heat oil in a large heavy-bottomed pot, add vegies and sauté gently for 5 minutes.

Add bones, peppercorns, bay leaves and parsley and toss for a few more minutes.

Add liquid and bring to boil. Skim off foam and simmer for 20 minutes skimming frequently.

Turn off heat and stand for another 20 minutes, before straining.

Beef Stock

(makes 3 litres)

1 kg (about 2 lb) beef brisket
4 kg (8 lb 12 oz) veal or small beef bones including
    knuckles & marrow bones
100 g (3^1/$_2$ oz) ghee
100 g (3^1/$_2$ oz) honey
3 large carrots, unpeeled & chopped
4 leeks, washed & chopped
2 celery stalks, chopped
a handful of mushroom peelings & stalks
6 garlic cloves, chopped
1 bottle dry white wine
2 large onions, skin on & halved
parsley stalks
2 bay leaves
12 whole black peppercorns
2 x 800 gm (26 oz) cans diced tomatoes, drained

Preheat oven to 200°C (400°F).

Coarsely chop brisket and put in a large roasting tray with bones. Melt ghee and honey, brush all over and cook in oven until lightly browned. Then put in a stock pot.

Add vegies to the roasting tray and sauté until lightly brown. Then add wine and reduce until almost evaporated. Add to stock pot.

Roast onions, skin side down, until dark brown. Then add to pot along with cold water to about 10 cm (4 in) above contents. Bring to boil then simmer very gently, regularly skimming for 30 minutes.

Add rest of ingredients to pot and simmer for 4–5 hours, adding more water if bones become exposed. Strain, cool and refrigerate overnight. Next day, remove the layer of fat.

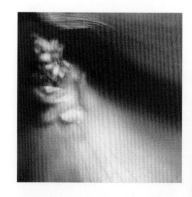

Vegetable Stock

(makes 2–3 litres)

2 leeks, washed & coarsely chopped
2 onions, coarsely chopped
6 tomatoes, washed & coarsely chopped
4 garlic cloves, chopped
60 g (2 oz) fresh herbs
2 lemons, sliced
4 litres (6^1/$_2$ pints) cold water
2 star anise
2 good slurps white wine
freshly ground salt & pepper

Put everything in a large pot and rapidly boil for 20 minutes. Cool, then strain through muslin and refrigerate.

'When making stocks, do not peel the vegies.'

Pesto

15 fresh basil leaves
1 garlic clove
2 tbsp freshly grated parmesan
olive oil
freshly ground salt & pepper

Whiz up in a blender or processor with enough oil to make a thinnish paste.

Mayonnaise

To make homemade mayonnaise, throw 2 eggs, 2 yolks, 1 tablespoon mustard and a pinch of salt into the food processor. Whiz up for 1 minute, then add 500 ml of any good oil, little by little, through the feeder tube. When all the oil is added, flavour to taste with fresh lemon juice and seasonings.

Aioli (Garlic Mayonnaise)

^{1}/$_2$ cup (4 oz) mayonnaise
3 tbsp (1^1/$_2$ fl oz) sour cream
1 tspn Dijon mustard
3 garlic cloves
a squeeze of lemon juice

Mix together.

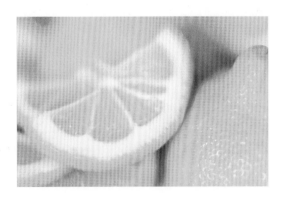

Glossary

Banana Leaves Briefly dipped in boiling water to soften them they are then used for wrapping food before cooking (foil can be substituted). Squares of unblanched leaves are also used for presentation purposes and are freely available in Asian markets.

Asian **Basil** There are three varieties commonly found in Asia (in most cases a small amount of a combination of chopped basil, mint and coriander can be used as a substitute). Thai Sweet Basil (Bai Horapha) has smooth dark green leaves and purplish flowers and is used in curries, soups and stirfries as well as raw, in salads in both Vietnam and Thailand. Lemon Basil (Duan Kemangi) is popular in both Malaysia and Indonesia where it is used as a garnish and a last minute addition to many dishes, in particular those involving seafood. Thai Holy Basil (Bai Ka-phrao) is sacred to the Hindi and is so named because it commonly grew around temples. It has notched, slightly pointed leaves, only releases its flavour when cooked and is traditionally used in stirfries and curries. All three can be sometimes found in specialist Asian markets and supermarkets.

Long or Snake **Beans** (Thaifak yao or Kacang Panjang) They have a mottled, bumpy skin which doesn't mean they are not fresh. Are often served raw in Thailand but I prefer them blanched in the style of Malaysia or Indonesia. Available at most markets, unlike normal beans they do not need to be strung.

Chinese **Celery Leaves** (Seldari or Khen Chaai) Not to be confused with normal celery, the stalk itself is rarely eaten. Instead the leaves are treated as a herb and have a pronounced flavour. Coriander would be a suitable substitute as would the leaves of celeriac. Seeds are available so you can also grow your own.

Chillies More than twenty varieties of chillies can be found in Asia. The hottest are the Phrik Khii Nuu or mouse or rat dropping chillies of Thailand and the Tavia Kerinyi of Indonesia (very similar to our birds eye chillies). The most common variety used is most probably the finger-length chilli known as the sky-pointing chilli which is medium hot (depending on whether you are Thai or not). They are available green (unripe), red (ripe) and dried. The milder banana chillies are traditionally served seeded and sliced as a garnish. In Bali, a very popular little number is the short, bulbous Tabia Balia which I noticed being used as a garnish too but maybe not for the fainthearted as 'hot' is a bit of an understatement. A good variety of chillies is available even in the chain supermarkets but some experimentation may be needed to discover the 'heat' that suits you.

Chinese Black Vinegar A rich malty, pungent vinegar traditionally made from glutinous rice, it is available from Asian markets.

Chinese Rice Wine (Shao Hsing) Has a rich, sweetish taste and is available in many chain supermarkets and all Asian supermarkets. A good quality dry sherry can be substituted.

Chorizo The most well known of the Spanish sausages, many different varieties are available, (smoked, fresh, semi-cured to name a few). But one thing they do all have in common is that they are well flavoured with paprika. They are available from specialist sausage makers and good delis.

Daikon Also know as Japanese radish or mooli (India), it is sweetish in flavour and is used widely, both raw and cooked, in Japanese, Indian and Chinese cooking. It is freely available.

Eggplant The Japanese eggplant is purple, long and slender and is also known as the Lebanese or Long Tom eggplant. It is freely available and less bitter than its larger counterpart. The Thai pea eggplant (Ma-Kheau Phuang) is small, firm and very bitter and is commonly used in curries. The Thai apple version (Ma-Kheau Phran) is round, also firm in texture but is not bitter while the Thai long eggplant (Ma-Kheau Yao) is skinny and green and is often used in stirfries. The Thai varieties can be sometimes found in specialist Asian markets but the Japanese variety can often be used as a substitute.

Asian **Fish Sauce** (Naam Plaa, Nuoc Mam, Patis) One of the basics of both Thai and Vietnamese cooking, this is a thin salty sauce made from an anchovy-like fish which is salted and left to ferment naturally. The resulting liquid is then strained and pasteurised. And while it really does stink in its natural form, thankfully the smell dissipates once cooked.

Galangal (Khaa, Laos) A pink rhizome from the ginger family, it is available in Asian markets. In some cases ginger can be substituted but in dishes like Thailand's Tom Khaa Gai you should maybe wait until you can get galangal itself because it is a prime ingredient.

Green Papaya or **Green Mango** The unripe fruit is most commonly grated and added to salads such as Thailand's Som Tom which is prepared in vast quantities throughout the country's markets and street stalls.

Harissa A fiery spice paste which originated in Tunisia, this is now a staple throughout Morocco, Algeria and many parts of North Africa. Freely available in tubes and jars in good delis, it is traditionally served at the table as an accompaniment as well as being used in cooking.

Jamon A cured ham in the Spanish style, its sweet, mellow flavour can be attributed to the fact that it has a longer than normal curing period. It is similar to prosciutto, which could be substituted.

Kaffir Limes (Luk Makrut, Jeruk Purut) The leaves and zest are frequently used in Thai (and sometimes Indonesian) cooking. The leaves should be shredded very finely before use but the juice, which is fairly sparse, is rarely used.

Kecap Asin See Soy Sauce.

Kecap Manis See Soy Sauce.

Lemongrass (Ta Khrai, Sereh) An intense fragrant herb, this is an absolute staple in Asian cookery. Discard the tough outer leaves before bashing with the flat side of a knife and slicing very finely. Add the white to soups, dressings and curry pastes while the tougher green part is often used to flavour drinks and teas.

Mirin Japanese rice wine, also known as sweet cooking sake. Its alcohol content is so low you will find it in Asian grocers rather than liquor stores.

Morning Glory Also known as water convolvulus, kangkong, ong choy and phak bung, it is a variety of water spinach which is sometimes available in Asian markets. In Australia it is grown around Darwin. Normal spinach could be substituted.

Palm Sugar Made by boiling the sap of the sugar palm, this is rich and aromatic with a slight caramel flavour. Thai Palm Sugar (Naamtaan Piip) is lighter than the Balinese version (Gula Bali) which is sweeter and suitable for desserts. While it is freely available, soft brown sugar can be substituted.

Preserved Mustard Greens (Kiam Chye) Available canned in Asian supermarkets, some brands are fairly salty so need a good rinsing in lots of cold water. (In Asia, preserved mustard greens are often sold by weight from large earthenware jars.)

Radicchio An Italian variety of chicory, its flavour is peppery and rather bitter and it can be used in a number of ways – chargrilled as an accompaniment to a simple grill or roast, tossed through pasta or risotto or, as is more common, tossed through a salad.

Asian **Rice Wine Vinegar** Not to be confused with mirin (Japanese rice wine) this is freely available in all Asian supermarkets. Sometimes can vary in strength so use with care.

Shrimp Paste (Trasi, Ka-pi, Belacan) A basic all over Asia, this is a pungent smelling paste which is made from salted, fermented shrimps. Always cooked, it is used in small quantities in curries, pastes and the like.

Soy Sauce Unless otherwise specified, I use light or Japanese soy (Kikkoman is my favourite). Dark soy is thicker and heavier with a touch of caramel. Kecap Manis is the Indonesian sweet soy (a decent substitute is dark soy plus a little soft brown sugar) while Kecap Asin is their thinner, saltier version.

Sambal Oelek An Asian chilli paste made from fresh chillies, vinegar and salt. One teaspoon equals about two small hot chillies.

Shallots Not to be confused with the spring (or green) onion which is often wrongly deemed to be a shallot. A mild member of the onion family, it is used extensively in Asian (and French) cooking. Red onion would be the best substitute. Deep fried shallots which are often used as a garnish in Thailand are available in all Asian markets.

Shiitake Mushrooms Also known as Chinese black mushrooms, they are available in most supermarkets and are more pronounced in flavour in their dried form. The stalks are always cut off and discarded and they need to be well soaked.

Smoked Paprika Before being ground, the peppers are dried over a fire which imparts a definite smoky flavour. It is available in good delis but normal paprika could be substituted.

Star Anise An attractive star-shaped spice with a distinctive aniseed flavour, available in most supermarkets.

Tamarind (Lunak, Ma-Khaam) The dark brown pod of the tamarind tree contains a sour pulp. Sold in block form, it is soaked before being strained and added to dishes as a souring agent. It's available in all Asian and many other supermarkets.

Turmeric A member of the ginger family and the base of Indian curry powders, it is sometimes found fresh in Asian markets. About 2/3 of a teaspoon of powdered turmeric equals 2 tablespoons of grated fresh.

Witloof Known as Belgian Endive in the States and chicory in Europe, it has a subtle bitterness. It can be braised or used raw in salads.

People & Places Index

Allen, Ruth 264
Anderson, Toby 129, 212
Antoines 124
Armstrong, Craig 100
Armstrong, Mark 268
Astle, Tony & Beth 124, 260
Aubergine 111, 157
Auckland 114, 115

Baddeley, Kent 134
Bali 133, 34
festivals 19
food 18–19, 35, 50, 55, 84, 85, 145, 183
Bangkok 5, 36, 37, 98, 140
Bates, Andrew 217
Bedi, Davinder 273
Berardo, Jim 89
Berardo's 89
Biron, George 25, 26, 28, 45, 226
Blackie, Michael 34
Brahimi, Guillaume 111
Britten, Des 222, 223
Brown, Alister 134, 136, 137
Brown, Marc 43
Brunetti, Eddie 89, 209
Buck, John 205
Burke, David 200

Canberra 111, 116, 230
Cape Panwa 15, 32, 81, 104, 131, 214, 246
Cardoso, Angel 28, 252
Carluccio, Antonio 153
Casa Iberica 28
Chris's 143, 151
Clark, Maxine 31
Coachman 222, 223, 224
Coolabine farmstead 30, 60, 163
Cox, Cameron 264
Curtain, Paul 130

Dalais, Jacqueline 122
David, Elizabeth 257
Daylesford 64, 65, 119, 182, 208, 217, 238
De Bertoli 153, 258
Dickinson, Michael 55, 272
Digger's Seeds 25
Doyle, Peter 128
Dunham, Dee 30

Eastwind Farm 179, 180
Eumundi 193
Evans, Len 46, 128

Fergusson, Peter 166
Fernleigh farm 184
Fitzpatrick, Donlevy 25
Fletcher, Don 260
Flowerdrum 142
Floyd, Keith 7
Fokker, Joe 75
Forell, Claude 25
Four Seasons resort 4, 57, 218
Frangos, Jim 119
Fraser Island 88

Garnisha 117, 209
Garrett, Diane 25
Granger, Bill 44
Gray, John 83

Great Barrier Reef Feast 46, 47, 49, 56, 91, 128, 188, 225, 250
Great Ocean Road 25, 97, 130, 132, 143, 252
Grosset, Jeffery 128
Grossi, Guy 182, 186

Hamilton, Te Huai 134
Hamilton Island 61
hangi 186
Harris, Iseta 238
Harvest Farm 66
Hay, Rob 73
Healesville Hotel 174
Hildreth, Deseree 134
Hill-Smith, Michael 128
Hilton Hotel 228
Howard, Peter 60
Hualamphong Restaurant 5
Humble, Simon 219

Jansz, Geoff 56
Johnson, Tiger 276

Kennedy, Michael 66
Kinloch Lodge 162
Klogan, Steve 136
Koh, Allan 128
Kuta 129

Lake House 64, 182
Lake Tarewa 100
Lake Wakatipu 160, 162
Langbein, Annabel 53
Lau, Gilbert 128, 142
Law, Digby 159
Lethlean, John 182
Lindsay, Geoff 128, 199, 250
Loenen, Rudy 275, 276
Logan, Steve 136
Logan Brown 134, 136
Lui, Anthony 128, 142

McConnell, Matt 60, 89
McCook, Lucinda 267
McDonald, Barry 80
McIldowney, Andrew 97
Maison Eureka 105, 170
Maison de Vanille 69
Mangan, Luke 228
Marchetti, Bill 7
Massoni, Leon 264
Mauritius 14, 54, 69, 70, 72, 105, 106, 107, 108, 201, 202, 272
dining out 122
food of 168, 171, 200
Miles, Phillip 25
Moore Wilson Fresh 134, 187, 219, 239
Mora, George & Mirka 264
Mosaic 118
Mouchel, Philippe 25
Mussillon, James 111
Nairn, Nick 153
Napier 94, 138, 188
New Zealand 75, 76, 150
a cook's tour 134
Hangi 186
Noosa 88, 89, 90

O'Donnell, Michael 146
Oberoi Hotel 54, 122, 123
Parker, Phil & Cath 73

Patong Beach 99
Perry, Neil 199
Pettavel 25
Phudon Prachum 246
Phuket 165
Poachers Pantry 31, 68
Pretty, Ruth 40, 134, 187
Purbrick, John 128

Queenstown 44, 73, 160

Robuchon, Joel 111
Rocco 260
Rospar, Laurent 111
Rotorua 186

Salans, Chris 118
Scott, Geoff 228
Season 90
Sebel Lodge 43
Sedaitis, Alby 111
Seed, Diane 153
Skelton, Gary 90
Skinner, Andrew 122, 123
Split Point Lighthouse 97, 253
Stein, Rick 46, 153
Stonyridge Winery 164
Sugar Beach Resort 14
Sukothai Hotel 37, 172, 177
Sunnybrae 25, 26–7

Talihmanidis, Chris 97, 143
Talihmanidis, Kosta & Pam 97
Te Mata Estate 205
Thailand 4, 5, 15, 57, 218
festivals 102
floating markets 78
food 80, 173, 176, 177, 178, 183, 195, 196, 199, 214
street food 36
table manners 198
Thomas, Ian 134
Thomas, Richard 41
Thompson, David 80, 98
Tolarno Bistro 264, 265

Van der Drift family 75
Van Senten, Paul 130

Wade, Paul 47, 128
Waka di Ume 210
Waka Padma Hotel 55
Walter Peak High Country Farm 44, 150, 158

Warren, Tim & Claire 117
Wellington 206
White, Stephen 164
Wolf-Tasker, Alla & Allan 64

Yarra Glen 166
Yarra Valley 41, 42, 43, 66
Yarra Valley Dairy 41, 42
Young, Christine 180

Recipe Index

abalone
    Abalone with Shiitakes, Snowpeas & Garlic 130
    see also paua
Aioli 111
anchovies
    Anchovy Butter 133
    Anchovy Vinaigrette 76
    Potato, Goat Cheese Feta & Anchovy Tortilla 30
apples
    Raw Tuna with Shredded Apple, Ponzu Dressing & Wasabi Flavoured Roe 49
    Thai Spicy Apple Salad 99
artichokes
    Noisettes of Lamb with Artichokes 153
Asian fish sauce 195
asparagus
    Asparagus with Mushrooms & Sherry Vinegar 242
    Gurnard with Asparagus, Mushrooms & Ponzu Dressing 94
    Smoked Peppered Sirloin and Pesto Asparagus Salad 68
Aubergine's Mixed Fish with Provencale Vegetables, Pesto & Aioli 111
avocado
    Avocado Salsa 53
    Mango & Avocado Salsa 31
    Prosciutto, Avocado & Orange Salad with a Hot Tomato Vinaigrette 68
Ayam Goreng (Balinese Fried Chicken) 211
Ayam Panggang Bumbu Merah (Chicken in Red Sauce) 210

Balinese Fried Chicken 211
Balsamic Glaze 75
bananas
    Banana Bread 267
    Banana Split Revisited 265
    Fried Bananas with Lime, Honey & Coconut 266
    Sticky Rice Pudding with Palm Sugar Syrup and Grilled Bananas 250
Barramundi with a Radicchio, Witloof and Walnut Slaw 91
Bashed Neeps 156
Basic Pizza Sauce 27
basil
    Beef with Thai Sweet Basil 173
    Japanese Herb Vinaigrette 128
    Minced Beef with Chilli, Garlic & Holy Basil 165
    Stir-fried Ground Pork with Thai Sweet Basil 177
batter, beer 234
BBQ Berry Puddings 253
BBQ Fennel Salad 92
BBQ Kumara 152
BBQ Prosciutto Wrapped Figs Stuffed

with Feta 42
BBQ Tuna with Pineapple Sambal 109
Be Celeng Base Manis (Fragrant Pork Stew) 183
beans
    Bullboar, Potato & White Bean Salad 65
    Green Bean & Corn Salad 117
    Squid & Snake Bean Salad Lawar 79
    Succotash with Scallops 126
beanshoots
    Stir-fried Beanshoots 140
beef
    Beef Patties with Coconut 50
    Beef Soup Noodles 20
    Beef Teriyaki with Cucumber Pickles 174
    Beef with Thai Sweet Basil 173
    Fillet of Beef 'Bourguignonne' 166
    Minced Beef with Chilli, Garlic & Holy Basil 165
    Oyster Sauce Beef with Smothered Chinese Cabbage 170
    Raw Beef Salad 83
    Rougaille de Boeuf 171
    Shakin' Beef 172
    Smoked Peppered Sirloin and Pesto Asparagus Salad 68
    Steak with an Eggplant and Capsicum Peperonata 164
    Steak & Smothered Onion Sandwich 162
    Steak & Sweet Potato Salad with a Tomato and Chilli Relish 70
    Taquitos of Porterhouse with Soft Goat Curd 163
    Thai Beef Salad 60
beer batter 234
beetroot
    Beetroot & Pepper Sauce 185
    Carpaccio of Beetroot with Baked Feta, Rocket, Walnuts & Pear 64
berries
    BBQ Berry Puddings 253
    Cherry Tomato, Jambu Air & Singapore Berry Salad 118
    Eton Mess 254
    Impossible Pie 256
    Strawberry Bruschetta 254
    Tipsy Berry Trifle 262
Bloody Mary Soup with Plumped Oysters 7
BLT Salad with a Poached Egg 66
Bombe Alaska 274
Bourride of Chicken 208
Braised Fennel Topping 27
Brandy & Lemon Butter Sauce 143
bread
    Banana Bread 267
    Lamb Pita Pockets 151
brioche

Ice Cream Stuffed Brioche with Chocolate Sauce 249
broccoli
    Orrechetti con Broccoli 182
broths
    Lemon and Harissa Broth 209
    Miso Broth 97
Bullboar, Potato & White Bean Salad 65
burgers
    Italian BBQ Vegie Burger 230
Burmese Style Pork Curry 176
butters
    Anchovy Butter 133
    Sage Butter 74
butties
    Paua Butties 137

cabbage
    Cabbage Rolls with Cheese Stuffing and a Fresh Tomato Sauce 226
    Smothered Chinese Cabbage 170
cakes
    Gingerbread Cake with Caramel Sauce 268
capsicum *see* red capsicum
caramel
    Caramel Sauce 268
    Caramelised Onion Topping 27
    Galangal & Palm Sugar Caramel 199
Carpaccio of Beetroot with Baked Feta, Rocket, Walnuts & Pear 64
Carrot & Parsnip Mash 154
casseroles
    Old-fashioned Chicken Casserole 204
    see also stews
caviar *see* salmon caviar
celery
    Light Celery Soup 17
cheese
    BBQ Prosciutto Wrapped Figs Stuffed with Feta 42
    Cabbage Rolls with Cheese Stuffing and a Fresh Tomato Sauce 226
    Carpaccio of Beetroot with Baked Feta, Rocket, Walnuts & Pear 64
    Chilli, Chicken & Cheese Soup 6
    Crab & Camembert Omelette 139
    Jamon, Roasted Capsicum & Cheese Toasties 44
    Muffin Melts 56
    Parmesan Crumbed Mushroom Steaks with a Coriander & Lime Tartare 231
    Parmesan & Garlic Croutons 125
    Pear, Goat Cheese & Honey Tart 247
    Potato, Goat Cheese Feta & Anchovy Tortilla 30
    Scrambled Eggs with Persian Feta 41
    Smoked Salmon Croque Monsieur 44
    Taquitos of Porterhouse with Soft Goat Curd 163
cheesecake

Lemon Cheesecake Between Leaves of Pastry 276
Cherry Tomato, Jambu Air &.Singapore Berry Salad 118
Chiang Mai Chicken Noodles 196
chicken
Balinese Fried Chicken 211
Bourride of Chicken 208
Chiang Mai Chicken Noodles 196
Chicken Chop Suey 201
Chicken, Coconut & Galangal Soup 15
Chicken Curry with Young Jackfruit 213
Chicken Fricassee Mauritian Style 202
Chicken with a Galangal & Palm Sugar Caramel 199
Chicken Mulligatawny 200
Chicken in Red Sauce 210
Chilli, Chicken & Cheese Soup 6
Fast Roast Chicken with Herby Juices 194
Glazed Honey & Soy Chicken 193
Gold Bags with Sweet Chilli Sauce 36
Green Chicken Curry 195
Grilled Bread with Smoked Chicken and a Mango & Avocado Salsa 31
Grilled Chicken with Sweet Chilli Sauce 214
New Wave Coq Au Vin 205
Noodles with Chicken & Vegies 216
Old-fashioned Chicken Casserole 204
Pot-roasted Chicken with Lemon and Harissa Broth 209
Roast Chicken Carbonara 192
Vietnamese Chicken Coleslaw 62
chicken livers
Tuscan Chicken Livers with Pesto Mash 206
chickpeas
Moroccan Lamb & Chickpea Soup 16
Spiced Chickpea Salad 89
chilli
Chilli, Chicken & Cheese Soup 6
Chilli & Galangal Sauce 110
Chilli-Lime Sauce 33
Chilli Paua 138
Mauritian Hot Chilli Eggs 54
Minced Beef with Chilli, Garlic & Holy Basil 165
Pipis with Chilli, Coriander & Ginger 146
Sweet Chilli Sauce 36, 96, 214
Tomato and Chilli Relish 70
Chinese celery
Chinese Celery Noodles 237
Fried Peanuts with Garlic and Chinese Celery 52
chocolate
Chocolate Sauce 249, 260
Elizabeth David's Chocolate & Orange Mousse 257
chop suey
Chicken Chop Suey 201
chorizo
Chorizo & Vegie Stew with a Baked Egg 28
Mushrooms & Chorizo 24
Potato & Chorizo Salad 88
Churros with Chocolate Sauce 260
chutney
Kiwi Fruit Chutney 159

cinnamon
Vanilla Bean & Cinnamon Syrup 258
clafoutis
Rhubarb Clafoutis 259
coconut 266
Beef Patties with Coconut 50
Chicken, Coconut & Galangal Soup 15
Fried Bananas with Lime, Honey & Coconut 266
coconut cream 131
coconut milk 4, 131
compote
Middle Eastern Fruit Compote with Banana Bread 267
coriander
Coriander & Lime Tartare 231
Coriander Raita 14
Pipis with Chilli, Coriander & Ginger 146
Yoghurt Coriander Sauce 238
corn
Corn Cakes with Cucumber Pickles 57
Green Bean & Corn Salad 117
Succotash with Scallops 126
Crab & Camembert Omelette 139
Creole Sauce 144
Creole Vindaye of Fish 105
Crepes Suzette 277
croque monsieur
Smoked Salmon Croque Monsieur 44
croutons
Parmesan & Garlic Croutons 125
Crudités with Salmon and an Anchovy Vinaigrette 76
Cucumber Pickles 57, 174
Cumi Cumi (Squid & Snake Bean Salad Lawar) 79
Cumin Lamb Steaks with BBQ Kumara 152
curries
Burmese Style Pork Curry 176
Chicken Curry with Young Jackfruit 213
Curried Dholl 'Soup' with Oysters & Coriander Raita 14
Curried Eggplant & Potato Pie 228
Dry Curry de Legumes 229
Green Chicken Curry 195
Mauritian Squid Curry 108
Mussel & Pineapple Curry 131
Pork Jungle Curry 178
Red Duck Curry 218
custard
Steamed Pumpkin Custard 246

dark miso paste 97
dates
Kahlua Poached Dates in Crisp Filo 264
David Thompson's Thai Passion 80
Deep Fried Fish with Three Flavoured Sauce 102
Des Britten's Pommes Dauphine 223
desserts
Banana Split Revisited 265
BBQ Berry Puddings 253
Bombe Alaska 274
Churros with Chocolate Sauce 260
Crepes Suzette 277
Elizabeth David's Chocolate & Orange Mousse 257
Eton Mess 254

Fried Bananas with Lime, Honey & Coconut 266s
Fruit 'Pizza' 263
Gingerbread Cake with Caramel Sauce 268
Golden Syrup & Orange Parfait 248
Hokey Pokey Ice Cream 270
Ice Cream Stuffed Brioche with Chocolate Sauce 249
Impossible Pie 256
Kahlua Poached Dates in Crisp Filo 264
Lemon Cheesecake Between Leaves of Pastry 276
Middle Eastern Fruit Compote with Banana Bread 267
Pear, Goat Cheese & Honey Tart 247
Pineapple with a Muscovado, Rum & Orange Sauce 272
Poached Peaches in a Vanilla Bean & Cinnamon Syrup 258
Rhubarb Clafoutis 259
Rocky Road Sundae 255
Sticky Rice Pudding with Palm Sugar Syrup and Grilled Bananas 250
Steamed Pumpkin Custard 246
Strawberry Bruschetta 254
Tipsy Berry Trifle 262
Vermicelli Kheer 273
Whiskey & Panettone Butter Pudding 271
Dill-flavoured Egg Salad with Smoked Salmon 48
doughnuts
Churros with Chocolate Sauce 260
dressings
Aioli 111
Coriander & Lime Tartare 231
Ponzu Dressing 49, 94
Spicy Lime & Vanilla Dressing 69
see also vinaigrettes
Dry Curry de Legumes 229
duck
Duck Breasts with Pomegranate Molasses & Orange 219
Duck, Noodle & Preserved Mustard Green Soup 10
Red Duck Curry 218
durian 84

eel
Smoked Eel with Watermelon and a Balsamic Glaze 75
eggplant
Curried Eggplant & Potato Pie 228
Eggplant and Capsicum Peperonata 164
Eggplant 'Lasagne' 232
Garlic Eggplant with Chinese Celery Noodles 237
Tuna with Roasted Eggplant & Tomato Vinaigrette 90
eggs
BLT Salad with a Poached Egg 66
Chorizo & Vegie Stew with a Baked Egg 28
Crab & Camembert Omelette 139
Dill-flavoured Egg Salad with Smoked Salmon 48
Indonesian Fried Rice with an Egg 55
Mauritian Hot Chilli Eggs 54
Scrambled Eggs with Persian Feta 41

Son-In-Law Eggs 32
Elizabeth David's Chocolate & Orange
  Mousse 257
Eton Mess 254
Exotic Potato Salad 115

Fast Roast Chicken with Herby Juices
  194
fennel
  BBQ Fennel Salad 92
  Braised Fennel Topping 27
  Fennel & Mushroom Salad with Truffle
  Oil 67
  Fennel Tarte Tatin 240
  Herb Crumbed Fennel with Red
  Capsicum Rouille 239
figs
  BBQ Prosciutto Wrapped Figs Stuffed
  with Feta 42
Fillet of Beef 'Bourguignonne' 166
fish
  Aubergine's Mixed Fish with Provencale
  Vegetables, Pesto & Aioli 111
  Barramundi with a Radicchio, Witloof
  and Walnut Slaw 91
  Creole Vindaye of Fish 105
  Deep Fried Fish with Three Flavoured
  Sauce 102
  Fish with Chilli & Galangal Sauce 110
  Fish with Rougaille de Tomate 106
  Fish Salad with a Spicy Lime & Vanilla
  Dressing 69
  Fish with a Warm Gazpacho Salad 101
  Gurnard with Asparagus, Mushrooms &
  Ponzu Dressing 94
  Italian Fish 'Soup' 8
  Lemon Flounder with an Exotic Potato
  Salad 115
  Mahi Mahi with a Potato & Chorizo
  Salad & Sauce Vierge 88
  Pan-fried Fish with a Pickled Lemon &
  Smoked Marlin Sauce 107
  Poached John Dory with a Vegetable
  Sauce 95
  Smoked Mackerel Fritters with Avocado
  Salsa 53
  Smoked Marlin Salad 72
  Snapper with a Green Vegetable Stew
  112
  Sour Fish Soup with Morning Glory 4
  Sour Hot Fish Salad 81
  Sour Spicy Fish Head Soup 21
  Spicy Steamed Fish 104
  Sybil Hewitson's Whitebait Patties 114
  see also salmon; squid; swordfish; trout;
  tuna
flying fish roe
  Raw Tuna with Shredded Apple, Ponzu
  Dressing & Wasabi Flavoured Roe 49
  Sautéed Watermelon with Scallops,
  Wasabi Flying Fish Roe & Pink
  Peppercorn Vinaigrette 124
Foodie's Feast 252
Fragrant Pork Stew 183
Fresh Tomato Sauce 226
fricassee
  Chicken Fricassee Mauritian Style 202
  Fricassee of Squab & Wild Forest
  Mushrooms 217
Fried Bananas with Lime, Honey &

Coconut 266
Fried Peanuts with Garlic and Chinese
  Celery 52
fritters
  Paua Fritters 136
  Pumpkin Rosemary Fritters with a
  Yoghurt Coriander Sauce 238
  Smoked Mackerel Fritters with Avocado
  Salsa 53
fruit
  Fruit 'Pizza' 263
  Middle Eastern Fruit Compote with
  Banana Bread 267
  Vegetable & Fruit Salad with Palm
  Sugar Syrup 84
  see also particular fruits

Gado Gado (Peanut Sauce) 85
Gaeng Pak Prik Muu (Pork Jungle Curry)
  178
galangal
  Chicken, Coconut & Galangal Soup 15
  Chilli & Galangal Sauce 110
  Galangal & Palm Sugar Caramel 199
Galloping Horses 37
garlic
  Aioli 111, 281
  Fried Peanuts with Garlic and Chinese
  Celery 52
  Garlic Eggplant with Chinese Celery
  Noodles 237
  Minced Beef with Chilli, Garlic & Holy
  Basil 165
  Parmesan & Garlic Croutons 125
George Biron's Pizzas 26–7
ginger
  Pipis with Chilli, Coriander & Ginger
  146
  Rice, Ginger & Green Vegetable Soup 5
Gingerbread Cake with Caramel Sauce
  268
glazes
  Balsamic Glaze 75
  Glazed Honey & Soy Chicken 193
Gold Bags with Sweet Chilli Sauce 36
Golden Syrup & Orange Parfait 248
Greek Cypriot Village Salad 160
Greek Lamb Salad 61
Greek Potatoes 157
Green Bean & Corn Salad 117
Green Chicken Curry 195
Green Lip Mussel Chowder 9
Green Papaya Salad 82
green peppercorns 178
Green Vegetable Stew 112
Grilled Bread with Smoked Chicken and a
  Mango & Avocado Salsa 31
Grilled Chicken with Sweet Chilli Sauce
  214
Grilled Pork Fillet with Sage, Lemon &
  Prosciutto 179
Grilled Salmon with Thai Spicy Apple
  Salad 99
Grilled Spiced Minced Seafood on
  Lemongrass Stalks 145
Grilled Swordfish with a Green Bean &
  Corn Salad 117
Gudeq (Chicken Curry with Young
  Jackfruit) 213
Gurnard with Asparagus, Mushrooms &

Ponzu Dressing 94
ham see jamon; prosciutto
harissa
  Lemon and Harissa Broth 209
Hashbrown Cakes with Sour Cream &
  Salmon Caviar 38
Hawy Thawt (Thai Mussel Cakes with
  Stir-fried Beanshoots) 140
herbs
  Fast Roast Chicken with Herby Juices
  194
  Herb Crumbed Fennel with Red
  Capsicum Rouille 239
  Herb Sauce 150
  Japanese Herb Vinaigrette 128
  Salsa Verde 119
  see also particular hrebs
Hokey Pokey Ice Cream 270
honey
  Fried Bananas with Lime, Honey &
  Coconut 266
  Glazed Honey & Soy Chicken 193
  Muffin Melts 56
  Pear, Goat Cheese & Honey Tart 247
  Simple Parsnip Soup with a little local
  honey 13
honeycomb 270
Hot Tomato Vinaigrette 68
Huey's Pizza Pie 45

ice-cream
  Banana Split Revisited 265
  Bombe Alaska 274
  Hokey Pokey Ice Cream 270
  Ice Cream Stuffed Brioche with
  Chocolate Sauce 249
  Rocky Road Sundae 255
Ikan Air Garam (Sour Spicy Fish Head
  Soup) 21
Ikan Bakar Rica (Fish with Chilli &
  Galangal Sauce) 110
Impossible Pie 256
Indonesian Fried Rice with an Egg 55
Italian BBQ Vegie Burger 230
Italian Fish 'Soup' 8

jackfruit 84
  Chicken Curry with Young Jackfruit
  213
jambu air apples
  Cherry Tomato, Jambu Air & Singapore
  Berry Salad 118
Jamon, Roasted Capsicum & Cheese
  Toasties 44
Japanese Herb Vinaigrette 128

Kacang Tojin (Fried Peanuts with Garlic
  and Chinese Celery) 52
Kaeng Hangleh Muu (Burmese Style Pork
  Curry) 176
Kaeng Khiaw-Waan Kai (Green Chicken
  Curry) 195
Kaeng Phet Pet Yaang (Red Duck Curry)
  218
Kaeng Som Pla Kup Phak Bung (Sour Fish
  Soup with Morning Glory) 4
Kahlua Poached Dates in Crisp Filo 264
Kai Yaang (Grilled Chicken with Sweet
  Chilli Sauce) 214
kebabs

Swordfish Kebabs with Spiced Chickpea Salad 89
Khai Luk Koei (Son-In-Law Eggs) 32
Khao Sawy (Chiang Mai Chicken Noodles) 196
Khao Tom (Rice, Ginger & Green Vegetable Soup) 5
Kiwi Fruit Chutney 159
kumara
    BBQ Kumara 152
    see also sweet potato

lamb
    Cumin Lamb Steaks with BBQ Kumara 152
    Greek Lamb Salad 61
    Lamb Cutlets with a Greek Cypriot Village Salad 160
    Lamb Pita Pockets 151
    Mini Lamb Roasts with Greek Potatoes 157
    Minute Steak of Lamb with a Herb Sauce 150
    Mixed Grill of Lamb with Kiwi Fruit Chutney 159
    Moroccan Lamb & Chickpea Soup 16
    Noisettes of Lamb with Artichokes 153
    Prosciutto-wrapped Lamb with Tomato Chutney and Bashed Neeps 156
    Pumped Lamb with Carrot & Parsnip Mash 154
Lamb's Fry Persillade 158
Lamb's Liver and Zucchini Salad with Sage Butter 74
lasagne
    Eggplant 'Lasagne' 232
leeks
    Seared Scallops with Angel Hair Pasta, Parma Ham & Leeks 129
lemon
    Brandy & Lemon Butter Sauce 143
    Grilled Pork Fillet with Sage, Lemon & Prosciutto 179
    Lemon Cheesecake Between Leaves of Pastry 276
    Lemon Flounder with an Exotic Potato Salad 115
    Lemon and Harissa Broth 209
    Lemony Veal Cutlets with Red Capsicum Relish 188
    Pickled Lemon & Smoked Marlin Sauce 107
lemongrass
    Grilled Spiced Minced Seafood on Lemongrass Stalks 145
lettuce
    BLT Salad with a Poached Egg 66
    Pork San Choi Bao 184
Light Celery Soup 17
light meals see starters, snacks and light meals
lime
    Coriander & Lime Tartare 231
    Fried Bananas with Lime, Honey & Coconut 266
    Pork & Lime Patties with a Chilli-Lime Sauce 33
    Spicy Lime & Vanilla Dressing 69
Little Popovers with Salmon Caviar & Sour Cream 40
liver

Lamb's Fry Persillade 158
Lamb's Liver and Zucchini Salad with Sage Butter 74
Lobster with a Brandy & Lemon Butter Sauce 143
Local Trout with Salsa Verde 119
lotus chips 47

Mahi Mahi with a Potato & Chorizo Salad & Sauce Vierge 88
Mango & Avocado Salsa 31
Mar Hor (Galloping Horses) 37
mashes
    Bashed Neeps 156
    Carrot & Parsnip Mash 154
    Pesto Mash 206
Mayonnaise 281
Mauritian Hot Chilli Eggs 54
Mauritian Spiced Scallops on a Palm Heart Salad 123
Mauritian Squid Curry 108
meat see beef; lamb; pork; poultry; sausages; veal; venison
Middle Eastern Fruit Compote with Banana Bread 267
Mie Jawa (Noodles with Chicken & Vegies) 216
Minced Beef with Chilli, Garlic & Holy Basil 165
Mini Lamb Roasts with Greek Potatoes 157
mint, Vietnamese 20
Minute Steak of Lamb with a Herb Sauce 150
Miso Broth 97
Mixed Grill of Lamb with Kiwi Fruit Chutney 159
Moo Phad Kapaw (Stir-fried Ground Pork with Thai Sweet Basil) 177
morning glory 4, 5
Moroccan Lamb & Chickpea Soup 16
mousse
    Elizabeth David's Chocolate & Orange Mousse 257
Muffin Melts 56
Muscovado, Rum & Orange Sauce 272
mushrooms
    Abalone with Shiitakes, Snowpeas & Garlic 130
    Asparagus with Mushrooms & Sherry Vinegar 242
    Fennel & Mushroom Salad with Truffle Oil 67
    Fricassee of Squab & Wild Forest Mushrooms 217
    Gurnard with Asparagus, Mushrooms & Ponzu Dressing 94
    Mushrooms & Chorizo 24
    Mushrooms à la Grecque 224
    Parmesan Crumbed Mushroom Steaks with a Coriander & Lime Tartare 231
    Sautéed Prawns with Pine Nuts & Shiitakes 142
    Scrumptious Mushrooms on Toast 225
mussels
    Green Lip Mussel Chowder 9
    Mussel & Pineapple Curry 131
    Mussels with Roasted Red Capsicum & Anchovy Butter 133
    Pasta with Mussels 132
    Thai Mussel Cakes with Stir-fried

Beanshoots 140
mustard greens
    Duck, Noodle & Preserved Mustard Green Soup 10

naam plaa 195
Nasi Goring (Indonesian Fried Rice with an Egg) 55
neeps
    Prosciutto-wrapped Lamb with Tomato Chutney and Bashed Neeps 156
Neua Phat Bai Hohrapha (Beef with Thai Sweet Basil) 173
New Wave Coq Au Vin 205
Noisettes of Lamb with Artichokes 153
noodles
    Beef Soup Noodles 20
    Chiang Mai Chicken Noodles 196
    Chicken Chop Suey 201
    Chinese Celery Noodles 237
    Duck, Noodle & Preserved Mustard Green Soup 10
    Noodles with Chicken & Vegies 216
    Noodle Salad with Prawns & Pineapple 78

oil, testing temperature 223
Old-fashioned Chicken Casserole 204
omelette
    Crab & Camembert Omelette 139
onions
    Caramelised Onion Topping 27
    Steak & Smothered Onion Sandwich 162
oranges
    Crepes Suzette 277
    Duck Breasts with Pomegranate Molasses & Orange 219
    Elizabeth David's Chocolate & Orange Mousse 257
    Golden Syrup & Orange Parfait 248
    Muscovado, Rum & Orange Sauce 272
    Orange Mascarpone 253
    Prosciutto, Avocado & Orange Salad with a Hot Tomato Vinaigrette 68
Orrechetti con Broccoli 182
oysters
    Bloody Mary Soup with Plumped Oysters 7
    Curried Dholl 'Soup' with Oysters & Coriander Raita 14
Oyster Sauce Beef with Smothered Chinese Cabbage 170

palm hearts 72
Palm Heart Salad 123
palm sugar
    Galangal & Palm Sugar Caramel 199
    Palm Sugar Syrup 84, 250
panettone
    Whiskey & Panettone Butter Pudding 271
Pan-fried Fish with a Pickled Lemon & Smoked Marlin Sauce 107
papaya
    Green Papaya Salad 82
    Pawpaw Salsita 116
paprika
    Pork Cutlets with Smoked Paprika & Sherry Vinegar 180
parfaits

Golden Syrup & Orange Parfait 248
Parmesan Crumbed Mushroom Steaks
  with a Coriander & Lime Tartare 231
Parmesan & Garlic Croutons 125
parsley
  Lamb's Fry Persillade 158
parsnips
  Carrot & Parsnip Mash 154
  Simple Parsnip Soup with a little local
  honey 13
pasta
  Orrechetti con Broccoli 182
  Pasta with Mussels 132
  Roast Chicken Carbonara 192
  Seared Scallops with Angel Hair Pasta,
  Parma Ham & Leeks 129
  Spaghetti with Zucchini Flowers 233
pastries
  Kahlua Poached Dates in Crisp Filo 264
  Lemon Cheesecake Between Leaves of
  Pastry 276
  see also tarts
patties
  Beef Patties with Coconut 50
  Pork & Lime Patties with a Chilli-Lime
  Sauce 33
  Sybil Hewitson's Whitebait Patties 114
paua 134
  Chilli Paua 138
  Paua Butties 137
  Paua Fritters 136
Pawpaw Salsita 116
pea eggplants 178
peaches
  Poached Peaches in a Vanilla Bean &
  Cinnamon Syrup 258
peanuts 50
  Fried Peanuts with Garlic and Chinese
  Celery 52
  Peanut Sauce 85
peanut butter 85
pears
  Carpaccio of Beetroot with Baked Feta,
  Rocket, Walnuts & Pear 64
  Pear, Goat Cheese & Honey Tart 247
peperonata
  Eggplant and Capsicum Peperonata
  164
Pesto 282
Pesto Mash 206
Phad Krapow Neua (Beef with Thai
  Sweet Basil) 173
pickles
  Cucumber Pickles 57, 174
  Pickled Lemon & Smoked Marlin Sauce
  107
pies
  Curried Eggplant & Potato Pie 228
  Impossible Pie 256
pine nuts
  Sautéed Prawns with Pine Nuts &
  Shiitakes 142
pineapple
  Mussel & Pineapple Curry 131
  Noodle Salad with Prawns & Pineapple
  78
  Pineapple with a Muscovado, Rum &
  Orange Sauce 272
  Pineapple Sambal 109
Pink Peppercorn Vinaigrette 124
Pipis with Chilli, Coriander & Ginger 146

pita
  Lamb Pita Pockets 151
pizza
  Basic Pizza Sauce 27
  Braised Fennel Topping 27
  Caramelised Onion Topping 27
  Fruit 'Pizza' 263
  George Biron's Pizzas 26–7
  Huey's Pizza Pie 45
Pla Neua Sot (Raw Beef Salad) 83
Plaa Neung (Spicy Steamed Fish) 104
Plaa Thawt Sahm Rot (Deep Fried Fish
  with Three Flavoured Sauce) 102
Plaa Thawt Sahm Rot (Three Flavoured
  Sauce) 102
Poached John Dory with a Vegetable
  Sauce 95
Poached Peaches in a Vanilla Bean &
  Cinnamon Syrup 258
Polenta Pasticciata 236
pomegranate
  Duck Breasts with Pomegranate
  Molasses & Orange 219
pomelo 84
Ponzu Dressing 49, 94
poritake 47
pork
  Burmese Style Pork Curry 176
  Fragrant Pork Stew 183
  Galloping Horses 37
  Grilled Pork Fillet with Sage, Lemon &
  Prosciutto 179
  Orrechetti con Broccoli 182
  Pork Cutlets with Smoked Paprika &
  Sherry Vinegar 180
  Pork Jungle Curry 178
  Pork & Lime Patties with a Chilli-Lime
  Sauce 33
  Pork San Choi Bao 184
  Stir-fried Ground Pork with Thai Sweet
  Basil 177
potatoes
  Bullboar, Potato & White Bean Salad
  65
  Curried Eggplant & Potato Pie 228
  Des Britten's Pommes Dauphine 223
  Exotic Potato Salad 115
  Greek Potatoes 157
  Hashbrown Cakes with Sour Cream &
  Salmon Caviar 38
  Pesto Mash 206
  Potato & Chorizo Salad 88
  Potato, Goat Cheese Feta & Anchovy
  Tortilla 30
Pot-roasted Chicken with Lemon and
  Harissa Broth 209
poultry see chicken; duck; squab
prawns
  Noodle Salad with Prawns & Pineapple
  78
  Prawn, Trout & Sesame Toasts 43
  Sautéed Prawns with Pine Nuts &
  Shiitakes 142
preserved citrus rind 97
prosciutto
  BBQ Prosciutto Wrapped Figs Stuffed
  with Feta 42
  BLT Salad with a Poached Egg 66
  Grilled Pork Fillet with Sage, Lemon &
  Prosciutto 179
  Prosciutto, Avocado & Orange Salad

with a Hot Tomato Vinaigrette 68
  Prosciutto-wrapped Lamb with Tomato
  Chutney and Bashed Neeps 156
  Ruth Pretty's Rack of Cervena wrapped
  in Prosciutto with Roasted Tomatoes
  187
  Seared Scallops with Angel Hair Pasta,
  Parma Ham & Leeks 129
Provencale Vegetables 111
puddings
  BBQ Berry Puddings 253
  Sticky Rice Pudding with Palm Sugar
  Syrup and Grilled Bananas 250
  Whiskey & Panettone Butter Pudding
  271
Pumped Lamb with Carrot & Parsnip
  Mash 154
pumpkin
  Pumpkin Rosemary Fritters with a
  Yoghurt Coriander Sauce 238
  Steamed Pumpkin Custard 246

Radicchio, Witloof and Walnut Slaw 91
Ragout of Seafood with Creole Sauce
  144
raita
  Coriander Raita 14
Raw Beef Salad 83
Raw Tuna with Shredded Apple, Ponzu
  Dressing & Wasabi Flavoured Roe 49
red capsicum
  Eggplant and Capsicum Peperonata
  164
  Jamon, Roasted Capsicum & Cheese
  Toasties 44
  Mussels with Roasted Red Capsicum &
  Anchovy Butter 133
  Red Capsicum Relish 188
  Red Capsicum Rouille 239
  Roasted Red Capsicum & Anchovy
  Butter 133
  Warm Gazpacho Salad 101
Red Duck Curry 218
Red Sauce 210
relish
  Red Capsicum Relish 188
  Tomato and Chilli Relish 70
Rempah (Beef Patties with Coconut) 50
Rhubarb Clafoutis 259
rice
  Indonesian Fried Rice with an Egg 55
  Rice, Ginger & Green Vegetable Soup
  5
  Sticky Rice Pudding with Palm Sugar
  Syrup and Grilled Bananas 250
rice paper
  Salmon Pan-fried in Rice Paper with
  Sweet Chilli Sauce 96
Roast Chicken Carbonara 192
Roasted Red Capsicum & Anchovy Butter
  133
Roasted Tomatoes 187
rocket
  Carpaccio of Beetroot with Baked Feta,
  Rocket, Walnuts & Pear 64
Rocky Road Sundae 255
rosemary
  Pumpkin Rosemary Fritters with a
  Yoghurt Coriander Sauce 238
Rougaille de Boeuf 171
Rougaille de Tomate 106

rouille
 Red Capsicum Rouille 239
Rujak (Vegetable & Fruit Salad with Palm Sugar Syrup) 84
Ruth Pretty's Rack of Cervena wrapped in Prosciutto with Roasted Tomatoes 187

sage
 Grilled Pork Fillet with Sage, Lemon & Prosciutto 179
 Sage Butter 74
salads
 BBQ Fennel Salad 92
 BLT Salad with a Poached Egg 66
 Bullboar, Potato & White Bean Salad 65
 Carpaccio of Beetroot with Baked Feta, Rocket, Walnuts & Pear 64
 Cherry Tomato, Jambu Air & Singapore Berry Salad 118
 Crudités with Salmon and an Anchovy Vinaigrette 76
 Dill-flavoured Egg Salad with Smoked Salmon 48
 Exotic Potato Salad 115
 Fennel & Mushroom Salad with Truffle Oil 67
 Fish Salad with a Spicy Lime & Vanilla Dressing 69s
 Greek Cypriot Village Salad 160
 Greek Lamb Salad 61
 Green Bean & Corn Salad 117
 Green Papaya Salad 82
 Lamb's Liver and Zucchini Salad with Sage Butter 74
 Noodle Salad with Prawns & Pineapple 78
 Palm Heart Salad 123
 Potato & Chorizo Salad 88
 Prosciutto, Avocado & Orange Salad with a Hot Tomato Vinaigrette 68
 Radicchio, Witloof and Walnut Slaw 91
 Raw Beef Salad 83
 Scallop Salad with Parmesan & Garlic Croutons 125
 Smoked Eel with Watermelon and a Balsamic Glaze 75
 Smoked Marlin Salad 72
 Smoked Peppered Sirloin and Pesto Asparagus Salad 68
 Sour Hot Fish Salad 81
 Spiced Chickpea Salad 89
 Squid & Snake Bean Salad Lawar 79
 Steak & Sweet Potato Salad with a Tomato and Chilli Relish 70
 Thai Beef Salad 60
 Thai Spicy Apple Salad 99
 Tofu & Vegetable Salad with Peanut Sauce 85
 Tuna Tataki 47
 Vegetable & Fruit Salad with Palm Sugar Syrup 84
 Vietnamese Chicken Coleslaw 62
 Warm Gazpacho Salad 101
salam leaves 213
salek 84
salmon
 Crudités with Salmon and an Anchovy Vinaigrette 76
 Grilled Salmon with Thai Spicy Apple Salad 99

Salmon in Miso Broth 97
Salmon Pan-fried in Rice Paper with Sweet Chilli Sauce 96
see also smoked salmon
salmon caviar
 Hashbrown Cakes with Sour Cream & Salmon Caviar 38
 Little Popovers with Salmon Caviar & Sour Cream 40
salsa
 Avocado Salsa 53
 Mango & Avocado Salsa 31
 Pawpaw Salsita 116
Salsa Verde 119
sambal
 Pineapple Sambal 109
sambal oelak 17
sandwiches
 Smoked Salmon Croque Monsieur 44
 Steak & Smothered Onion Sandwich 162
Sangkaya Fuk-Thong (Steamed Pumpkin Custard) 246
Sate Lilit (Grilled Spiced Minced Seafood on Lemongrass Stalks) 145
Sauces (savoury)
 Basic Pizza Sauce 27
 Beetroot & Pepper Sauce 185
 Brandy & Lemon Butter Sauce 143
 Chilli & Galangal Sauce 110
 Chilli-Lime Sauce 33
 Coriander & Lime Tartare 231
 Creole Sauce 144
 Fresh Tomato Sauce 226
 Herb Sauce 150
 Peanut Sauce 85
 Pickled Lemon & Smoked Marlin Sauce 107
 Red Sauce 210
 Rougaille de Tomate 106
 Salsa Verde 119
 Sauce Vierge 88
 Sweet Chilli Sauce 36, 96, 214
 Sweet & Sour Sauce 34
 Three Flavoured Sauce 102
 Vegetable Sauce 95
 Yoghurt Coriander Sauce 238
sauces (sweet)
 Caramel Sauce 268
 Chocolate Sauce 249, 260
 Muscovado, Rum & Orange Sauce 272
sausage
 Bullboar, Potato & White Bean Salad 65
 Chorizo & Vegie Stew with a Baked Egg 28
 Mushrooms & Chorizo 24
 Potato & Chorizo Salad 88
Sautéed Prawns with Pine Nuts & Shiitakes 142
Sautéed Watermelon with Scallops, Wasabi Flying Fish Roe & Pink Peppercorn Vinaigrette 124
savoiardi 262
scallops
 Mauritian Spiced Scallops on a Palm Heart Salad 123
 Sautéed Watermelon with Scallops, Wasabi Flying Fish Roe & Pink Peppercorn Vinaigrette 124
 Scallop Salad with Parmesan & Garlic

Croutons 125
Seared Scallops with Angel Hair Pasta, Parma Ham & Leeks 129
Steamed Scallops with Japanese Herb Vinaigrette 128
Succotash with Scallops 126
Scrambled Eggs with Persian Feta 41
Scrumptious Mushrooms on Toast 225
seafood
 Abalone with Shiitakes, Snowpeas & Garlic 130
 Crab & Camembert Omelette 139
 Grilled Spiced Minced Seafood on Lemongrass Stalks 145
 Lobster with a Brandy & Lemon Butter Sauce 143
 Pipis with Chilli, Coriander & Ginger 146
 Ragout of Seafood with Creole Sauce 144
 see also mussels; paua; prawns; scallops
Seared Scallops with Angel Hair Pasta, Parma Ham & Leeks 129
sesame
 Prawn, Trout & Sesame Toasts 43
 Sesame Seared Tuna with Cherry Tomato, Jambu Air & Singapore Berry Salad 118
Shakin' Beef 172
shiso 128
Silverbeet 'Minestra' 12
Simple Parsnip Soup with a little local honey 13
Smoked Eel with Watermelon and a Balsamic Glaze 75
Smoked Mackerel Fritters with Avocado Salsa 53
Smoked Marlin Salad 72
Smoked Peppered Sirloin and Pesto Asparagus Salad 68
smoked salmon
 Dill-flavoured Egg Salad with Smoked Salmon 48
 Smoked Salmon Croque Monsieur 44
Smothered Chinese Cabbage 170
snacks see starters, snacks and light meals
Snapper with a Green Vegetable Stew 112
snowpeas
 Abalone with Shiitakes, Snowpeas & Garlic 130
Som Tam (Green Papaya Salad) 82
Son-In-Law Eggs 32
soups
 Beef Soup Noodles 20
 Bloody Mary Soup with Plumped Oysters 7
 Chicken, Coconut & Galangal Soup 15
 Chilli, Chicken & Cheese Soup 6
 Curried Dholl 'Soup' with Oysters & Coriander Raita 14
 Duck, Noodle & Preserved Mustard Green Soup 10
 Green Lip Mussel Chowder 9
 Italian Fish 'Soup' 8
 Light Celery Soup 17
 Moroccan Lamb & Chickpea Soup 16
 Rice, Ginger & Green Vegetable Soup 5

Silverbeet 'Minestra' 12
Simple Parsnip Soup with a little local honey 13
Sour Fish Soup with Morning Glory 4
Sour Spicy Fish Head Soup 21
Vegetable 'Bouillabaisse' 2
Sour Fish Soup with Morning Glory 4
Sour Hot Fish Salad 81
Sour Spicy Fish Head Soup 21
soursop 84
Spaghetti with Zucchini Flowers 233
Spiced Chickpea Salad 89
Spicy Lime & Vanilla Dressing 69
Spicy Steamed Fish 104
spring rolls
Vegetarian Lumpia Rolls with Sweet & Sour Sauce 34–5
squab
Fricassee of Squab & Wild Forest Mushrooms 217
squid
Mauritian Squid Curry 108
Squid & Snake Bean Salad Lawar 79
starters, snacks and light meals
BBQ Prosciutto Wrapped Figs Stuffed with Feta 42
Beef Patties with Coconut 50
Chorizo & Vegie Stew with a Baked Egg 28
Corn Cakes with Cucumber Pickles 57
Dill-flavoured Egg Salad with Smoked Salmon 48
Fried Peanuts with Garlic and Chinese Celery 52
Galloping Horses 37
George Biron's Pizzas 26–7
Gold Bags with Sweet Chilli Sauce 36
Grilled Bread with Smoked Chicken and a Mango & Avocado Salsa 31
Hashbrown Cakes with Sour Cream & Salmon Caviar 38
Indonesian Fried Rice with an Egg 55
Jamon, Roasted Capsicum & Cheese Toasties 44
Little Popovers with Salmon Caviar & Sour Cream 40
Mauritian Hot Chilli Eggs 54
Muffin Melts 56
Mushrooms & Chorizo 24
Pork & Lime Patties with a Chilli-Lime Sauce 33
Potato, Goat Cheese Feta & Anchovy Tortilla 30
Prawn, Trout & Sesame Toasts 43
Raw Tuna with Shredded Apple, Ponzu Dressing & Wasabi Flavoured Roe 49
Scrambled Eggs with Persian Feta 41
Smoked Mackerel Fritters with Avocado Salsa 53
Smoked Salmon Croque Monsieur 44
Son-In-Law Eggs 32
Tuna Tataki 47
Vegetable & Fruit Salad with Palm Sugar Syrup 84
Vegetarian Lumpia Rolls with Sweet & Sour Sauce 34–5
Steak with an Eggplant and Capsicum Peperonata 164
Steak & Smothered Onion Sandwich 162
Steak & Sweet Potato Salad with a Tomato and Chilli Relish 70

Steamed Pumpkin Custard 246
Steamed Scallops with Japanese Herb Vinaigrette 128
stews
Chicken Mulligatawny 200
Chorizo & Vegie Stew with a Baked Egg 28
Fragrant Pork Stew 183
Green Vegetable Stew 112
Sticky Rice Pudding with Palm Sugar Syrup and Grilled Bananas 250
Stir-fried Beanshoots 140
Stir-fried Ground Pork with Thai Sweet Basil 177
stock
beef 280
chicken 280
fish 280
vegetable 281
strawberries
Eton Mess 254
Strawberry Bruschetta 254
Succotash with Scallops 126
sundaes
Rocky Road Sundae 255
swedes
Bashed Neeps 156
Sweet & Sour Sauce 34
Sweet Chilli Sauce 36, 96, 214
sweet potato
Steak & Sweet Potato Salad with a Tomato and Chilli Relish 70
sweetcorn see corn
swordfish
Grilled Swordfish with a Green Bean & Corn Salad 117
Swordfish Kebabs with Spiced Chickpea Salad 89
Swordfish with Pawpaw Salsita 116
Sybil Hewitson's Whitebait Patties 114
syrups
Palm Sugar Syrup 84, 250
Vanilla Bean & Cinnamon Syrup 258

Taquitos of Porterhouse with Soft Goat Curd 163
tarts
Fennel Tarte Tatin 240
Pear, Goat Cheese & Honey Tart 247
tatsoi 70, 75
Thai apples
Thai Spicy Apple Salad 99
Thai Beef Salad 60
Thai Mussel Cakes with Stir-fried Beanshoots 140
Thai Spicy Apple Salad 99
Thai Tongue Twister 98
Three Flavoured Sauce 102
Thung Tong (Gold Bags with Sweet Chilli Sauce) 36
Tipsy Berry Trifle 262
toasts
Jamon, Roasted Capsicum & Cheese Toasties 44
Prawn, Trout & Sesame Toasts 43
Scrumptious Mushrooms on Toast 225
Smoked Salmon Croque Monsieur 44
Strawberry Bruschetta 254
Tofu & Vegetable Salad with Peanut Sauce 85
Tom Khaa Gai (Chicken, Coconut &

Galangal Soup) 15
tomatoes
Basic Pizza Sauce 27
Bloody Mary Soup with Plumped Oysters 7
BLT Salad with a Poached Egg 66
Cherry Tomato, Jambu Air & Singapore Berry Salad 118
Creole Sauce 144
Fresh Tomato Sauce 226
Hot Tomato Vinaigrette 68
Red Sauce 211
Roasted Tomatoes 187
Rougaille de Tomate 106
Sauce Vierge 88
Tomato and Chilli Relish 70
Tomato Vinaigrette 90
toppings (pizza)
Braised Fennel Topping 27
Caramelised Onion Topping 27
tortillas
Potato, Goat Cheese Feta & Anchovy Tortilla 30
Taquitos of Porterhouse with Soft Goat Curd 163
trifle
Tipsy Berry Trifle 262
trout
Local Trout with Salsa Verde 119
Prawn, Trout & Sesame Toasts 43
Whole Rainbow Trout with Moroccan Flavours 100
truffle oil 67
Fennel & Mushroom Salad with Truffle Oil 67
tuna
BBQ Tuna with Pineapple Sambal 109
Raw Tuna with Shredded Apple, Ponzu Dressing & Wasabi Flavoured Roe 49
Sesame Seared Tuna with Cherry Tomato, Jambu Air & Singapore Berry Salad 118
Tuna with a BBQ Fennel Salad 92
Tuna with Roasted Eggplant & Tomato Vinaigrette 90
Tuna Tataki 47
turnips
Prosciutto-wrapped Lamb with Tomato Chutney and Bashed Neeps 156
Tuscan Chicken Livers with Pesto Mash 206

vanilla
Spicy Lime & Vanilla Dressing 69
Vanilla Bean & Cinnamon Syrup 258
veal
Lemony Veal Cutlets with Red Capsicum Relish 188
Veal Scaloppine with Lemon & Sage 186
vegetables 35
Chicken Chop Suey 201
Chorizo & Vegie Stew with a Baked Egg 28
Crudités with Salmon and an Anchovy Vinaigrette 76
Dry Curry de Legumes 229
Green Vegetable Stew 112
Noodles with Chicken & Vegies 216
Provencale Vegetables 111
Rice, Ginger & Green Vegetable Soup 5

Tofu & Vegetable Salad with Peanut Sauce 85
Vegetable 'Bouillabaisse' 2
Vegetable Fritto Misto 234
Vegetable & Fruit Salad with Palm Sugar Syrup 84
Vegetable Sauce 95
see also particular vegetables
vegetarian
Asparagus with Mushrooms & Sherry Vinegar 242
Cabbage Rolls with Cheese Stuffing and a Fresh Tomato Sauce 226
Curried Eggplant & Potato Pie 228
Des Britten's Pommes Dauphine 223
Eggplant 'Lasagne' 232
Fennel Tarte Tatin 240
Garlic Eggplant with Chinese Celery Noodles 237
Herb Crumbed Fennel with Red Capsicum Rouille 239
Italian BBQ Vegie Burger 230
Mushrooms à la Grecque 224
Parmesan Crumbed Mushroom Steaks with a Coriander & Lime Tartare 231
Polenta Pasticciata 236
Pumpkin Rosemary Fritters with a Yoghurt Coriander Sauce 238
Scrumptious Mushrooms on Toast 225
Spaghetti with Zucchini Flowers 233

Vegetable Fritto Misto 234
Vegetarian Lumpia Rolls with Sweet & Sour Sauce 34–5
venison
Ruth Pretty's Rack of Cervena wrapped in Prosciutto with Roasted Tomatoes 187
Venison with Beetroot & Pepper Sauce 185
Vermicelli Kheer 273
Vietnamese Chicken Coleslaw 62
Vietnamese mint 20
vinaigrette
Anchovy Vinaigrette 76
Hot Tomato Vinaigrette 68
Japanese Herb Vinaigrette 128
Pink Peppercorn Vinaigrette 124
Tomato Vinaigrette 90

walnuts
Carpaccio of Beetroot with Baked Feta, Rocket, Walnuts & Pear 64
Radicchio, Witloof and Walnut Slaw 91
Warm Gazpacho Salad 101
wasabi 49
water apples 84
Sesame Seared Tuna with Cherry Tomato, Jambu Air & Singapore Berry Salad 118
watermelon

Sautéed Watermelon with Scallops, Wasabi Flying Fish Roe & Pink Peppercorn Vinaigrette 124
Smoked Eel with Watermelon and a Balsamic Glaze 75
Whiskey & Panettone Butter Pudding 271
whitebait 114
Sybil Hewitson's Whitebait Patties 114
Whole Rainbow Trout with Moroccan Flavours 100
witloof
Radicchio, Witloof and Walnut Slaw 91
wontons
Gold Bags with Sweet Chilli Sauce 36

Yam Plaa Yaang (Sour Hot Fish Salad) 81
Yang Pla Yum Poodza (Grilled Salmon with Thai Spicy Apple Salad) 99
yoghurt
Coriander Raita 14
Yoghurt Coriander Sauce 238

zucchini
Lamb's Liver and Zucchini Salad with Sage Butter 74
Warm Gazpacho Salad 101
zucchini flowers
Spaghetti with Zucchini Flowers 233

Picture credits

The full-page food shots throughout are by Greg Elms.

The shots on the following pages are by Greg Elms:
ii, iv, v, vi, vii, 17, 41, 46, 56, 86-87 (New Zealand), 120-121 (New Zealand), 132, 137, 148-149 (New Zealand), 153, 158, 165, 182, 183, 192, 204, 205, 212, 224, 247, 249, 262, 265.

The location shots throughout have been supplied by Dreampool Productions.

The food pictures on the following pages are used with permission from of Digital Vision: 9, 12, 27, 31, 33, 42, 43, 48, 49, 52, 67, 72, 75, 90, 91, 96, 97, 104, 106, 108, 109, 116, 117, 123, 131, 133, 139, 143, 150, 152, 157, 159, 163, 171, 179, 185, 186, 187, 193, 194, 218, 219, 223, 225, 230, 233, 236, 253, 256, 257, 258, 262, 263, 272, 274, 280, 281.

The following images are used with permission from Lonely Planet Images:

Pages x-1
Fishing boat silhouetted at sunset in Jimbaran Bay, Bali, Indonesia, by Richard I'Anson
Pages 22-23
Driving through the Barabool Hills outside Geelong, Australia, by Richard I'Anson
Pages 58-59
Domaine Chandon Vineyard, Yarra Valley, Australia, by John Hay
Pages 190-191
Rural workers toil in the fields in Flic en Flac, Mauritius, by Jean-Bernard Carillet
Pages 220-221
Rice terraces in eastern Bali, Indonesia, by James Lyon
Pages 244-245
City of Canberra from Mt Ainslie, Australia, by Rob Blakers
Pages 278-279
Traders at a floating market in Bangkok, Thailand, by Greg Elms

The photos on page 18 (bottom right), 19 (bottom) and 110 are used with permission from George Krawat.

The photos on pages 248 and 255 are from the author's private collection.

The photos on the following pages are used with permission as noted:
46 (Len Evans), 66 (Healesville Hotel), 135 (Logan-Brown), 222 (Des Britten), 273 (Davinder Bedi).

Other books

The Huey Diet
A new flavoursome approach
to sensible, healthy eating.

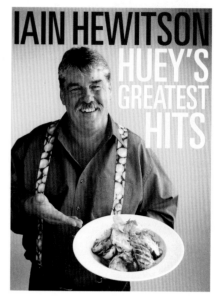

Huey's Greatest Hits
A bumper collection of the most
requested recipes from
Iain Hewitson's popular TV shows.

Huey's Best Ever Barbecue Recipes
Easy-to-prepare, no fuss meals that introduce
you to a whole new way to barbecue.

Tales & Recipes from a Travelling Cook
The Huey classic – jam-packed with recipes, hints,
tips and hilarious travel anecdotes.

www.hueyscookingclub.com